ON-DEMAND CULTURE

WITHDRAWN

ON-DEMAND CULTURE

DIGITAL DELIVERY AND THE FUTURE OF MOVIES

CHUCK TRYON

RUTGERS UNIVERSITY PRESS
New Brunswick, New Jersey, and London

Library of Congress Cataloging-in-Publication Data
Tryon, Chuck, 1970–
On-demand culture : digital delivery and the future of movies / Chuck Tryon.
p.   cm.
Includes bibliographical references and index.
ISBN 978-0-8135-6110-3 (hardcover : alk. paper) — ISBN 978-0-8135-6109-7 (pbk. :
alk. paper) — ISBN 978-0-8135-6111-0 (e-book)
1. Motion pictures.   2. Digital media—Influence.   3. Interactive multimedia.
4. Motion pictures—Distribution—Social aspects.   I. Title.
PN1994.T7175 2013
384'.8—dc23   2012033373

A British Cataloging-in-Publication record for this book is available from the British
Library.

Visit our website: http://rutgerspress.rutgers.edu

Manufactured in the United States of America

CONTENTS

ACKNOWLEDGMENTS

Writing this book has been both challenging and invigorating. Given that new technologies and movie distribution strategies emerge almost daily, the pace of change invariably seems to surpass the ability to research and document those changes. At the same time, I have been excited not only to observe this moment of media in transition but also to be connected to a vast scholarly network of researchers who have helped me to engage with this material. This project grew out of a moment of transition in film culture—the "indie crisis" that was addressed in Mark Gill's 2008 Los Angeles Film Festival keynote address—and seeks to trace how different groups within the movie industry are adapting to the changes introduced by digital delivery. I am grateful to all of the colleagues and friends who have helped me through this process.

Feedback on some of my written work from Charles Acland, Julia Lesage, Karen Lury, and Janet Wasko proved incredibly helpful as I was wrestling with many of the ideas in this book. Recent research with Max Dawson through the Connected Viewing Initiative has also helped me to look more specifically at highly localized media consumption practices. Discussions with the guys from the Riot Film Collective in a café in Madrid also proved helpful in my thinking about crowdsourcing and crowdfunding. Conversations with colleagues both at conferences and online consistently had an impact on my thinking. In particular, I would like to thank Pat Brereton, Jason Sperb, Jason Mittell, Derek Kompare, Elissa Nelson, Chris Becker, Nick Rombes, Rachel Thibault, Tim Anderson, Alissa Perren, Jennifer Holt, Amanda Lotz, Jonathan Gray, Jeffrey Jones, Ethan Tussey, Kim Owczarski, Henry Jenkins, Bill Wolff, Anne Helen Petersen, Brian Faucette, Yannis Tzioumakis, Eric Hoyt, Nina Huntemann, Catherine Grant, Matt Payne, Chris McConnell, Scott Eric Kaufman, Bob Rehak, Drew Morton, Steven Shaviro, Julie Levin Russo, Christopher Lucas, Tama Leaver, Richard Edwards, David Bordwell, Geoffrey Long, Michael Newman, Elana Levine, Edward O'Neill, Noel Kirkpatrick, Karen Petruska, Girish Shambu, Miriam Ross, Geoff King, David Gurney, Ted Friedman, Patrick Vonderau, Paul McDonald, Jihoon Kim, Skye Dent, Aymar Jean Christian, Josh Braun, Aynne Kokas, and Daniel Marcus.

My colleagues from Fayetteville State University, especially Sonya Brown, Sarah Frantz, Brenda Hammack, Eric Hyman, Ed McShane, Micki Nyman, Dean Swinford, Carole Weatherford, and Alison Van Nyhuius, have consistently provided advice, suggestions, and support regarding the ideas in this book. I am also grateful for the support and enthusiasm I have received from Rutgers University

Press. Leslie Mitchner, in particular, has offered advice and steady encouragement for my work.

Friends and family continue to offer support and guidance. Mike Duvall, Jim Hansen, Renée Trilling, Lara Vetter, and George Williams comprised part of my first genuine scholarly network and continue to be steadfast in providing friendship and advice. My parents, Charles and Glenda Tryon, and sister Kristen have never stopped providing encouragement and support, and my new extended family, Angela Blake, Russell Blake, Richie LaPierre, Erika LaPierre, Yasmine Haddad, and Ramsey Haddad have all graciously welcomed me into their lives. Finally, this book was written during a time of profound personal transition. Just days before I received my copies of my first book, I met my amazing wife, Andrea Biondi, who has offered a number of wise and skeptical observations about the future of movie distribution and has been unshakably patient, supportive, and enthusiastic about my work, but who also knows when I should step away from the computer and embrace the world around me. I will always treasure our time together, whether we are in a plaza in Barcelona, a mountaintop in Bogota, a beach in Costa Rica, or a café in North Carolina. No matter what, I know that we will always just keep walking together.

Sections of this book have been published elsewhere. Part of chapter 3 was published as "'Make Any Room Your TV Room': Digital Delivery and Media Mobility," in *Screen* 53.3 (Fall 2012). Part of chapter 5 appeared as "Redbox vs. Red Envelope, or What Happens When the Infinite Aisle Swings through the Grocery Store" in the fall 2011 issue of the *Canadian Journal of Film Studies*. Finally, the section of chapter 7 focusing on *The Age of Stupid* appeared in the 2011 issue of *Jump Cut* as "Digital Distribution, Participatory Culture, and the Transmedia Documentary." I am also grateful to all of the anonymous readers who provided feedback on my work. Their comments sharpened my arguments considerably. I have also benefited from discussions of the ideas of this book in my personal blog, *The Chutry Experiment*, in the web magazine *AlterNet*, and in scholarly networks such as In Media Res, the University of Wisconsin's Antenna blog, and Hacktivision. I am also grateful for the feedback I received at invited lectures at Georgia State University, at the Colombia Film Week seminar in Bogota, and at Dublin City University, as well as during conference presentations at the Society of Cinema Studies, Media in Transition, and the Marxism and New Media Conference at Duke University. This book also benefited indirectly from research I conducted through the Connected Viewing Initiative sponsored by the University of California, Santa Barbara.

ON-DEMAND CULTURE

INTRODUCTION:
ON-DEMAND CULTURE
Digital Distribution and the Future of Cinema

IN MAY 2012 COMEDIAN Mark Malkoff embarked on an unusual challenge when he sought to watch as many Netflix streaming movies as possible over the course of a single month. Reasoning that he wanted to get the best value possible for his $7.99 per month subscription, Malkoff managed to watch 252 movies—approximately eight per day—bringing his cost per film to an impressively low three cents per day. Malkoff's well-publicized stunt, which was happily embraced by Netflix, served as unofficial advertising for the company, especially when Malkoff touted the wide selection of movie titles. In interviews, Malkoff emphasized that the existing catalog of streaming movies could last several lifetimes and added that the service's recommendation algorithms typically suggested titles that fit his tastes.[1] Malkoff's experiment was also deeply connected to the social media tools that have shaped movie culture, with Malkoff actively promoting his project on Twitter and Facebook, where he would also solicit recommendations from fans and followers. Finally, Malkoff demonstrated that he could watch Netflix titles on a variety of devices and in multiple locations, at one point watching *St. Elmo's Fire* (1985) on his iPhone while actor Andrew McCarthy pulled him along in a wagon through Central Park. Although Malkoff's performance pushed the possibilities of digital delivery to their logical extreme, it illustrated many of the key questions facing both producers and consumers of media content.

This book addresses the continued changes that are taking place within the realm of media distribution and consumption, especially as we seek to make sense of an emerging "on-demand culture," one that provides viewers new forms of immediate access to movies and television shows, even while introducing a number of potential constraints. Although many observers have read these changes as democratizing media distribution, arguing that they offer people a wider range of options to watch movies and television, these distribution practices also contribute to a more fragmented, individualized media culture. These new modes of access—whether online streaming services such as YouTube or Netflix, digital downloads at iTunes, the Redbox kiosks at nearby grocery stores, tablet computers, iPhones, set-top boxes such as Roku players or gaming systems such as the Playstation 3, or movie theaters offering digitally projected 3D movies—are all engaged in redefining how audiences access and consume motion picture entertainment, destabilizing what Adrian Johns has referred to as "the business of culture."[2] At the same time, despite the seemingly unlimited choices made available through these online catalogs, users often face bewildering limitations, as video-on-demand (VOD) services compete over streaming rights to movies while internet service providers and cell phone services seek to limit the amount of data consumers use to watch video. In discussing his Netflix binge, Malkoff frankly acknowledged that he benefited from an internet subscription that provided him with unlimited bandwidth, even joking that his internet service provider was likely "mad" at him.[3]

This focus on distribution in the digital era offers a corrective to address what Philip Drake calls one of "the least widely understood aspects of the contemporary Hollywood film industry."[4] In fact, these new distribution models often expose some of the contradictions between the manufacturers of hardware (DVD players, video game players, set-top boxes, tablets and cell phones, internet-connected and 3D television sets, laptop computers) and the producers of media (the movies, videos, video games, and television shows themselves), as well as between the producers and retailers, such as Walmart, Blockbuster Video, and Amazon. The very idea of the film text, in particular, is transformed in the digital era, turning a tangible artifact—a filmstrip—into digital code. As David Bordwell bluntly reminds us, "films have become files."[5] Implied in this analysis is the recognition that the media industries have sought, with limited success, to shape the uses and practices associated with the digital distribution of entertainment, both through advertising and public service announcements and through less visible techniques, such as data caps and geo-blocking. Meanwhile, anti-piracy discourses, not to mention tighter controls over digital rights management, serve to dissuade even legitimate forms of copying, sharing, and "bootlegging" of movies.[6]

At the same time, this book has grown out of a sense of ambivalence about how digital media have reshaped the film industry in a time of rapid industrial change. When I finished my first book in 2009, Hulu was a relatively new player in digital delivery, and few people were discussing the role of Redbox kiosks in reshaping DVD distribution. Although many independent filmmakers were experimenting with day-and-date distribution, major studios were somewhat reluctant to shorten the four-month window that provided theaters with exclusive rights to show new movies. Film festivals were only beginning to discuss the benefits of making some of their movies available via VOD or streaming video. Finally, the revived attempts to use 3D as a means to encourage moviegoing as an activity were only just beginning, while audiences that initially made *Avatar* (2009) one of the highest-grossing films of all time now seem indifferent to 3D, viewing it as just another price point.

Thus, digital distribution raises new questions about how, when, and where we access movies and what this model means for entertainment culture. Digital media seem to promise that media texts circulate faster, more cheaply, and more broadly than ever before, leading to utopian accounts that imagine the potential for television shows or movies to be available anywhere. This is the promise articulated by digital utopians such as Chris Anderson, who argued in *The Long Tail* that media aggregators, such as iTunes, Netflix, and Amazon.com, would thrive on selling niche content rather than focusing solely on blockbuster hits. Even though digital storage costs are relatively minimal compared with other methods of distribution, allowing retailers such as Amazon to store titles that are purchased only a few times a month, Anderson's argument generally understates the production costs required to make a feature-length film or ongoing televised or web series. And although a number of niche films have found an audience online, the persistent availability of movies through different VOD services has altered their value, often with the result that consumers have felt less urgency to own copies of individual films, taking away one of the primary sources of income for moviemakers, a situation that has been especially damaging to independent producers.[7]

Anderson's discussion of the "long tail" is an example of what Vincent Mosco would describe as part of the "digital sublime," the idea that the internet would level all boundaries that limit access and participation, thereby democratizing culture.[8] In Anderson's argument, long-tail retailers offer what appears to be unlimited access, as well as the idea of unlimited mobility. Thanks to digital storage and streaming access, we can take our digital libraries with us and consume selections from them at our convenience, creating a culture characterized by various forms of media mobility. No longer are we wedded to the broadcast schedule or dependent upon proximity to a video store. Further, as Mosco argues, the introduction of new technologies is often accompanied by utopian promises of greater access, broader political participation, and increased choices. But despite these promises, true choice and mobility are often greatly exaggerated. This discrepancy can be confirmed by a look back at one of the most recent new media technologies to gain widespread adoption: cable television. As Sarah Banet-Weiser, Cynthia Chris, and Anthony Freitas argue, "Cable TV, on the brink of a boom in the 1970s, promised TV audiences a new media frontier, an expansive new variety of entertainment and information choices."[9] Viewers were offered a wide array of channel choices and an escape from the "oligopolistic" stranglehold of the major broadcast networks. Further, the increased number of channels was supposed to open up new opportunities for independent broadcasters to produce content that could be tailored to niche audiences that might have been underserved by the networks. However, as Banet-Weiser, Chris, and Freitas point out, cable television eventually became central to television's commercial interests, with most cable channels being owned by one of the major media conglomerates.

Thus, although digital delivery may open up new spaces for independent producers or new forms of access for consumers, we need a more careful examination of how video circulates online. In fact, the current era of media distribution is one that might best be understood within the concept of "platform mobility." I define platform mobility as encompassing the ongoing shift toward ubiquitous, mobile access to a wide range of entertainment choices. Platform mobility entails far more than the mere technological changes that allow mobile access. It also includes the social, political, and economic changes that make mobile access more desirable, as discourses such as advertisements for cell phones both promote and appeal to desires for mobile connectivity. Within this culture of platform mobility, we also encounter the individualized consumer, one who is ostensibly capable of controlling his or her viewing experience, whether that entails starting a movie on one platform and continuing it on another, watching a movie on a mobile device, or accessing digital libraries through various streaming platforms and digital downloads from anywhere an internet connection is available. In all cases, access to entertainment is promoted as mobile, persistent, and interactive, allowing the user far more control than in the past. At the same time, users can remain in constant contact with friends and family through cell phones, text messaging, and even social media.

Although mobile devices seem to multiply the locations where we can access movies and television shows—think about the stereotypical commuter watching movies on her iPhone, the student curling up in her dorm room with an iPad, or the father entertaining his children with cartoons while waiting to board an airplane—they also contribute to a great deal of uncertainty as consumers attempt to navigate a wide range of platforms and services where they can access the movies they would like to watch. Despite the promises of ubiquitous and immediate access to a wide range of media content, digital delivery has largely involved the continued efforts of major media conglomerates to develop better mechanisms for controlling where, when, and how content is circulated. Thus, the forms of platform mobility suggested here—watching movies on iPhones or continuing a television show on a separate platform—are, to some extent, a means of controlling what I call content mobility, that is, the ability for content to circulate among users. In fact, home video has always been characterized by a relative degree of mobility, given that videocassettes turned movies into tangible, portable objects that could be carried home from a video store, shared with friends and family, or sent through the mail, while VCRs helped to set the stage for time-shifting, a concept that has become commonplace in the era of digital video recorders (DVRs) and other forms of on-demand viewing.[10] Thus, many of the current practices associated with on-demand viewing have their origins in past delivery formats.

PERSONALIZED MEDIA

These notions of individualized, fragmented consumption shape media choice in complicated ways. Media consumers now have the ability to craft deeply personalized media environments, consuming texts based on personal tastes, interests, and politics. As I write this passage in North Carolina, I am listening to a streaming feed of the Seattle-based community radio station KEXP over the internet, although I could plug my favorite bands into Pandora and create a "channel" of music that is seemingly personalized to my tastes. Later tonight, I may indulge my sports fandom and watch an Atlanta Braves game on MLB TV, Major League Baseball's streaming service that allows users to watch virtually any televised game on a laptop, while my wife watches a Boston Red Sox game over that same internet connection across the table from me, unless one of our teams happens to be playing against a team blacked out in our location. Although my wife and I usually watch *The Daily Show* and *The Colbert Report* as they are broadcast before we go to bed, when we are too tired, we can catch up by going to the shows' websites to watch or, more likely, to Facebook, where we can find embedded videos in our news feeds, which we will often share with our friends. Or our family might instead view a television series or movie via my Netflix account, which we could choose to watch either via my computer or through a Wii video game player hooked up to our television set, unless we planned ahead to have that DVD mailed to our home. In most cases, though, my wife's daughter and our exchange student daughter are likely to binge-watch shows like *Glee* or *The Secret Life of the American Teenager* using their laptops or our iPad. Meanwhile, my wife and I may opt for an independent film on the living room television set.

Or I could stop at a café and watch that same movie on my Netflix app on my iPod touch, finishing it later through my Wii-connected television set, given that Netflix will remember exactly where I left off. Or I could use the Roku player hooked to my office television to watch older shows on Hulu and Crackle or movies on Netflix. If I'm in the mood for an art-house film, I could go to

Mubi.com or Fandor and pay for streaming access to one their titles, while stopping to comment on threaded blog discussions about favorite directors or an upcoming film festival. If it's the right time of year, I could go to YouTube or to my cable service's VOD selections and watch a film playing at the Sundance Festival without standing in line in the snow. If the film intrigues me, I can even participate in virtual question-and-answer sessions with the director. On occasion, when I forget to bring a copy of the movie I'm teaching in class, I will rent access to the film through Vudu or Amazon, unless those services are blocked on my campus computer. That being said, my family members are still frequent moviegoers, and unless we have planned well ahead, we will typically check movie times, watch trailers, or buy tickets on our iPhone using the Flixster app, often while sitting in a restaurant. Once we have identified a movie, we may have to decide whether to see it in 3D, IMAX, or, given our cost-conscious tendencies and aesthetic preferences, 2D. I can seek advice about what movie I should see using Twitter or Facebook. I'm also likely to post tweets while watching a television show, especially a live show like the Academy Awards, carrying on a running dialogue with several friends scattered across the country or globe. In all of these cases, the inexpensive, immediate access to entertainment content seems to promise unlimited choice, illustrating that the challenges of on-demand culture are not limited to one medium. In addition, we can choose to watch on at least four different kinds of screens—laptops, iPads, television sets, or, in rare cases, our mobile phones—and through several different platforms, depending on which is most convenient and usually which is most affordable.[11] As these anecdotal examples illustrate, media consumption has also become deeply individualized, with users able to access the movies and television shows they want in pretty much any location with an internet connection. But even though these practices may be individualized, they are shaped by our specific viewing contexts and reinforced by the media environment that we collectively produce through decisions about hardware purchases, through shared or contested tastes, and even through our geographic location.

The different connected viewing practices used by my family help to illustrate another principle of platform mobility. Rather than watching through a single internet-connected device, we consume media on a variety of devices, including iPhones, tablets, and laptops, as well as through DVD players and set-top boxes. We also use a range of subscription video-on-demand (SVOD) and electronic sell-through (EST) services, and very rarely we might watch a movie using our cable company's premium video-on-demand (PVOD) service. In this sense, Henry Jenkins is correct to argue against what he calls the "black box fallacy," the idea that video content will be piped into a single device in the living room.[12] To explain these new forms of convergence, Sheila Murphy has offered the concept of the "box of wires," the idea that many of us maintain boxes or cabinets containing various wires, connectors, wireless routers, adapters, power cords, and other tools that allow "media to jump from platform to platform." And although we may connect wirelessly, most of us still depend on electrical chargers and other devices that eventually require us to plug in.[13]

Given the diversity of changes taking place within the media industries, scholars face a difficult challenge in mapping the social, technological, and industrial transformation that is taking place. I will address some of the ways in which digital delivery is affecting television, but I am especially intrigued by how it is reshaping the film industry. Digital delivery offers the promise of ubiquitous access across multiple sites; however, it also challenges the cultural role of movie consumption as a social activity. As Charles Acland argues, this shift is especially true of the activity of moviegoing itself. With a seemingly unlimited array of options for watching movies—from plush home theater systems to mobile media that ostensibly offer the convenience of watching anytime and anywhere—the trip to the movie theater now seems less vital. In response, theaters and movie studios are creating enticements—including 3D projection and gimmicks such as Robert Rodriguez's use of scented cards to promote *Spy Kids 4: All the Time in the World* (2011)—to encourage audiences to see a movie on the big screen in a collective environment.[14] But in keeping with the idea that films have become files, audiences are also confronted with choosing not merely when to watch a movie or in what theater but also in what format and to consider whether viewing the film in 3D or in IMAX is worth the surcharge. More crucially, digital delivery is altering the practices of home consumption, with the discourses of platform mobility and individualized consumption leading to a situation in which consumers are now far less likely to purchase collectible, physical formats such as the DVD or Blu-Ray.

These changes in distribution may offer viewers a wide range of viewing options, but they take place within a media industry that has developed a carefully structured business model designed to maximize profit. Any consideration of the film industry must take into account the effects of media consolidation, especially the vertical and horizontal integration of distribution. As Thomas Schatz has noted, the flurry of mergers in the 1980s and 1990s helped to establish what he calls "Conglomerate Hollywood," in which six companies take in more than 85 percent of movie revenues while supplying more than 80 percent of all primetime television shows.[15] Writing in 2008, Schatz described how the studios fit neatly within larger media conglomerates, providing them with lucrative content that could be disseminated via a wide variety of platforms, whether in theaters, on DVD, on premium or basic cable channels, or through VOD in hotels or at home. Schatz further argued that, despite massive budgets and despite periodic complaints about box office slumps, most films were virtually guaranteed to make a profit, thanks in large part to the wide range of delivery options, at least before the collapse of the DVD market in 2008. In fact, Schatz observed that by the early 2000s, movies playing in theaters frequently served as "loss leaders," given the massive marketing budgets and delivery costs required to launch a franchise film. Instead, media conglomerates were increasingly turning toward cable, DVD, and other forms of delivery. However, by 2012, as I was completing this book, the studios were confronting a significant challenge in that DVD sales, once crucial to the profitability of Hollywood films, were declining rapidly.[16] Instead, consumers were becoming far more likely to pay for temporary access to films, whether that involved a DVD rented from a kiosk, streaming access, or video-on-demand through their cable companies. This shift in practices is consistent with the trends toward increased mobility and toward more flexible forms of entertainment consumption.

Although digital delivery is often treated as a technological inevitability, it is important to consider the economic, political, and legal infrastructures that shape the distribution of media content. The most crucial change has been in the arena of media deregulation. Jennifer Holt points out that "consolidation and integration in the new era [are] now being engineered across industries, gradually uniting film, cable, and broadcast properties with a number of distribution pipelines and exhibition outlets across a variety of media."[17] Holt and others have been attentive to the ways in which the deregulation of media ownership has produced conditions in which a single organization might include a cable company, a movie studio, cable channels, and a wide range of other media holdings. Perhaps the best example of this kind of synergy is the January 2011 merger between cable giant Comcast, the largest multiple system operator (MSO) in the world with over 23 million cable subscribers and 17 million internet subscribers, and NBC Universal, which includes a major movie studio, Universal, and a network, NBC, along with several prominent cable channels, including Bravo, CNBC, MSNBC, Syfy, and the USA Network. The merger created a massive $30 billion corporation, one that controls not only the production but also the distribution of entertainment content.

As Holt observes, the merger produced a media company that is fully integrated horizontally and vertically, providing both the infrastructure for delivery, the cable wires going into millions of homes and businesses, and the content that is delivered, the movies and television shows that are consumed on a variety of devices. More crucially, as Holt argues, "new delivery platforms and the convergence of distribution technologies have rendered the language and objects of regulation inadequate at best, and media industries have long outgrown the dimensions and arbiters of current policy."[18] Although the merger was allowed, regulators expressed some concern about it, noting that the company might be able to stifle content provided to online video distributors such as Hulu and Netflix. In fact, Comcast was forced to relinquish "management rights" to

Hulu, although it continued to maintain a minority stake in the online video hub, which is co-owned by News Corp., Disney, and NBC Universal.[19] These new ownership models, Holt concludes, have produced a "crisis" for regulators seeking to protect the interests and needs of consumers.[20] Thus, although digital delivery tools seem to open up new forms of consumption, distribution, and exhibition, we must also consider the role of media ownership in shaping how we access movies and television series.

These new distribution practices also have the potential to shape our very understanding of the film or television text. As Schatz argues, franchise filmmaking encourages the development of an "expanding textual system," in which the movie is just a small part, a phenomenon vividly described by Henry Jenkins in his discussion of convergence culture, in which "the art of storytelling has become the art of world-building, as artists create compelling environments that cannot be fully explored or exhausted within a single work or even a single medium."[21] This form of world-building can also encourage forms of enduring engagement as fans are provided with more opportunities to explore a story world in detail. Warner Brothers, for example, drew in the participation of thousands of Batman fans with its "Why So Serious" alternate-reality game (ARG), building a much deeper culture of anticipation around an already popular character. However, even though media producers may generate content that encourages ongoing attention, contemporary fan culture also draws immediate responses. As Matt Hills points out, blogs and discussion forums that focus on contemporary television shows may actually help to generate what he calls "just-in-time fandom," by which fans are more deeply drawn into the rhythms of the broadcast schedule so that they can participate in discussions of specific episodes immediately after they air.[22] Thus, digital delivery tools alter the temporal rhythms of media consumption in complex, often unpredictable ways.

"THE VELOCITY OF MOTION PICTURES"

Movie distribution is now characterized by new, more accelerated distribution models in which movies move quickly from theaters (if they play on the big screen at all) to VOD and DVD before landing in DVD remainder bins at big-box stores or, perhaps more likely, archives of videos available for streaming, whether through a subscription service, such as Netflix, or through a pay-per-view option, such as those offered by Mubi.com, Vudu, or Amazon. Charles Acland argues that we should be attentive to "the velocity of motion pictures as they move from screen to screen, format to format, and hence from a cultural circuit of relative exclusivity to other more accessible circuits."[23] These new forms of circulation have produced a number of inconsistencies as users seek out inexpensive alternatives for viewing movies and television shows. The rapid movement of movies through multiple platforms ensures that viewers who are unwilling to pay premium prices to see a movie in the theater may be able to wait just a few months to see the same film via a kiosk or on streaming video. Persistent online availability ultimately diminishes the urgency of seeing a movie on the big screen, particularly if there is no compelling reason to do so. In turn, this persistent availability potentially decreases the value of the film text, providing consumers with less incentive to purchase expensive DVDs or Blu-Rays. Questions of velocity also affect the television industry, as networks and cable channels constantly negotiate when and where audiences can access recent or past episodes of specific shows. The practice of watching off of the normal broadcast schedule, known as time-shifting, profoundly altered how people watch, allowing them to catch up on episodes of shows they may have missed or to binge-watch favorite programs, a practice that becomes almost automatic through Netflix, which now directs users to follow-up episodes of whatever show they happen to be watching through its Post-Play feature. Of course, Netflix simply automates and accelerates a practice that has been available—in some form—since the earliest phase of home video. As Frederick Wasser notes, movie rentals themselves—Wasser is talking about videocassettes, but the same principle applies to digital delivery—also serve as a form of time-shifting, freeing audiences from concerns about limitations on their leisure time.[24] Thus, for both television and film, time-shifting and other forms of on-demand viewing are becoming a crucial means of engagement, even as those processes have intensified in the digital era.

New distribution tools have further altered these dynamics, changing points of access and modes of consumption. DVRs and DVD box sets, for example, allowed users to binge on shows, consuming an entire season's worth of programming in a matter of days or weeks, rather than waiting for reruns. At the same time, streaming services such as Hulu and Netflix allowed the networks to experiment with releasing television shows on the web almost immediately after their original broadcast date rather than waiting for the end of a season or even the end of a show's run before making them available in a systematic way. Such practices potentially further upset the social rituals of viewing television, altering the "water cooler" status of certain popular shows, although this effect is somewhat mitigated by social media tools such as Twitter and check-in services such as GetGlue that reward and encourage live viewing. Thus, digital delivery serves to extend the logic of "product choice" and "time flexibility" that Frederick Wasser associated with videocassettes.[25]

These new flexible forms of digital delivery are also connected to what David Harvey describes as "flexible labor," the idea that employees are expected to work irregular schedules, snatching brief moments of leisure and in many cases taking work home.[26] As Manuel Castells argues, "skilled labor is required to manage its own time in a flexible manner, sometimes adding more work time, at other times adjusting to flexible schedules, in some instances reducing working hours, and thus pay."[27] The notion of flexible labor is reflected in cultural accounts of the multitasker, the individual capable of dividing her attention between two or more tasks, juggling multiple demands. The dispersed workday also leads to a fragmentation of leisure time, contributing to what Max Dawson and Lynn Spigel refer to as "flexible leisure."[28]

In addition to thinking about the temporal shifts in the window system—the speed at which movies circulate across various platforms—I also argue for paying closer attention to the spatial changes associated with digital delivery. In my first book, I began to take note of the ways in which Netflix, Apple, Hulu, and other companies were starting to take advantage of increasing broadband access in order to develop a system for delivering movies and television shows digitally. However, given the global scope of the entertainment industry, it is crucial to recognize the intersections of the local and the global when it comes to digital delivery. This analysis requires careful attention to a variety of political, logistical, and cultural factors that influence how audiences access movies across a range of countries. By comparing different media infrastructures, we can gain a better understanding of how different media economies ensure competition, foster local production, and protect consumers. In addition, looking at local cultures can also provide us with a more thorough understanding of how movies and television shows circulate across borders, especially as companies such as Netflix and Hulu seek to expand beyond U.S. borders, while other companies, such as the streaming service Mubi.com, seek to foster the development of a globalized collective of cinephiles who can access movies while on the go.[29] In addition, those same movie lovers can connect, through blogs and forums, with people who share similar tastes in movies. Thus, film collectives may become defined less by the local multiplex and more by shared interests in a genre or filmmaker.

PLATFORM MOBILITY AND INDIVIDUALIZED CONSUMPTION

In an era of digital media, it's not just texts that circulate. So do screens. The ability to watch television, videos, and movies on the go has become a major selling point of iPhones, iPads, and similar connected mobile devices. However, even though critics have examined the ways in which these new media devices have become associated with the discourses of mobility, less attention has been paid to the ways in which these technologies are also associated with the production of fragmented, often deeply individualized media consumers. As Acland observes, "individualism rules the world of entertainment. The contemporary environment of mobile, hand-held and personalized technological trinkets is a most astounding manifestation of this common sense."[30] This sense of individualism comes across in the structures and practices of mobile devices. Anne Balsamo points to the role of the iPhone in allowing individual users to immerse themselves in the "flow of media," where they can watch movies, make purchases, and even write back, a process that allows for the creation of "a sense of self" pieced together from all of the fragments of this media culture. In turn, these traces can be reflected back to us though directed advertising that often uncannily identifies our interests, our desires, and our previous journeys through a wider media culture.[31]

As a result, these new distribution, circulation, and exhibition tools are not merely changing the ways in which the media industries seek to create new forms of profitability. They also alter the very nature of everyday life. As Steven Shaviro explains it in his discussion of "post-cinematic affect": "Digital technologies, together with neoliberal economic relations, have given birth to radically new ways of manufacturing and articulating lived experience."[32] Shaviro argues that we continue to lack the "vocabulary" to describe the changes that seem to be defining twenty-first-century life. As he points out, one shift is the transition from what Michel Foucault referred to as a disciplinary society to one that is more readily associated with what Gilles Deleuze called a "control society," in which humans are no longer characterized by their visibility through confinement. Instead, control societies are marked by flexibility and by looser networks that allow and even encourage movement. Thus, even while we are granted the experience of free-flowing individualism, our behaviors and movements are constrained by the networks and channels available to us at any given time.[33]

These new forms of mobile, individualized consumption are reinforced throughout entertainment culture, not just through the technologies themselves but also in advertisements for a wide range of mobile devices and digital delivery tools. These advertisements, which often show individual consumers liberated from the constraints of time and space, not only sell the products depicted but also specific modes of liberated consumption. For example, an advertisement for a Verizon 4G phone invites the viewer to "become a high-octane version of you" while a hip young man, head leaning back and looking toward the heavens, seems to imagine the liberating potential of using a Verizon phone. One of the possibilities suggested in the advertisement is the ability to "stream your favorite director's cut without any buffering." Thus, users are congratulated for their good taste in movie consumption—only a true connoisseur would seek out a director's cut—but they are also presented with the idea that platform mobility will open up a wide range of communication options, empowering the user to remain fully engaged even while on the go.

The ability to carry around personalized screens has prompted a number of critics to worry about the decline of public space, producing what conservative columnist George Will referred to as a kind of "social autism."[34] As Anna McCarthy notes, such comments tend to obscure the complexity of how media technologies are used, whether smart phones and iPads or older technologies, such as television sets placed in shopping malls and other semi-public spaces. On the one hand, many of these complaints rely upon nostalgic and idealized notions of public space that often mask "contemptuous" attitudes toward the teenagers, parents with children, and retail employees who work, shop, and congregate in these spaces.[35] On the other hand, mobile devices are often used in spaces where public television screens already exist. Thus, rather than treating platform mobility as symptomatic of a decline in public life, this book argues for a more nuanced understanding of how platform mobility fits into, and in some cases reshapes, the ways in which viewers find, watch, share, and discuss movies and television shows.

Although the intersections between the film industry and the new media are often marked by the rhetoric of novelty and anticipation—the promises of fast, cheap, and ubiquitous content—some users are often reluctant to embrace new technologies, ensuring that the adoptation of these tools is far from seamless. As Lucas Hilderbrand argues, "new media reveal continuities, collaborations, and periods of coexistence as technologies change. New technologies do not necessarily kill media when they upgrade the devices."[36] Thus, in addition to studying the mobile technologies that now seem to have captured the cultural imagination, I also consider older technologies, such as the standard DVD player, that are often taken for granted. In fact, one of the most important "innovations" in home video has been the emergence of Redbox, the rental kiosk system that may, on the surface, appear to be essentially non-technological in that it weds two familiar technologies and practices, video rentals and vending machines. However, Redbox depends upon incredibly fast internet connections to process the thousands of credit card transactions made on any given night.

This project seeks to unpack the technological, social, and economic implications of the shift to digital delivery. As I was writing this book, several of the major studios announced that they would stop producing film prints of their movies and rely exclusively on digital projection. If films have become files, to use Bordwell's evocative phrase, what happens to the place of movie theaters as both social institutions and sites of commerce? If DVDs are supplanted by digital copies stored on a user's hard drive or in the cloud, what happens to the practices of DVD collecting that have been crucial to the profitability of most movies? If movies can be viewed anywhere with an internet connection, what happens to the value of exclusive screening events, such as film festivals? These questions all speak to the shifting definition and value of the film text in the era of media mobility.

CHAPTER SUMMARIES

This book addresses the ongoing conflicts over digital delivery and its role in reshaping the movie and television industries. In particular, it considers the ways in which new delivery systems are caught up in a wider culture of mobility. Although media scholars, including Raymond Williams, Lynn Spigel, and Anne Friedberg, have traced a much longer history of intersections between media and mobility, this book argues that contemporary media platforms actively solicit an individualized, fragmented, and empowered media consumer, one who has greater control over when, where, and how she watches movies and television shows. However, this offer of liberation from the viewing schedule is often accompanied by increased surveillance, giving studios, streaming video services, and social media companies more precise information for their efforts to market directly to those individualized viewers. Thus, one of the implicit goals of this book is to make sense of how the idea of mobility functions in discussions of digital delivery, whether that entails the ability of content to migrate from one platform to another or the physical mobility of consumers who can take their video libraries with them.

Chapter 1, "Coming Soon to a Computer Near You," explores the implications of new models of digital delivery. Tools such as VOD, streaming video, and digital downloads have all been promoted in terms of their ability to provide fast, inexpensive, and ubiquitous access to movies, but the implications of these models for the film industry and consumers are less than clear. In fact, despite the claims about platform mobility, viewers often found themselves unable to access specific titles, as different subscription VOD services sought to compete over streaming rights. At the same time, streaming video prompted consumers to rethink their viewing practices.

The second chapter, "Restricting and Resistant Mobilities," looks at some of the tensions that have emerged over digital delivery by framing those discussions around the question of how content circulates. Although digital delivery has often been promoted as offering unprecedented forms of mobility, users sometimes encounter limitations on how and where they can access content. Many of these issues center on conflicts over digital rights, as distributors seek to create formats that restrict informal practices of sharing that were often legal in the era of physical media such as DVDs and VHS tapes. Thus, this chapter looks at industry efforts to foster digital sales through the UltraViolet initiative, as well as attempts to combat piracy. Finally, the chapter considers how consumers have begun to challenge or work around traditional delivery formats, often by creating highly individualized programming schedules and rejecting expensive cable subscriptions through a process known as cord-cutting. Although cord-cutting remains a relatively uncommon practice, I argue that it represents a cutting-edge practice that may further unsettle traditional delivery models.

The third chapter, "'Make Any Room Your TV Room,'" extends this logic by looking at a series of advertisements for mobile devices to show how they offer the contradictory promise that individualized consumption will enhance family harmony. Drawing from Lynn Spigel's insightful readings of 1950s-era advertisements for television sets, this analysis examines the transition from collective family viewings in front of a shared television screen to a multiplicity of individualized screens. Significantly, almost all of the advertisements for mobile devices show an individual consumer begin to watch a movie on one platform and finish that movie on a second (or even third) device. At the same time, family members are differentiated through social media tools that allow them to develop individualized viewing sites.

Chapter 4, "Breaking through the Screen," builds upon the discourses of media mobility to examine the role of 3D projection in redefining moviegoing as an activity. Although 3D is most frequently discussed in terms of its aesthetics, it can be better understood through its relationship to digital delivery. To be sure, 3D offers an attractive tool for encouraging audiences to view moves in theaters. However, digital delivery also allows us to reconceptualize the film text, turning it into a file that can be altered and updated. These discussions were initially framed by the popular debates about James Cameron's 2009 film *Avatar,* which became both a critical and box office success and spurred other studios to plan 3D movies. As these discussions spilled out into Hollywood trade publications and newspaper editorial pages, Cameron's film invited speculation about the future of film narrative. In addition, this chapter will address industry rhetoric that has framed 3D as an economic and financial success by considering how figures such as Cameron became defined as techno-auteurs who manage to tell compelling stories while also revolutionizing movies as a medium, thus reworking more traditional concepts of the auteur in film scholarship. Furthermore, Cameron's status as someone engaged in creating idealized movie experiences served to promote 3D television, thus reinforcing narratives of technological revolution.

The fifth chapter, "Redbox vs. Red Envelope," examines the initial industry reaction to the DVD kiosk company and its role in reshaping the DVD distribution business, even while contributing to the ongoing devaluation of home video. Unlike Netflix, which has become the paradigmatic "long tail" distributor, Redbox typically offers a limited selection of top hits, and most kiosks hold approximately six hundred DVDs, rather than the thousands available via Netflix. Redbox's rapid growth in 2009 and 2010 confounded industry insiders, and it was perceived as a potential threat to the normal DVD revenue streams sought by Hollywood studios. It also challenges arguments about the value of owning a film text (or even access to that film text). In this sense, Redbox seems to offer a corrective to arguments that we are inevitably moving completely away from physical media.

Digital delivery has affected more than how we watch movies. It also influences how we promote, discuss, and share them. Thus, chapter 6 extends the focus on digital delivery by examining the ways in which social media have been used to promote and discuss movies. On the one hand, Twitter, Facebook, and other social media websites allow users to engage in conversations about movies they love; on the other, social check-in services, such as GetGlue, build upon the discourses of media mobility to encourage users to imagine themselves as a global moviegoing audience. This active, energized audience is often eager to participate in the marketing of movies to a wider audience, usually for free, allowing them a much greater sense of participation in the entertainment industry.

The following two chapters bring together these questions about digital delivery and social media to look at how these phenomena have shaped independent filmmaking. Digital delivery has proven especially troubling for indie filmmakers, due to declining DVD sales and to a far more uncertain and competitive theatrical distribution system. Chapter 7, "Indie 2.0" examines how discourses of "independence" have been transformed by the emergence of digital distribution. In particular, this chapter focuses on how independent filmmakers have begun tapping into the energies of socially networked movie fans, many of whom have expressed willingness to support projects and filmmakers they admire. This inclination has led to a dramatic rise in the practices of crowdsourcing, by which audiences contribute their talents to the production or promotion of a film, and crowdfunding, through which audiences make donations to support the production of a film. I will consider a range of case studies, including Kevin Smith's *Red State*, Nina Paley's *Sita Sings the Blues*, and Franny Armstrong's *Age of Stupid*, to argue that the practices of creating or participating in new distribution models bring about new relationships between producers and consumers.

The final chapter, "Reinventing Festivals," addresses the transformed role of the film festival in promoting independent and documentary films. Beginning in 2009 at the Tribeca, Sundance, and South by Southwest film festivals, filmmakers increasingly made their content available online through streaming video or on VOD, often while the festivals were still taking place. The creation of a "virtual" festival that existed alongside the physical festival complicates the sense of exclusivity typically associated with seeing movies at these events but is consistent with festival organizers' desires to produce audiences who are aware of the latest movies. In addition, these online festivals contribute to what Charles Acland has described as the "felt internationalism" of the global movie-consuming audience, as users interact with each other through social media in order to share reactions to films as soon as they hit the screen, whether big or small.[37] More crucially, these endeavors help to support the illusion that digital delivery is expanding consumer choice. In fact, rather than expanding our movie consumption options, these festival platforms arguably merely accelerate the distribution schedule, increasing the "velocity" at which movies circulate and collapsing the traditional distribution windows that independent and low-budget films typically followed.

The arguments in this book reflect my own ambivalence about the ways in which digital delivery has altered the media industries. I am conscious of the ways in which discourses of media mobility have contributed to new modes of watching, using, and engaging with movies and television shows, and these changes may have significant implications for social and political life. As Acland observes, "the organization of how, when, and under what conditions people congregate is a fundamental dimension of social life."[38] These questions are especially urgent in the era of platform mobility, when the practices and economics of watching or buying a movie are in the process of being redefined.

1 ▶ COMING SOON TO A COMPUTER NEAR YOU

Digital Delivery and Ubiquitous Entertainment

IN AN INTERVIEW discussing the closure of all of the Blockbuster Video stores in Canada, Kaan Yigit, president of Solutions Research Group, commented that "this is the Netflix decade for movies. Kids growing up will hardly ever know there was a time you actually went to a store to get a movie."[1] Yigit's comments underscored the perceived mobility of movies and television shows across a variety of platforms and devices, a shift that seemed to make trips to the video store unnecessary. These changes in film distribution—formerly associated with physical copies of DVDs sold at big-box retailers or rented from local video stores—have altered not only the economics of the movie industry but also the perceived value of movies themselves, creating even deeper interconnections between the movie industry and digital hubs such as Apple, Amazon, Netflix, and Facebook. At the same time, the role of retailers such as Walmart, Target, and Best Buy is changing dramatically. Rather than just selling physical media, Walmart has been making a gradual effort to position itself in the digital marketplace, both through its digital delivery service, Vudu, and its participation in a cloud-based movie storage service, UltraViolet. Yet, even though the electronics and entertainment industries have made significant efforts to promote digital delivery, the persistence of the DVD as a format cannot be underestimated. As of 2011, 92 million homes continued to have at least one DVD or Blu-Ray player, with two-thirds of those homes having more than one. Another 46 million homes had video game consoles that could play DVDs. Finally, digital delivery accounted for only 13 percent of home video spending in 2010, suggesting that physical media remain a preferred way for people to watch movies.[2]

What has changed is the perceived concept and value of the textual artifact, whether that is a movie or television show. This shift in perspective is shaped by the increased mobility associated with digital delivery and the speed with which texts now circulate (or in some cases fail to circulate) across digital platforms. In this sense, platform mobility alters not only the economics of the film industry but also the practices of consumers seeking a few minutes' entertainment.

This chapter explores the ways in which digital delivery reworks traditional models of distribution. Any account that seeks to explain these transitions comes up against a number of terminological difficulties. Although it would be tempting to describe digital movie delivery as "post-theatrical," the use of day-and-date distribution, in which movies are released simultaneously in theaters, on DVD, and through video-on-demand (VOD), complicates any strict distribution timeline. More crucially, the timing and location of distribution is altered, as trips to the video store or movie theater are replaced by a variety of delivery mechanisms that allow users to purchase or rent movies anytime and anywhere, producing new forms of audience mobility. However, even while digital delivery services offer promises of ubiquitous access, there are a number of significant limits that constrain when and where users can watch movies. Thus, while this chapter surveys the variety of formats and distribution patterns that have emerged in the era of digital delivery, I am also conscious of the degree to which new delivery models may not fulfill every promise of access, convenience, and affordability. In addition, I am attentive to the fact that digital delivery is not an entirely new practice. Although it has become more viable thanks to increasingly fast broadband, the widespread acceptance of platform mobility is the result not merely of technological factors but also of cultural changes.

These changes are most commonly associated with a transformed infrastructure, in which the internet has become a site for renting, purchasing, and downloading movies, often for instantaneous viewing. These distribution practices came to include a range of methods—streaming video, digital downloads, electronic sell-through (EST), and VOD—and many services also offered "digital lockers" that would allow customers to store movies in the cloud, so that they would no longer have to worry about losing a physical copy or about seeing an older format sink into obsolescence. These services have been affiliated with a wide range of online retailers, video sharing sites, and social networking hubs, as well as being available as applications through mobile devices such as cell phones and iPads. As a result, users' modes of access have changed considerably, moving from a relatively stable domestic, post-theatrical distribution system associated with physical media—whether VHS tapes or DVDs—to one that is marked by profound uncertainty and unpredictability. In addition to delivering movies and television shows in a wide range of formats, digital delivery systems also experimented with a number of different pricing models, illustrating even further uncertainty about how users would access entertainment. While movie studios continued to encourage consumers to pay for permanent ownership of a movie or television show—whether on a physical format or in a digital locker—consumers generally opted to pay for temporary access to a movie through rental or subscription services, often known as subscription video-on-demand (SVOD). They were far less likely to purchase DVDs or any other form of physical media. As a result, many distributors, especially television networks, sought to create artificial or temporary forms of scarcity that would increase demand for purchasing media products by making television shows or movies temporarily unavailable.

This chapter looks at a wide range of movie distribution practices, beginning with pay-per-view movies through cable television and some of the early experiments with digital delivery through internet-based services such as DivX and MovieFlix. Although many of these early initiatives failed, they help to illustrate Hollywood's earliest attempts to reach busy consumers at home, even while the studios sought to retain control over the amount of time users might have to watch a given movie, which might, in turn, help them to control the degree to which those movies might be shared. I then focus on the current digital delivery ecosystem, which continues to be marked by instability and experimentation, especially given that the interests of the studios and the interests of content aggregators, such as Netflix, Amazon, and Hulu, may not be aligned. Thus, rather than a singular "celestial jukebox," to use Chris Anderson's formulation, we have a series of discrete streaming megaplexes, which for the most part offer only incomplete access to the full catalog of movie and television titles. At the same time, these industry changes often take place with such rapidity that it is difficult to document them. Thus, this chapter attempts to make sense of some of the key strategies that have been used to transition from physical media such as DVDs to digital delivery systems ranging from streaming video to electronic sell-through. Instead of a single dominant platform, we are witnessing the proliferation of platforms, devices, and strategies, so that the landscape of digital delivery remains far from settled.

These changes can be measured by the flow of traffic online and the debates over bandwidth between cable services such as Comcast and video rental services such as Netflix, which became one of the most significant sources of bandwidth use on the internet. In fact, by March 2011, Netflix was regarded as the largest source of internet traffic in the United States, accounting for 29.7 percent of all peak downstream traffic, while similar sites like BitTorrent and YouTube used 10.4 percent and 11 percent, respectively. Overall, real-time entertainment, which includes both streaming video and streaming music options, constituted nearly half of all downstream traffic, while web surfing accounted for only

17 percent.[3] In this sense, digital media provided a persistent form of flexible entertainment.

In discussions of these services, they are frequently described in terms of their ability to break the barriers of geographic tyranny, providing audiences with new forms of access to films they normally wouldn't see. In a *New York Times* article on the Independent Film Channel's (IFC) decision to distribute Hong Kong action director Johnnie To's *Vengeance* (2009), for example, the IFC on-demand service is depicted as a means of allowing movie buffs to discover new talents: "a new conduit is opening for Mr. To and other foreign and independent directors who struggle to have their work seen in theaters in the United States outside of urban centers such as New York and Los Angeles."[4] Similarly, the origin story for the streaming movie site and social network Mubi (formerly The Auteurs) emphasizes the inability to access quality movies online legally. Mubi founder Efe Cakarel frequently reports in interviews that he realized the need for Mubi when he was unable to track down a version of Wong Kar-Wai's *In the Mood for Love* (2000) to fill the time during a long layover at the Tokyo airport.[5] In both cases, films are characterized as increasingly mobile and audiences as becoming more cosmopolitan, seeking access to a wide range of entertainment, often while in transit from one location to another.

At the same time, there is widespread debate within the industry about how much audiences are willing to pay for entertainment. Although Chris Anderson's concept of the "long tail" is based on the idea of unlimited shelf space and virtually frictionless forms of distribution, it quickly became evident that bandwidth and other costs—including the initial production costs of making a movie or television show—made digital delivery far more complex than it might have initially appeared. In addition, competition over rights often determines what content might be available at a given time, as content producers seek to maximize the value of their movies and television series. Thus, although digital delivery seemed to hold out the promise of unlimited choice, audiences were often confronted with the difficulty of navigating a frequently changing menu of choices as movies and television shows migrate from one platform or service to another.

In one of his characteristically blunt industry analyses, David Poland tracks not only the proliferation of hardware but also the shifting grounds associated with software—the television and movie content that viewers are now encouraged to purchase. As Poland points out, streaming rights can expire at sites such as Netflix, often without warning, making it difficult to keep up with what is available and what isn't, changes that complicate the anything, anytime, anywhere promises associated with long tail marketing. In fact, these "access problems" inspired the creation of the website Instawatcher to track literally hundreds of Netflix titles that are due to expire.[6] The site allows users to search for specific titles and even alerts visitors to some of Netflix's most popular current titles. The implied point of Instawatcher is that our access to streaming versions of movies may be contingent and temporary rather than permanent. This impermanency leaves Poland to conclude, with a characteristic stab at fantasies of ubiquity: "How much anything/anywhere is enough? When does everyone who is not in puberty get to too much/too many places?"[7]

Poland's arguments about the complications associated with digital delivery would only be reinforced in September 2011, when Starz announced that it would no longer provide streaming rights for movies and television shows to Netflix, cutting deeply into its streaming catalog at precisely the moment the service instituted significant price increases for monthly subscriptions. Although Netflix had historically been marketed and discussed in terms of its ability to offer a wide selection of content at a comparatively low price, by September 2011 the company could offer very little streaming content from the major studios, requiring customers to pay for a significantly more expensive DVD-and-streaming subscription if they wanted to see films made by Universal, Fox, Warner Bros., Disney, and Sony, as well as Dreamworks films made after 2010.[8] Although Netflix's access to streaming rights eventually changed, the end of the Starz deal illustrates the degree to which SVOD catalogs are contingent and often somewhat more limited than video stores, especially when it comes to new releases, a situation that often makes it difficult to find legal versions of streaming titles.

HISTORIES OF MEDIA MOBILITY

Although digital delivery has been treated in the entertainment press as a new phenomenon, it is important to consider the longer history of pay-per-view (PPV) entertainment, whether that content was delivered through cable television services or online. As Janet Wasko notes, subscription television services were approved in 1968 by the Federal Communications Commission and began operating in the 1970s, garnering 1.7 million subscribers by 1984. By the mid-1980s, subscribers could watch programs on PPV, permitting them to pay for specific programs, particularly event screenings such as boxing matches, concerts, and Wrestlemania events. This programming proved incredibly lucrative for cable companies, earning them $2.5 billion in 2002 alone. Movie studios made extensive use of PPV, recognizing it as a viable alternative to rentals at a video store because it allowed consumers to access and purchase movies without leaving home. In fact, as Wasko notes, a special PPV screening of *Star Wars* drew in 1.5 million consumers who paid $8 per television set to watch the movie, although premium events like Wrestlemania could cost as much as $49.99.[9] The primary limitation to PPV was that broadcasters would show the movie or television episode at the same time to everyone who ordered it, unscrambling the channel only after the content was purchased and thus making it difficult for viewers to watch at their own convenience, which is what made live events more attractive to cable companies.

One of the most prominent early attempts at digital movie delivery was the use of Digital Video Express (DivX), a studio initiative by which customers would pay US $4 to purchase a DivX title on a disc programmed to be viewable for up to forty-eight hours, approximately the same cost as a rental at a bricks-and-mortar video store. The user could call to pay an additional amount for the right to view the film for two more days. Finally, users could also arrange for an unlimited number of views by paying another fee, creating what Paul McDonald referred to as a "peculiar hybrid of sell-through and rental video models."[10] The service launched in 1998, primarily through the electronics chain Circuit City, with initial tests in Richmond and San Francisco, and within less than a year 87,000 DivX capable players were sold, with approximately 400 titles available through the service.

Like other future services, such as Netflix and Redbox, DivX was marketed as an alternative for movie viewers who did not have time to stop at video stores to return movies. The "expiration date" allowed users to let their right to access a film terminate rather than having to pay for late fees, and they could dispose of used discs after they were done with them rather than returning them to a store. However, the format also introduced a number of other limitations. For example, DivX discs did not contain the extras that were popular with many consumers of DVDs, so that users had only a limited form of interactivity with the disc itself. More crucially, as McDonald points out, the system was essentially "closed." That is, DivX discs could not be played on standard DVD players, and the hardware costs for DivX players were substantially higher than those for DVD players. Thus, as McDonald concludes, "without the added features or widescreen presentation, DivX actually seemed like DVD only less. DivX offered copyright holders such as the Hollywood majors greater control over video consumption but it was precisely that control which consumers rejected."[11]

This conflict over DivX is instructive in that it anticipates more recent experiments in digital delivery. As McDonald notes, the temporary viewing window gave studios far greater control over the circulation of their content, allowing them to circumvent some of the problems they had faced with video piracy and with what he calls "ownership issues caused by the first sale doctrine."[12] Because the "first sale doctrine" entitles people to sell or share physical media, purchasers of books, CDs, and DVDs can resell those texts or loan them to others. Formats such as DivX disrupted that practice by permitting only a single user to watch a movie. Further, given that studios controlled the distribution pipeline, they could easily take films out of circulation. Many of these problems have resurfaced in the era of digital delivery, as customers have begun to use models that allow temporary access—video-on-demand, streaming video—rather than paying for enduring ownership rights, whether through a physical copy or through a "copy" of the film stored in the cloud, although these protections might be circumvented if, for example, college roommates or parents and children were to share passwords for their subscriptions.

Ultimately, these early attempts at marketing the digital delivery of movies and television shows helped to establish many of the practices that are still in place. Wasko documents a number of independent sites that experimented with digital delivery, most notably SightSound Technologies and MovieFlix. SightSound began operating in 1999, and by January 2001 it was offering a limited selection of movies produced by independents, including Miramax, with the company offering downloads of Miramax's *Guinevere* for $3.49 for a twenty-four-hour viewing window. However, by 2001 SightSound was struggling to stay in business. MovieFlix, by contrast, worked on a subscription basis, charging $5.95 per month for access to a small catalog of independent and public-domain films. Thus, MovieFlix anticipated the Netflix model of monthly subscriptions and also encountered the challenges that companies such as Netflix face when it comes to securing rights to streaming or downloaded content.[13]

Other early services included CinemaNow, which was owned by Lionsgate and continues to operate as Best Buy's online distribution service. When it first launched in June 2001, users could access streaming movies for $2.99 for a two-day window. Like MovieFlix, CinemaNow initially offered a relatively limited catalog of approximately 1,200 films.[14] One of the most influential models was Movielink, a pay-per-rental service formed and owned by Sony Pictures Entertainment, Universal Studios, Paramount Pictures, MGM, and Warner. Users could download movies for prices ranging from $1.99 to $4.99 and could watch the movies as often as they liked over the course of a twenty-four-hour window. After purchase, the movies would be available on the customer's computer hard drive for thirty days before being automatically deleted if they went unwatched. Although studios were involved in the launch, the service initially offered only 170 titles.[15] Despite these limitations, the service did anticipate one potential "future" for digital delivery, the possibility of direct sales from the studios to consumers, an approach used by Apple's iTunes store, Amazon, and Vudu, among others. However, Movielink faced a number of technological and ideological barriers. Most notable were a number of compatibility issues. Movies could play only on Intel-based PCs running Windows 2000 or later and Windows Media Player, thus limiting the service's consumer base considerably. The service was eventually purchased by Blockbuster Video, which sought to take control of what was then one of the largest online libraries of Hollywood films. But Blockbuster shut down Movielink in 2008, and as of July 2012 the domain redirects potential customers to Blockbuster's streaming video service.

These examples show that digital delivery is not an entirely new phenomenon. In fact, it had been technologically feasible, at least on a limited scale, by the late 1990s. However, many of these services struggled until the emergence of Apple's iTunes and Netflix, suggesting that new technologies and formats may be adapted only fitfully and gradually and that the development of new distribution tools does not guarantee that they will be accepted until a cultural need for them emerges.

CABLE TELEVISION

The debates about new platforms have played a role in the reception of earlier media as well, especially when familiar media, such as film and television, are repackaged into new delivery formats. Even though "repackaging" can provide new modes of access—think of the role of DVD extras in fostering the growth of an informed, educated film audience—consumers often resist these new formats, especially when they upset traditional perceptions of the value of a text or medium. This reluctance extended to cable television when it was first introduced and popularized. As John McMurria argues, consumers were less than uniform in their acceptance of cable, noting that "the prospect of having to pay for television programs was not universally embraced."[16] Not surprisingly, when the concept of pay television was introduced in the mid-1950s, some of its most vocal opponents were movie theater owners, who had already been stung by the challenges raised by suburban sprawl and broadcast television. At the same time, network television executives expressed concerns about increased competition. However, as McMurria also notes, promoters of cable television initially argued that pay television would serve a cultural good, providing access to quality programming, whether public lectures or symphonic music, in much the same way that advocates of the digital delivery of movies and television shows have argued that it will increase choice and opportunities to access niche content.[17] Such claims ultimately proved difficult to sustain, especially given that many cable channels were purchased by the broadcast networks themselves; at the same time, many cable channels focused on obtaining cheap programming to fill broadcast time, leaving many of the public service promises unfulfilled.

But the rise of cable television, along with the growth of video distribution in the 1980s, set the stage for the vast increase in the value of film libraries. As Jennifer Holt points out, several studios had unwisely sold off the negatives of many of their films in the 1950s, failing to anticipate their eventual value. Paramount, for example sold 750 films for $50 million to MCA in 1958, while Warner sold the rights to more than 700 films to United Artists for just $30 million.[18] In some limited cases, studios even allowed rights to certain films to expire, thus permitting them to fall into the public domain, including Howard Hawks's screwball comedy classic *His Girl Friday* and Frank Capra's Christmas fable *It's a Wonderful Life.*[19] With the rise of cable television and video distribution, these libraries were transformed into the source of significant profits for major studios. Their value was reflected in the frenzy of media mergers and acquisitions in the 1980s and 1990s, when cable channels gobbled up the broadcast rights to studio libraries, such as Ted Turner's high-profile purchase of the MGM library in the 1980s. Soon after, in 1993, Turner purchased independents New Line and Castle Rock Entertainment, allowing him to broadcast their content on his many cable channels, including TNT, TBS, and TCM. Later, the joining of Time Warner and Turner in 1996 created what Holt describes as "an unprecedented merging of media assets spanning film, cable, broadcast, music, publishing, sports, and journalism."[20] As a result, Holt concludes, cable television in the 1980s and 1990s became the film industry's most predominant "archivist," storing films and classic television series and controlling their broadcast rights.[21] In some cases, these "archives" even allowed older movies to be rediscovered, thanks to repeat broadcasts on channels such as TCM and AMC, gaining them greater attention than they might have received from a DVD re-release.

More recently, many digital delivery services have begun imitating and even competing with cable television in terms of how they obtain and manage rights to films and television shows. Netflix seemed to be challenging industry norms when it acquired syndication rights to shows such as AMC's critically acclaimed drama *Mad Men*, with the first four seasons of the show becoming available in July 2011, a deal that followed up the acquisition of exclusive syndication rights for the show in Canada.[22] In fact, Netflix CEO Reed Hastings frequently compared Netflix's practices with cable television, and even suggested that his primary competition was not another streaming service but HBO, especially the premium channel's mobile service, HBO Go.[23] Given that Netflix emulated the practices of cable channels in acquiring content for redistribution, Hastings's comparison was not entirely inaccurate, especially given the company's aspirations to produce and program original content. In this sense, the movement toward streaming television content also reflects past models of television distribution, that is, the role of re-runs and syndication in shaping the temporal flow of television broadcasting, even as streaming alters the primary location where the distribution takes place.[24] As a result, although online libraries such as Netflix and Hulu may provide users with access to numerous titles, they also potentially change the distribution timing of many prominent television shows and movies in complex ways, in part by altering the speed with which content is made available for repeat or catch-up viewing.

To some extent, these changes were anticipated by practices associated with cable television. Perhaps the most significant shift was the role of the digital video recorder (DVR) in enabling viewers to arrest and redirect the flow of shows they might have missed for subsequent viewing, often while zapping through commercials. Even though this potential for time shifting was available for VCR users, DVRs enhanced the ability to play back and store programming, making it easier for viewers to engage in more intense analysis of a specific show, a practice that became commonplace with puzzle shows such as *Lost*.[25] Further, as Derek Kompare argued in his discussion of television box sets, drawing from Raymond Williams's famous argument about television as flow, the DVD box set of a television series served as a means of "packaging flow," in that viewers could use DVDs to go back and watch shows consecutively, often within weeks after a show's season had ended or just in time for a new season to begin. Such practices seemingly provided viewers with far greater control over their limited leisure time. In fact, as Shawn Shimpach noted, these new storage formats turned television from a form associated with "temporal scarcity" into one that allowed viewers to invest more time and attention in their favorite shows and movies.[26]

These new distribution models arguably help to shape the kinds of narratives available to producers, allowing for more intensive forms of viewing by creating shows that encourage, if not require, repeat viewings in order to grasp all of the plot nuances. In addition, television viewers who encounter a program several episodes or seasons after it has already begun can easily catch up on past episodes in sequence. Thus, while Netflix and Hulu may be altering when and where content can be found, their practice of acquiring streaming rights to recent television shows is consistent with older industry strategies, such as reruns and syndication, even while creating interfaces that allowed menu-driven interactivity by which users, rather than flipping channels, can "flip through" menus of options via VOD, subscription-based services, or even EST options.

STREAMING MULTIPLEXES

As digital delivery became a viable option for studios and consumers, there were a number of attempts to distribute movies and television shows through online channels and on a variety of platforms and devices. As a result, connected viewing built upon a variety of technological, social, and legal factors, each with unique characteristics that addressed specific kind of viewers. Rather than a singular, universal viewer, platform mobility addressed highly individualized viewers who could personalize when and where they watch. The most dominant player in the subscription marketplace was Netflix, which could boast 24 million U.S. memberships in June 2012 and approximately 26 million worldwide, making it the leading VOD service, despite complaints about a lack of popular movies available in its streaming catalog.[27] Although Netflix received the most attention, other services also sought to become involved in distribution. Apple, for example, rented movies and television shows through its iTunes store starting in January 2008 and followed up by selling movies beginning in March 2009. Alongside of Apple and Netflix, gaming systems also opened up markets for selling movies. In fact, Microsoft sold movies through its Xbox 360 gaming platform, and Sony had more modest sales through the PS3. In addition to gaming systems, consumers could use internet-connected set-top boxes that offered a variety of subscription-based and even free streaming services, including Hulu, which also had a premium subscription service, SnagFilms, and Crackle, which offered movies and television shows for free if users were willing to sit through a small number of advertisements. These ad-supported services provided comparatively inexpensive access to movies and television shows, even if their catalogs were somewhat limited. Crackle, for example, gained attention by obtaining streaming rights to a small number of older television shows, including *Seinfeld* and *227*, and a limited selection of movies.

Although a small number of leading players dominated the VOD market, other companies sought to identify niches where they could profit from the possibilities associated with online video. One example of this form of streaming media was YouTube, which has gradually evolved from a website primarily identified with postings by amateur users into a site that offers a mix of professional and amateur content. In 2008 YouTube launched its "Screening Room," a channel devoted to promoting independent and low-budget films. The Screening Room showed eight new independent short films every month for free, with filmmakers getting a small cut of the advertising revenue generated by banner and sidebar ads on the film's YouTube page. This initiative allowed YouTube to continue to define itself as a champion of independent content while also potentially attracting a niche audience of independent film fans willing to invest a short amount of time in a lesser-known movie. The Screening Room's debut was headlined by *Are You the Favorite Person of Anybody?*, which was written by performance artist Miranda July and directed by Miguel Arteta (best known for the independent film *Chuck and Buck*). The film had previously appeared in 2006 in Wholphin DVD Magazine. The debut also featured a range of award-winning short films, including Torill Kove's *The Danish Poet*, which had been nominated for an Oscar for best Animated Short.[28]

Also in 2008, YouTube created its own video rental service, initially signing a contract with Lionsgate for streaming rights to a number of that company's films, including the *Saw* franchise and *Dirty Dancing*, as well as television shows such as *Weeds*.[29] The initial agreement relied upon the existing YouTube advertiser model, in which the service and the studio would share a cut of advertising revenue generated by page views. Later, that approach evolved into a pay-per-view model in which users would pay for temporary streaming access, an a la carte model that was not unlike a movie rental, but with the convenience of downloading the movie straight to a computer. YouTube also partnered with several major film festivals, including Sundance, to distribute movies and, in some cases, live concerts and panels associated with the events. By June 2012, YouTube had struck deals with a number of studios, including Paramount, providing the website with nearly 9,000 titles available for rental. These changes ultimately turned YouTube and its parent company, Google, more explicitly into distributors of professional media content, even while the streaming video company retained its reputation as a service primarily associated with short, "bite-sized" entertainment produced by both amateurs and professionals.[30] More crucially, this evolution illustrated that YouTube and Google had largely resolved the conflicts over the presence of copyrighted material on their site. In particular, Paramount's parent company, Viacom, had a longstanding $1 billion lawsuit against YouTube alleging copyright infringement due to clips—many of them featured in remixes and mashups—containing scenes from Paramount movies. But with the deal, Paramount joined Sony Pictures Entertainment, Warner Bros., Universal Pictures, and Walt Disney Studios in selling or renting movies through YouTube.[31]

Like YouTube, online retailer Amazon pursued a similar hybrid VOD and EST approach, creating a tiered system that provided users with a variety of options to rent or purchase immediate access to a relatively small selection of titles (approximately 5,000 as of February 2011, and 9,000 by August 2011).[32] Amazon customers could choose from one of three options. First, they could purchase a three-day rental of a streaming video for $3.99, approximately the same cost as renting the movie from a bricks-and-mortar video store or a kiosk such as Redbox. Alternatively, they could purchase a download of that same movie for $12, with small surcharges for watching the content in high-definition (HD) formats. Finally, Amazon offered a subscription service that would entitle any consumer who purchased an Amazon Prime account (other than the free accounts given to students) to unlimited rentals. As with other streaming services, the consumer could access the movie on a variety of platforms, including computers and mobile devices. The Amazon Prime service was created, in part, to encourage users to purchase directly from Amazon rather than their third-party sellers and showed that in some cases digital delivery of movies could be used as an enticement to purchase other goods or services. But the Amazon Prime subscription service, like other forms of digital delivery was constrained by legal limitations, in that the service was unavailable to Amazon customers living outside the United States, reinforcing the role of geo-blocking in curtailing access to certain forms of content.[33]

In January 2011, in order to reach markets outside the United States, Amazon purchased the European video rental service LoveFilm, which operates in several European countries, including the United Kingdom, Germany, Sweden, Norway, and Denmark. Like Netflix, the subscription service offers a combination of DVDs by mail and streaming video and maintains a deep catalog of films and television shows, with more than 70,000 physical DVD and Blu-Ray titles and 7,500 streaming videos available. Further, like Netflix, LoveFilm appeals to the discourses of platform mobility, allowing users to watch on their computers as well as through their Playstation3 game consoles. At the time of purchase, the service had more than 1.6 million online customers and partnerships with a number of studios, including MGM, Warner Bros., and Disney. LoveFilm also allowed non-members to rent new releases for prices ranging from £2.49 to £3.49. This wide variety of choice, in terms of both the selection of films and the locations where they could be viewed, led Dan Sabbagh to reinforce one of the more popular metaphors for digital delivery, as he enthused that LoveFilm "turns every home into a multiplex."[34]

Even Walmart, the world's largest retailer of physical DVDs, opted to invest in the digital delivery of movies by purchasing the online movie site Vudu. Although one journalist characterized Walmart as the "largest distrib outlet in the film biz," lagging DVD sales forced the company to reconsider its practice of selling DVDs as a "loss leader" in order to draw consumers into stores to make more expensive purchases.[35] The Vudu player allowed users to rent or buy digital downloads, with rentals typically costing around $3.99, depending on the rental window, and purchases of new movies usually costing about $15.99. Like Amazon, Vudu also offered users the opportunity to watch movies in a variety of formats, including HD, either on a computer or on a television set, providing many of the same mobile features associated with other players. Users could also choose a number of search options, including rating, format, and genre, as well as studio and even language. Viewers were given some limited choice in terms of the length of the rental window, ranging from twenty-four hours to one week, although most films were available for a two-day window. Walmart ultimately managed to capture a significant share of the streaming market. Less than a year after it purchased Vudu, it became the third-largest online video store, with a 5.3 percent share of the movie download business. That number placed it well behind Apple's iTunes, which continued to dominate the business with a 65.8 percent share, but it was ahead of other competitors, including Amazon and Sony's Playstation Store. Walmart benefited strongly from Vudu's existing distribution deals with a number of major studios, which obviated the need to negotiate new deals.[36] Eventually Vudu also became a key player in the studio initiative UltraViolet, which sought to encourage consumers to purchase digital copies of new movies that could be stored in the cloud and watched through a variety of devices.

Google, Amazon, and Walmart joined a number of new media companies, including Apple, Facebook, and Netflix, in reshaping the networks through which media content is delivered. As a number of critics have observed, these changes dramatically altered the Hollywood economy. The variety of distribution practices also underscored the fact that there would likely be no single delivery model that would dominate the home and mobile markets, leading to complications in how movies are distributed and exhibited. However, the more crucial shift entailed alterations in viewing practices. Most notably, users were far less likely to purchase copies of films or television shows for home collections, whether physical or digital, choosing instead to pay for temporary access for a single viewing, whether through a subscription or an on-demand service. In this sense, the various streaming and on-demand catalogs became a kind of shared collection that could be accessed, albeit only in limited circumstances. This notion contributed to a significant alteration in the perceived value of a film text, given that it became increasingly difficult for studios to market DVDs or to sell upgrades to the Blu-Ray format, despite promises of a better image. By extension, movie watching became a more informal practice, one that required even less commitment than renting a title from a bricks-and-mortar store. In all cases, streaming, VOD, and EST did not simply change how movies were purchased or rented; instead, they changed the perception of the film and television text and altered the behaviors of consumers and the business practices of the industry itself.

ONLINE CINEPHILIA

As some of my examples suggest, digital delivery considerably alters how, when, and where we access movies. Given the complications raised by digital rights and the lack of certainty that content would be available, film fans were often faced with significant challenges when it came to tracking down specific titles. These challenges were especially acute for cinephiles who sought out older movies, international art films, and documentaries. Often there were sudden shifts in where users could find content. This problem was powerfully illustrated when the popular DVD distributor Criterion abruptly ended its contract with the streaming site Mubi.com in order to provide its movies through the streaming service Hulu, which was then owned by NBC Universal, News Corp., and Disney. Hulu had established a solid reputation as an over-the-top subscription service offering on-demand programming supported, in some cases, by limited commercial interruptions. The company was most commonly associated with its catalog of recent episodes of current television shows, including *30 Rock*, *The Office*, and *Saturday Night Live*. The latter show, in particular, benefited from web distribution, given that users could often catch individual segments rather than watch the entire show, a practice that allowed *SNL* to revitalize itself as a site of pointed, often humorous political commentary, especially during the 2008 election, when Tina Fey impersonated Republican vice presidential candidate Sarah Palin.[37] Thus, the decision to purchase Criterion's catalog came as a significant surprise.

In February 2011 Hulu acquired streaming rights to more than 800 Criterion titles, of which 150 were made available to Hulu Plus subscribers almost immediately, with about 800 total planned to be available within a few months.[38] Meanwhile, non-subscribers were able to see a narrower selection of titles through Hulu's free service. But this deal, negotiated by a delivery system typically associated with television content and disruptive advertisements, seemed designed to entice cinephiles away from Netflix. The deal between Hulu and Criterion was exclusive, which meant that Netflix would no longer be able to stream these titles, thus altering Netflix's reputation as a primary source of canonical cinema and setting the stage for ongoing complaints about Netflix's streaming catalog.[39] This type of deal suggests that, despite claims about a giant celestial megaplex in the computing cloud, in which we will have comparatively easy access to the history of film, what we will have instead is something closer to a range of competing miniplexes, each with access to a limited range of content, with frequently changing marquees depending on what content is available at what price at any given time. Even after signing the Hulu deal, Criterion continued to emphasize DVDs as its "core business," rooted in the company's history of producing collectible artifacts, whether DVDs or laser discs.[40] At the same time, the Hulu deal was promoted as a means of expanding the archive by using digital storage to make it feasible for Criterion to offer films that had been too expensive to market as DVDs, making the deal even more appealing for internet cinephiles.

Unlike other content on Hulu, the Criterion films are not interrupted by advertising. As Matt Singer at the IFC blog surmised, Criterion's standards for streaming quality were very high, an expectation that would further promote Hulu as a service dedicated to quality cinema.[41] Hulu also made some of Criterion's popular supplemental features available online, something that typically had not been available through other VOD services. Responding to the announcement, David Poland suggested that Netflix had overreached in its pursuit of television shows and movies from major studios, paying too much for content that is likely to age quickly rather than focusing on content that would engage art-house fans. Poland added that there is little "customer loyalty" online, which means that people will migrate to content they desire rather than remain attached to a specific platform, such as Netflix, Hulu, or Redbox. However, despite these concerns about "loyalty," Netflix retained a large subscriber base.[42] Still, Poland's comments help to illustrate some of the challenges related to the flexible distribution models that movie fans would now be forced to negotiate. Although Netflix has often been seen as a dominant player in the era of digital delivery, deals such as the one between Hulu and Criterion show that no single platform or delivery system is guaranteed to control the market or even to retain an association with specific types of movies or television shows. At the same time, although Netflix initially stood out as a service associated with vast selection and convenience, this reputation was subject to change, given the degree to which content circulates among different platforms.

Thus, one of the more significant aspects of this deal is the degree to which it alters Hulu's place in the digital distribution ecosystem, changing it from a service primarily defined by its television holdings to one that is at least somewhat focused on fostering (and profiting from) internet cinephilia. At the same time, it indicates that many movies are simply shifting from one celestial multiplex to another one just a few clicks away. In fact, while Hulu worked toward diversifying its movie holdings, Netflix began looking more like a traditional cable channel, albeit one without a linear broadcast schedule, a perception that Netflix CEO Reed Hastings often reinforced in interviews about the company. Users could access and consume movies or entire runs of older television series, leading some observers to suggest that Netflix's main competition was the premium cable channel HBO.[43] This perception of Netflix as analogous to a cable channel was reinforced when the company paid for the right to exclusive distribution of the American adaptation of the British miniseries *House of Cards*, starring Kevin Spacey, with the initial episode to be directed by David Fincher, who had previously made *Fight Club* and *The Social Network*. The British miniseries had been popular with regular Netflix users, making an American adaptation an attractive opportunity for the company in its efforts to provide original content unavailable on other services. Later, Netflix deepened its investment in original content by reviving the critically acclaimed cult television series *Arrested Development* five years after the Fox Network canceled it. The show's return furthered Netflix's attempt to emulate the HBO model of combining exclusive access to popular movies with a limited amount of original content. However, as Time Warner CEO Jeffrey Bewkes pointed out, the perpetual availability of content on Netflix made it difficult to sell that content to other distributors, such as cable channels, thus devaluing one of the primary distribution windows: "Once you put it on Netflix, you really can't sell it anywhere else."[44]

Like Netflix, Hulu also moved to distribute web series and even to produce original content. During the 2008 Writers Guild of America strike, Hulu hosted Joss Whedon's *Dr. Horrible's Sing Along Blog*, with three episodes released two days apart in July 2008. The series starred Neil Patrick Harris as a supervillain who sought to build a Freeze Ray that would stop time. The series was built upon the premise that Dr. Horrible had a video blog where he discussed his schemes with his online audience. Unlike most Hulu content, the series was distributed internationally, and it became a web sensation, creating interest not only in the web series format but also in Hulu as an important distributor of what Sheila Murphy refers to as "quality" video content.[45] In August 2011, Hulu started distributing *Day in the Life*, a series by documentary filmmaker Morgan Spurlock, best known for *Super Size Me* and *The Greatest Movie Ever Sold*. Like his previous works, *Day in the Life* featured Spurlock as a participant, with the film-maker following a well-known public figure over the course of a day. The original deal called for six episodes focusing on subjects ranging from Virgin Group CEO Richard Branson to Black Eye Peas front man will.i.am. The series not only allowed Hulu to identify itself with a marketable persona in Spurlock but also permitted the company to keep 75 percent of the advertising revenue, rather than giving back a large chunk of it to the television networks and filmmakers that had provided the content.[46] Even as Hulu and Netflix moved more deeply into the realm of programming, there were still differences between digital delivery platforms and cable channels. Most notably, Hulu and Netflix were not required to fill slots in a broadcast schedule. Instead, they could focus on marketing, promoting, and delivering content, whether it was purchased through subscriptions, bought as individual programs, or subsidized by advertising shown before and during individual programs.

Finally, a number of other companies sought to capture niche audiences, most notably the audience for independent and documentary films. While the Independent Film Channel focused on building a large catalog of VOD movies, which were made available through cable menus, a number of streaming sites created services specializing in niche content. These services relied upon a variety of payment models. One of the most prominent services, Mubi.com, allowed users to view movies either by using a $12 monthly subscription or by paying $3 per film. Mubi specifically sought to appeal to online cinephiles through its efforts to curate series associated with specific film festivals, directors, genres, or national cinemas, though the service could offer only a small number of titles in each country, depending upon the digital rights it had obtained. In fact, as Mubi founder Efe Cakarel acknowledged, "a principal challenge [for the video service] has simply been to convince rights holders that Internet distribution is a viable business."[47] But Mubi was understood not solely as a distribution platform. Although Cakarel emphasized Mubi's role as a curator of art-house cinema, he also highlighted the role of social media—including the website's blog, The Notebook—as a means of building a global movie-loving audience that would assist in the viral marketing of the films available on the site.[48]

Similarly, SnagFilms promoted itself as a site for easy access to streaming documentaries. The service used an advertiser-supported model in which viewers would be required to watch two or three short advertisements over the course of a feature-length documentary. Snag also aligned itself—initially at least—with a philanthropic mission. Users of the site could "donate their pixels" by placing a widget on their website, typically in a blog post, where they could share the film with others.[49] By making the films available for free, SnagFilms was able to characterize itself initially as an outreach tool, one that could allow documentary filmmakers to address a socially networked, activist audience. This perception was reinforced by Marcy Garriot, producer of *The Least of These* (2009), a documentary about imprisoned immigrant children, who argued that SnagFilms offered a means to "start a conversation across the country about a film."[50] SnagFilms eventually expanded its focus to include a selection of independent feature films, some of which would require viewers to pay to watch. But like Mubi, SnagFilms built upon an audience that was actively engaged with movies and the social and political cultures associated with them.

FAMILY ENTERTAINMENT

Although it is tempting to focus on forms of original content that are designed to attract tech-savvy movie fans, much of the content available on distribution sites is targeted at working parents seeking an online version of the electronic babysitter that had, in the past, been supplied by television and, later, by VCRs and DVD players. Streaming sites and digital downloads provide busy parents with on-demand access to a wide range of content that can keep their children entertained—and in some cases educated. The role of child and teenage audiences has been crucial to the major studios for some time. As industry observer Edward Jay Epstein noted, children and teens could be expected to "use television sets for hours on end, either to watch programs on cable channels and networks or to play movie videos, music videos and games."[51] These products, as Epstein points out, can then be used to market and promote toys, clothing, and other forms of related merchandise, expanding the profitability of an entertainment franchise.

Epstein later expanded this argument, detailing Hollywood's "Midas formula," a set of characteristics that were likely to guarantee financial success. He traced the phenomenon to Disney's *Snow White and the Seven Dwarfs*, which was originally released in 1937. In particular, Epstein noted that successful films were often adapted from familiar children's stories, serials, or comic books and typically featured youthful protagonists, fairy tale plots, and characters that could easily be licensed for toys and video games.[52] More crucially, Epstein emphasized that younger audiences were often quite happy to engage in repeat viewings of their favorite television shows and movies, revisiting familiar characters and plots. Similarly, as Jeff Ulin pointed out, the sell-through market for videos and DVDs benefited enormously from the "goldmine" of children's entertainment before the rise of digital delivery. "[I]t does not take brain surgery," as he bluntly argued, "to recognize as a parent that buying a cassette for $20 that your kids will watch seemingly a hundred times is a good investment."[53] In fact, as Ulin goes on to note, VHS and DVD allowed studios, especially Disney, to invest in cheap sequel properties associated with popular media franchises, which could be marketed directly to families with small children. These spin-offs, which Ulin called "video sequels," typically recycled the plots and characters of popular animated films, including *Aladdin, Beauty and the Beast, Pocahontas, Hercules*, and *The Little Mermaid*.[54] These repeat viewings, whether watching the same film over and over or revisiting familiar characters, play a crucial role in film and television consumption. Further, as Barbara Klinger argues, this emphasis on repetition can be tied to a need for familiarity, one that can provide viewers, especially younger audiences, with a greater sense of "comfort and mastery."[55] As a result, children's programming has always played a crucial role in home video and continues to offer an attractive market in the era of digital delivery.

This recognition of the crucial role of children's content led several digital media portals to focus on obtaining rights to children's content and even to tailor their platforms to children. Amazon, for example, invested heavily in children's media, acquiring rights to several seasons of the PBS show *Sesame Street*, as well as a number of children's films, including *Babe* and *Jetsons: The Movie*.[56] Less visibly, Netflix secured rights to content popular with teenagers and older children, including several ABC Family shows, such as *Pretty Little Liars* and *The Lying Game*, as well as the popular network series *Glee*. Like Amazon, Netflix invested heavily in content for children and younger teens, purchasing rights to shows such as *Yo Gabba Gabba, SpongeBob SquarePants*, and *iCarly*, as well as a range of children's movies. In addition, Netflix worked to create interfaces that would allow children to navigate the site and find their favorite shows more easily. In the "Just for Kids" section, the site offered a bar across the top of the page featuring a row of clickable characters from popular children's shows. When a child clicked on a character, she would be directed to a list of episodes available on streaming video.[57] Netflix's "Just for Kids" interface proved that younger audiences could be addressed not merely through content but also through the ways in which platforms and devices were structured. In fact, Microsoft attributed much of its success as a streaming video platform to what Aresh Amel called the "Kinect effect," the motion controller that made the system more "family friendly." In some cases, such as Kinect Sesame Street, television incorporated interactive elements, in which popular Muppets, including Cookie Monster and Elmo, seem to respond positively when children perform specific tasks.[58] Such user-friendly interactive features helped to naturalize the Xbox, even while allowing it to become useful as a device for streaming video content, allowing the game player to function as a set-top box for receiving television and movie content.

PREMIUM VOD

Declining DVD sales led to a number of attempts to entice customers to seek other entertainment options. Even as these new delivery systems potentially altered the financial prospects of the major studios, they also challenged historical perceptions of the role of moviegoing in daily life. Although studios used 3D exhibition as a way to draw audiences back into theaters, digital delivery continued to raise the prospect that the social aspects of theatrical exhibition were endangered. In March 2011 the chairman of the Motion Picture Association of America, former U.S. senator Christopher Dodd, stated that several major studios, including Warner, Sony, Universal, and Fox, would release a small number of films through VOD just sixty days after their theatrical debut for a premium rental price of $30 per movie. This move signaled an accelerating departure from the more traditional distribution pattern, in which the DVD is released four to six months after a film's theatrical debut. Although Dodd eventually took a more conciliatory tone with theater owners, emphasizing that movies are usually not made to be watched on "small screens," the debate about premium VOD seemed to crystallize the ways in which digital delivery is altering the film industry. Dodd promoted premium VOD as an alternative that could help to alleviate the problems of physical distance and mobility for "families with young children, senior citizens, the disabled, and those living in remote areas."[59] In particular, Dodd implied that the continued transition to digital media seemed to offer audiences new forms of access, even if such claims were somewhat disingenuous, given that most people in the United States live only a short drive from a movie theater, although premium VOD could potentially open up a wider range of choices for people living outside of big cities.

Naturally, theater owners complained that this acceleration would further undermine their exclusive window and worried that movie consumers would stay at home and wait for their desired viewings to become available through on-demand platforms, choosing convenience over the pleasures of collective, public consumption. No less an authority than *Avatar* (2009) director James Cameron weighed in on the controversy, lending his name to a letter distributed by the National Association of Theater Owners (NATO), an international organization representing chains and independent theater owners. In a *New York Times* interview Cameron commented, "I do feel it's not wise to erode your core business."[60] Cameron's remarks no doubt related to his practice of producing films identified with visual spectacle; however, the attempt to promote premium VOD also underscored the ways in which the home video market itself was changing. In fact, premium VOD seemed designed to make up for declining DVD sales.

To be sure, independent filmmakers and studios had been using a variety of VOD strategies for years. In 2005 Magnolia Pictures released Steven Soderbergh's *Bubble* using a "day-and-date" strategy, by which the film was released to theaters, on VOD, and on DVD on the same date.[61] This strategy has been extended to the point that, in some cases, movies appear on VOD before they reach theaters. 2929 Entertainment released the Kirsten Dunst–Ryan Gosling drama *All Good Things* via VOD several weeks before the film hit theaters in December 2010, a move that prompted further criticism from NATO. Despite this unorthodox distribution plan, 2929's Todd Wagner reported that the film made over $4 million in rentals through VOD, although it grossed less than $1 million theatrically.[62] Subsequently, a number of cable channels, including the Independent Film Channel, launched their own VOD services to offer independent films, many of which came out prior to or during a film's theatrical run. In addition, such cable service providers as Comcast and Time Warner Cable offered access to a wide range of independent films through their VOD offerings. Comcast, in particular, created what it called its Indie Film Club; it launched in October 2010 with the release of Edward Burns's *Nice Guy Johnny* simultaneously on VOD, on DVD, and through digital retailers such as iTunes.[63] As a result, a number of independent film distributors have argued that these on-demand and streaming options have served low-budget films better than theatrical distribution.[64] Although it is often difficult to get firm information about revenues from cable companies for on-demand rentals, Anthony Kaufman estimated that Pablo Proenza's *Dark Mirror* was purchased by approximately 110,000 to 120,000 households at a cost of $7 each. After the cable companies and the Independent Film Channel took their share, proceeds amounted to more than $200,000 through VOD. Similarly, Mumblecore filmmaker Joe Swanberg reportedly earned about $250,000 each from VOD rentals of his features *Hannah Takes the Stairs* and *Alexander the Last*.[65] Thus, there was some precedent that audiences were prepared to purchase movies through VOD, albeit on a relatively small scale.

Among the films included in the initial premium VOD test conducted by the studios were the Adam Sandler family comedy *Just Go With It* (2011) and the Liam Neeson action film *Unknown* (2011).[66] Notably, neither film was part of a major franchise, suggesting that studios were reluctant to experiment with a film that had a bigger budget or might have a larger built-in audience. But the VOD experiment allowed studios to investigate whether enough viewers might be willing to pay a specified amount—the equivalent of approximately three adult movie tickets—in order to see movies several weeks before they were available on DVD or in other streaming formats and without the incidental costs of a night at the movie theater.[67] Later, Universal attempted a similar experiment with the Ben Stiller and Eddie Murphy action comedy *Tower Heist* (2011), which it planned to release for $60 just three weeks after the theatrical premiere. However, despite Universal's decision to limit the test to just two cities, Atlanta and Portland, Oregon, complaints from theater owners, as well as pressure from the stars' agents, ultimately led the studio to drop the experiment.[68] Even though the studios' experiments remain inconclusive—the two test films showed only a modest drop in box office after being released on premium VOD—a number of entertainment pundits speculate that studios will continue to narrow the theatrical window and lower the price points in order to make premium VOD a viable alternative to seeing movies in the theater.[69]

Despite this uncertainty, entertainment critics still weigh in on the implications. Many are convinced that VOD will further erode the communal aspects of moviegoing that are central to popular understandings of film as a medium. Roger Ebert—a long-time champion of the big-screen experience—worries that VOD will lead to further social isolation: "The communal experience of moviegoing will be threatened. The erosion of community continues." Citing Robert D. Putnam's argument in *Bowling Alone* that Americans are retreating from communal institutions, Ebert asks rhetorically, "Who foresaw that we might also be seeing new movies alone?"[70] Ebert is not the first movie critic to claim that the social aspects of theaters are threatened. Still, his concerns ignore the fact that most movie viewers already consume most of what they watch through their home television set, whether on cable or DVD, and overlook the fact that many of the social aspects of movie culture have shifted to online forums, blogs, and social media sites. Such concerns reflect one of the perceived threats presented by platform mobility: the isolated, individualized media consumer.

However, within just a few short months of the premium VOD experiment, it was widely panned in the entertainment press as a failure. By July 2011, the major studios announced that they would discontinue future premium VOD releases for lack of consumer interest. One of the most notable examples of the weak sales for premium VOD was *Cedar Rapids* (2011), a Fox Searchlight comedy starring Ed Helms and John C. Reilly and directed by Miguel Arteta. The film performed modestly at the box office, grossing about $6.8 million domestically on a reported $10 million budget,[71] but the studio had hoped that the comedic premise would play better in homes. To the contrary, the film collected a total of 500 rentals nationwide, generating only about $15,000. As Patrick Goldstein observed, this amount was not significantly greater than what the movie might have made in one theater over the course of a single weekend.[72] Although the studios were quick to blame DirecTV for failing to market the film properly, industry observers pointed out that the model made little sense, given that many potential film offerings would be available just a few weeks later for purchase or rental on DVD. Further, premium VOD suffered because of the limited number of DirecTV subscribers who could access the service. According to Ben Fritz, only 6 million subscribers had the option of participating in the rental program.[73] Even with a larger potential consumer base, however, it was difficult to imagine that premium VOD would take off at a cost of $30 to $60 per rental. In essence, the failure of premium VOD reflected the ongoing problem of price facing studios in the era of digital delivery, especially as consumers began to seem more inclined to pay lower amounts for temporary, informal access rather than premium prices for appointment viewing.

CONCLUSION

Even as debates about digital delivery occupied the trade press, it was often difficult to judge how studios were adapting to the various forms of VOD. As Anthony Kaufman reported, little information about VOD numbers was provided publicly, in part because distributors and cable companies were reluctant to share it. Given the number of available formats through which films could be rented or sold, such information as per-screen averages was difficult to interpret.[74] Thus, although a number of key narratives about digital delivery began to emerge in 2011, there was some uncertainty about how audiences were using it. Still, the enduring perception was that digital delivery provided users with more choices and more flexibility in consuming media content. But in fact, a number of real restrictions and limitations determined when and where users could access movies. To address these concerns, the following chapter looks at the tensions between what I call restricting and resistant mobilities. On the one hand, digital delivery, I suggest, is shaped by the methods through which access is limited, whether this involves temporal restrictions, such as a "window" that provides exclusive distribution rights, or spatial restrictions, such as limitations on where a viewer can watch. On the other hand, audiences have cultivated a wide variety of legal and illegal, or authorized and unauthorized, strategies to work around these limitations.

2 ► RESTRICTING AND RESISTANT MOBILITIES
Negotiating Digital Delivery

THIS CHAPTER OFFERS a more extended exploration of the issues related to the practices and the business of digital delivery. It starts with the observation that, despite the promises of digital utopians, on-demand culture is characterized not by universal access but by the process of limiting and restricting when and where content is available. Thus, although a number of film critics and cultural observers have fantasized about the possibility of a "celestial multiplex," most online collections are incomplete, providing users with only partial catalogs that are subject to frequent change. This sense of incompleteness is exacerbated by ongoing conflicts over streaming rights. In addition, local and regional differences often affect which movies are available and in which formats, once again challenging the perceived mobility of a film text. Although digital delivery may potentially allow movies to circulate freely, conflicts over rights lead to practices such as geo-blocking, by which movies may be available for streaming in the United States but not in Canada. Or a company's rights to stream a movie may expire. As a result, users have adopted a wide range of practices—many of them illegal—to cultivate more individually satisfying and inexpensive viewing experiences.

Thus, this chapter examines what I call "resistant mobilities," activities that defy the practices promoted by the entertainment industry. In addition to more obviously illegal activities, such as video piracy, this chapter also explores practices such as cord-cutting, in which users discontinue their cable subscriptions, choosing instead to watch movies and television shows through alternative formats, including fully legal services such as subscription video-on-demand (SVOD), network websites, digital downloads, and other formats. In all cases, digital delivery fed into a perception that content was mobile, available for purchase or rental on demand and in a variety of formats. This content mobility ushered in more fragmented and individualized viewing experiences.

RESTRICTING MOBILITY: ULTRAVIOLET AND THE CHALLENGES OF DIGITAL OWNERSHIP

As movie studios and television stations began to see a growing demand for digital delivery, they also began to recognize that online delivery could provide a more stable audience stream than the struggling DVD market and that they could increase the price Netflix and Hulu would have to pay to obtain media content. In addition, several television networks, many of which actually had an ownership stake in Hulu, made the decision to withhold recent episodes of new television shows from the service. At one time, Hulu served as a secondary option for fans who missed a single episode of a specific show. Because Fox, ABC, and NBC would regularly post episodes on Hulu immediately after they aired, fans could use Hulu in much the same way they would use a DVR to catch up with shows off the normal broadcast schedule so that they could continue to participate in cultural conversations about those shows on Twitter, Facebook, and online forums. However, in August 2011 Fox set up an authentication system that would require Hulu users to demonstrate that they were subscribers to selected pay-television services—originally this option was exclusively available to Hulu Plus and DISH Network subscribers—before they could view an episode of a recent television show; otherwise they would be forced to wait eight days to watch.[1] While such a move was treated as a response to the rise of cord-cutting—the practice of dropping costly cable or satellite television subscriptions and instead patching together entertainment packages through online delivery—it also potentially had the effect of altering points of access to popular television shows and potentially changing the temporal rhythms of the fan cultures that watch and discuss these shows. Some critics speculated that the new policy could lead to increased piracy as enthusiastic viewers sought to keep up-to-date with other fans.

These changes reflect an ongoing effort to negotiate the value of media content for both the media industries and the consumers. In other words, studios and distributors were forced to consider how much audiences would be willing to pay for these forms of immediate, ubiquitous access to a wide range of content, especially when a consumer's media interests might be distributed over a range of delivery platforms. For example, a movie buff searching for a few days' entertainment might be forced to juggle between two or more services, watching Richard Linklater's *Dazed and Confused* on Netflix one day and catching a favorite Fellini film on Hulu Plus the following day. Meanwhile, she might have to go over to Amazon to purchase streaming rights to an episode or two of *Sesame Street* to entertain her daughter during a long car trip. Just a few weeks later, many of those entertainment options might have changed, prompting her to consult Walmart's Vudu or Apple's iTunes, where a movie download might be available for purchase only.

In an attempt to capitalize on this uncertainty, a number of studios joined forces to create the digital delivery service UltraViolet, which was meant to revive the practice of buying and collecting movies, rather than renting them or paying for some other form of temporary access. Although DVDs were promoted as a sell-through item, the practice of purchasing DVDs began to decline in 2004 and plummeted rapidly in 2010. By January 2011, there was widespread discussion of what would "replace" the DVD.[2] According to The Wrap, total disc sales declined 13 percent in 2010, dropping from $10.06 billion to $8.73 billion, numbers that remained relatively steady in 2011, when combined disc sales totaled approximately $8.8 billion. There was a significant increase in sales of downloaded movies, with total sales increasing 37 percent to $285 million, but those numbers hardly offset the decrease in physical media sales, whether on DVD or Blu-Ray.[3] Even media companies that traditionally market to children, such as Disney, saw a distinct decline in DVD sales in 2010, with Disney reporting a 14 percent decline in home entertainment revenue during the first three months of 2010.[4] More crucially, UltraViolet provided studios with an alternative that would allow them to distribute content straight to consumers rather than working through a middleman such as Netflix, Hulu, or even Apple's iTunes. As David Poland observed, "There will come a tipping point [when] studios and library owners see the potential for more profit in making their product available directly and not through Netflix, which cannot afford to keep expanding their slice of the market or to pay the kind of rates it is now paying for a slice of the market."[5] UltraViolet would offer studios one channel through which they could control the circulation and purchase of content.

The UltraViolet service—essentially a digital locker in the computing cloud where a user's movies could be stored and accessed via a wide range of devices—brought together all of the major studios, with the exception of Disney, which later announced plans for its own streaming video service, and several major cable providers and technology companies, including Comcast, Nokia, and Microsoft, suggesting that there was quite a bit of cross-industry support for this form of digital delivery. One other exception to this industry consensus was Apple, which declined to join the Digital Entertainment Content Ecosystem (DECE), the consortium of companies that created UltraViolet, most likely because it would compete with Apple's lucrative movie sales through its iTunes library. This decision made it difficult for users to access UltraViolet movies through Apple devices, including iPhones and iPads, which were commonly used for enabling platform mobility.[6] Given the industry consensus, the studios hoped that UltraViolet would mitigate the format wars that had shaped the early rollout of videocassettes, while also protecting against formatting problems that prevented movies from being played on multiple devices. Thus, despite the lack of participation from Apple, the service was promoted as offering greater convenience for users who might want to consume movies while on the go.

UltraViolet initially allowed up to six users to join a single account, a unit that was often referred to as a "family" of users, essentially redefining family as a group of consumers and further entrenching digital delivery as a family-friendly format. These six users could purchase enduring rights to the movies of their choice, allowing them to register discs purchased through UltraViolet or to buy movies on the cloud for digital download or streaming viewing. Movies could then be viewed on up to twelve different "authorized" devices, and consumers would have the flexibility to authorize and de-authorize devices, ostensibly making it possible to upgrade versions of a film even when devices become obsolete. DECE hoped that users would view UltraViolet as a simplified form of managing their digital movie collections, one that would provide them with greater control over when, where, and how they watch. By allowing content to be downloaded to multiple devices, UltraViolet promised users that, as technology improves, they would not be forced to replace their home media collections, as they were forced to do in the past in the transition from VHS to DVD, for example, or even from DVD to Blu-Ray. As part of this offer to protect against obsolescence, UltraViolet encouraged users to upload their existing DVD collections to the cloud. The service would then confirm that the consumer owned the movie and would place a "copy" of that title in his or her digital locker; users would also be required to register with every studio from which they had purchased a movie.[7] Once the movie was in the user's locker, he or she could access it from as many as twelve devices and would be allowed to retain a copy of the movie for up to three technological upgrades. In fact, users could authorize and de-authorize devices when they replaced older machines, as long as the user was listed on the account. Further, cloud storage would protect against the potential for lost, stolen, or damaged discs, as well as hard drive crashes that might cause the loss of valued movies. Perhaps even more compelling for the movie studios, UltraViolet's unlimited storage would allow consumers to purchase movies without worrying about filling up crowded computer hard drives.

However, UltraViolet also functioned as a form of controlled consumption, shaping when and where users would be able access their collections while also "swaddling" users' content in digital rights management (DRM) software that would prevent them from copying their movies or sharing them with others, a technique that was policed in part by demanding that users submit multiple log-ins in order to consume movies they already owned. To view *Moneyball*, for example, users would have to log in to both the Ultraviolet and the Columbia websites. Watching Steven Spielberg's *The Adventures of Tintin* would require that users create an additional log-in with Paramount. By restricting access to those individuals who are on an UltraViolet account, this policy represents a significant shift from the era of physical media, when the "first sale doctrine" allowed users to share VHS tapes or DVDs with others.[8] These forms of sharing might prove difficult under the DRM tools designed to prevent copying or loaning movies to others.

The first movie to be released with UltraViolet technology was the summer blockbuster *The Green Lantern*, which came out in October 2011 in three different versions: a Blu-Ray 3D combo pack retailing for $40.99, a basic Blu-Ray combo pack selling for $35.99, and a widescreen 2D DVD version that cost $28.98. However, only the Blu-Ray versions contained the UltraViolet digital copy, implicitly requiring users to upgrade to Blu-Ray if they wanted to take advantage of the UltraViolet service. Once users purchased the disc, they would have two years to activate a redemption code that would allow them to unlock their digital copy. The code would entitle them to unlimited streaming for three years and would allow them to download up to three copies of the film. After three years, as Marc Hachman discovered, consumers would have to pay a renewal fee, suggesting that viewers were essentially purchasing a "three-year lease" on the movie, although buyers would continue to own any physical copies they had purchased or downloads they had made of the movie.[9]

These attempts to market digital ownership were expanded when UltraViolet established an arrangement with Walmart's Vudu to allow users to buy movies through that site and store them in the cloud. These promises of platform mobility were further promoted when Walmart, often described as the world's largest DVD retailer, agreed to partner with UltraViolet to aid consumers in obtaining digital rights to their existing DVD collections. In order to take advantage of the service, people could bring their DVD collections to their local Walmart and pay $2 to purchase digital rights to each title, $5 if the consumer wanted to upgrade to a high-definition version. Thus, Walmart was essentially asking consumers to pay a second time in order to obtain streaming access to films they already owned. In addition, Walmart would continue to face the challenge of marketing the concept of "going digital" to consumers who were unaccustomed to paying for something as immaterial as cloud storage, which many were unable to distinguish from digital copies stored directly on a computer hard drive. Finally, despite the attempts to market UltraViolet as a service compatible with the needs of families, Disney films were unavailable on the service, in part due to Disney's vigilant protection of its digital rights, making UltraViolet less than ideal as a mobile babysitter, while raising the possibility that a service designed for greater convenience would actually lead to more confusion and frustration.[10]

This form of cloud storage raises a number of complications for the ownership of media content. As Wheeler Winston Dixon points out, cloud storage provides content companies enormous control over how users can access movies and television shows. Dixon offers the example of the conflict between Sony and Netflix: Sony demanded that Netflix remove its streaming titles, citing Netflix's "explosive subscriber growth," even though Netflix had obtained rights to those movies through its purchase of content from Starz. Thus, movies that might have enticed some consumers to pay for Netflix subscriptions were, briefly at least, made unavailable.[11] As this example shows, competing forms of digital ownership may actually reduce points of access to movies and television shows. Dixon concludes that digital storage is by no means a guarantee of permanent access, especially given that digital formats constantly need to be upgraded, maintained, or transferred to new platforms, raising questions about how these costs will be subsidized and by whom.[12] Further, given that disc sales were being supplanted by rentals, whether of streaming videos from Netflix or physical discs from Redbox, it was less than clear whether consumers were interested in obtaining ownership rights.

STREAMING GOES GLOBAL

Although many digital delivery services were available only in the United States, a number of companies sought to offer inexpensive digital movie delivery in other countries, further illustrating the existence of a globalized, cosmopolitan film culture. In turn, these services help to illustrate the challenges of making universal claims about the future of digital delivery. In fact, individual countries often presented unique legal, economic, and organizational challenges. But in all cases, digital delivery companies sought to appeal to a mobile movie-loving audience that wanted to see their favorite cinematic masterpieces wherever they happened to be at any given time. Services such as Jaman and Mubi catered to this global audience by offering movies paid for through subscriptions, through individual rentals, or in some cases through advertising. Jaman's origin story, like Mubi's, begins with the desire for mobile access to international art cinema. As Jaman founder Gaurav Dhillon asked, "Why couldn't a really good film made in Europe be enjoyed by somebody in India?"[13] Like Mubi, Jaman was able to obtain rights to films from a number of independent distributors, including Trust Film, Dreamachine, and Fortune Star in Europe and Fortissimo in Asia, providing it with access to films directed by Bernardo Bertolucci, Wim Wenders, Woody Allen, David Cronenberg, and Takeshi Kitano, as well as hundreds of Bollywood titles.[14] Eventually, Jaman built a catalog of more than 7,000 films, although only half of them were available in the United States, and attracted 1.8 million registered users worldwide. The United Kingdom accounted for 29 percent of the users, while 26 percent resided in North America and 23 percent in India, with most users identified as young males aged eighteen to twenty-four.[15] Notably, according to Jon Silver, Stuart Cunningham, and Mark David Ryan, the Bollywood films were most often consumed in the United States and the Middle East, a reflection of how cultural taste may be becoming increasingly dispersed, as well as the lack of availability of those films in theaters outside of India.[16]

Later, Netflix, took advantage of increasing broadband access to make its streaming video service available in a number of other countries. Hulu eventually joined Netflix both in expanding into Latin America and Europe and in acquiring local content that could appeal to international audiences. In July 2011 Netflix, which had already moved into Canada, announced a massive expansion of the service into forty-three countries in Central America, South America, and the Caribbean. The decision to target Latin America was attributed to the specific media infrastructure in many of these countries, including broadband and pay television penetration rates, as well as a perception of growing interest in moviegoing. Of course, Netflix and Hulu were simply joining a mass of competing services across the globe. By some estimates, there were more than 300 online distribution sites at the time, though many of those are now defunct.[17]

Unlike the traditional Netflix DVD-by-mail service, Latin American customers would be offered streaming-only accounts. According to the *Los Angeles Times*, there were an estimated 40 million broadband internet subscribers in Latin America, many of whom did not have pay television service.[18] In fact, broadband penetration often exceeded household pay television subscription rates in many countries: 22 percent of all Latin American homes had pay television, while 24 percent had broadband access. In individual countries, these distinctions were often more pronounced. Brazil, for example, had 16 percent pay television penetration, while 23 percent of homes had broadband. Similarly, Ecuador only had an 8 percent pay television subscription rate, while 67 percent of homes had broadband access. By contrast, in the United States over 90 percent of homes had some form of pay television, leading observers to suggest that in Latin America Netflix could serve as a substitute for cable instead of a supplement to it.[19]

Many observers saw Netflix's entrance into the Latin American market as consistent with efforts to combat video piracy. It was hoped that the monthly subscription services would help to curtail the global pricing problem that made it difficult for movie fans outside the United States to purchase or rent legal versions of DVDs or digital downloads. In fact, Netflix CEO Reed Hastings frequently stated that some of Netflix's main competitors were not DVD retailers such as Walmart or Best Buy but pirate sites such as BitTorrent.[20] Subscriptions in most Latin American and Caribbean countries cost approximately US $7–9 per month. However, when adjusted for the comparative purchasing power of people living there, these prices are considerably steeper than they initially appear. As Janko Roettgers observed, a $9 monthly subscription rate for Netflix in Brazil would be the equivalent of $60 in the United States. However, because Netflix was marketing primarily to middle-class families already paying for internet access, the price may have been more manageable, especially for consumers frustrated with the poor quality of many bootlegged copies of films.[21]

Given that Netflix is based in the United States, there was some concern about whether the company would be attentive to the local interests of the countries involved. To address the need for local content, Netflix made deals with TV Azteca and Grupo Televisa of Mexico and Globo of Brazil.[22] The initial Latin American launch also provided subscribers with streaming access to hundreds of titles from Miramax, the onetime independent label that had been purchased by Disney, only to be sold off by the studio in 2010 to Filmyard Holdings because the company's titles had declined in value. One complaint about the content was that the American movies distributed in some Latin American countries were dubbed, prompting a number of movie buffs to request the option to view films in their original English format with subtitles in the local language of their country.[23] As in many other countries where streaming services had launched, there were concerns that broadband caps could pose significant limits to the "unlimited" accounts. In Brazil, for example, some internet service providers (ISPs) had data caps of 10 GB per month, enough to allow users to watch approximately fifteen to twenty movies and television shows per month if they used their data for that purpose only. Notably, Netflix subscribers living in the United States could use their subscriptions when abroad, although they would be limited to the content available locally. Thus, although the Netflix expansion seemed to promise

TABLE 1   Initial Monthly Costs for Netflix Subscriptions in Latin America, September 2011

Country	Monthly Subscription Cost (local currency)	Monthly Subscription Cost (in U.S. dollars)
Brazil	$14.99 BR	$8.92
Argentina	39 pesos	$9.27
Uruguay, Paraguay, Bolivia	N/A	$7.99
Chile	3,790 pesos	$8.12
Colombia	14,000 Col	$7.79
Venezuela, Peru, Ecuador	N/A	$7.99
Mexico	99 pesos	$7.82
Central America, Caribbean	N/A	$7.99

SOURCE: Jeremy Kay, "Netflix Kicks Off LatAm Expansion with Brazilian Launch," *Screen Daily*, September 5, 2011, http://www.screendaily.com/.

the potential of more flexibility and mobility, the reality was somewhat more complicated, leaving consumers with limited choices in terms of the amount of content they could watch, as well as a limited catalog to choose from.[24]

Similarly, Hulu announced in October 2011 that it was acquiring rights to content designed to appeal to Spanish-speaking audiences living in the United States, most notably a major agreement with the Spanish-language station Univision.[25] Later, Hulu made deals with eleven other prominent providers of Spanish-language programming, potentially turning the site into an important hub for access to telenovelas, variety shows, and other forms of content popular with Latino audiences living in the United States. As Janko Roettgers observed, such a move reflected not only changing demographics but also recognition that Latino audiences were some of the more avid viewers of online video. In fact, according to a Nielsen study, Latinos watch an average of six hours and twenty-two minutes of online video per month while white audiences watch approximately three hours and foty-four minutes.[26]

In July 2011 *Variety* reported that Netflix had plans to expand into Spain and the United Kingdom, starting in early 2012.[27] Given the media infrastructure in those two countries, the move was considered to be an astute entryway into Western Europe. In the United Kingdom, Netflix would compete with Love-Film, a similar DVD-by-mail and streaming service owned by Amazon. It would also vie for attention with the BBC's iPlayer, which provided streaming access to recently broadcast television shows and movies. Spain would also prove to be an interesting test case for Netflix, given its reputation as a hotbed of media piracy, based in part on the country's looser piracy laws. However, Netflix would also be entering a video distribution environment in which there was little existing direct competition, potentially positioning itself as an authorized and presumably inexpensive alternative to free downloads.[28]

At around the same time that Netflix was launching in Latin America, Hulu began streaming service in Japan. Its initial plan offered unlimited on-demand access to Hulu's television and movie catalog for 1,480 yen ($19) per month, with content coming primarily from such American distributors as CBS, Sony Pictures Entertainment, and Twentieth Century Fox. Content from Japan and other Asian countries was to be added later.[29] These changes suggest that Hollywood productions will increasingly be identified with digital delivery, as subscription services expand outside of the United States. It remains unclear, however, whether such content will be available legally to the vast majority of people across the globe or whether streaming services will perpetuate the "global pricing problem" that reinforces the sale of pirated DVDs or illegal downloads from pirate websites. Further, it remains uncertain whether these streaming services will cater to the needs of local citizens, providing them with easy access to locally and globally produced content.

RESISTANT MOBILITIES: PIRACY AND
PEER-TO-PEER SHARING

The various modes of digital delivery are designed in part to provide media con-glomerates with greater control over the distribution, circulation, and exhibition of their movies. Although some experiments, such as DirecTV's PVOD efforts were less than successful, they illustrate the ways in which distributors are seek-ing to use what Vincent Mosco refers to as the internet myths of freedom and mobility to promote delivery methods that in fact give them greater control over how consumers use the movies they watch. Users of UltraViolet's digital storage, for example, may find it more difficult to loan movies to friends, a commonplace practice in the DVD era and one that is protected under the first sale doctrine. To this end, it is also worth thinking about how texts are mobile in ways that may resist the interests of the major studios and cable companies, namely, through video piracy and cord-cutting.

To some extent, the practice of piracy is related to the changed perception of what DVDs and other texts ought to cost, a shift informed by the cheap availabil-ity of movies from rental services such as Redbox and Netflix, as well as the ease of sharing video files online. Piracy researcher Joe Karaganis concludes that the practice has little to do with issues of intellectual property and can be attributed instead to what he calls a "global pricing problem."[30] Karaganis and the other authors of *Media Piracy in Emerging Economies* offer ample evidence that enter-tainment commodities are overpriced for countries such as Bolivia, India, and China; as we have already seen, pricing affected the decisions made by Netflix as it entered the Latin American marketplace. However, pricing is only one fac-tor. Piracy is also, in an international context at least, an access problem, shaped by a range of institutional, legal, and economic factors. For example, American films face a quota system in China that allows only twenty major foreign films to be distributed annually (an additional forty independent films per year are also permitted). Christopher Dodd, in his inaugural address as chairman and CEO of the Motion Picture Association of America (MPAA), highlighted this limitation as a major industry concern because, in effect, it requires Chinese audiences to obtain most U.S. releases through unauthorized versions.[31]

The quota system in China was altered in February 2012 to increase the num-ber of foreign films from twenty to thirty-four, provided that the additional four-teen were in 3D or IMAX formats. Studios would also receive 25 percent of the box office, rather than the 13 percent stipulated under the previous quota. The increase in the number of films reflected the ongoing emphasis on blockbuster franchises and depended on the growing affluence of China's middle class. As David Rosen noted, the number of theatrical screens in China doubled between 2006 and 2011 to 10,700, with most of those screens using digital projection, leading a number of observers to speculate that China would become one of the driving forces in shaping the U.S. film industry, a situation that could influence narrative and other creative choices made by Hollywood filmmakers. For example, the plot of the remake of *Red Dawn* (2012) was altered after production on the film was nearly completed to make the villains North Korean rather than Chinese, and several scenes from *Men in Black 3* (2012) that took place in Chinatown were shortened because of concern that they depicted Chinese characters in an offensive manner.[32] Thus, China's expansion of its quota system led to self-limitations on what Hollywood films could depict in an effort to appeal to Chinese audiences.

In addition to attacking the quota as a contributing factor to movie piracy, Dodd emphasized that there is indeed a "victim" in what is normally considered a "victimless crime," reminding audiences of the many below-the-line workers involved in the production of Hollywood films. Given that it is often difficult to generate concern about highly paid actors and executives, Dodd used the backdrop of a struggling U.S. economy, in which the unemployment rate was approaching 9 percent, and sought to characterize piracy not as an intellectual property crime but as a form of labor theft:

> It is critical that we aggressively educate people to understand that movie theft is not just a Hollywood problem. It is an American problem. Nearly 2.5 million people work in our film industry. The success of the movie and television business doesn't just benefit the names on theater marquees. It also affects all the names in the closing credits and so many more—middle-class folks, working hard behind the scenes to provide for their families, saving for college and retirement.... Those who steal movies and television shows, or who knowingly support those who do, don't see the faces of the camera assistant, seamstresses, electricians, construction workers, drivers, and small business owners and their employees who are among the thousands essential to movie making.

Dodd sought to make the wide range of jobs involved in motion picture production visible by suggesting that downloaders "do not see" these forms of essential labor or associate that work with supporting families. In addition, Dodd framed the issue of "stolen labor" as a national issue, one that specifically affected the U.S. economy, even though many major Hollywood films are shot abroad, in part to avoid the union wages that apply to many productions filmed in the United States.[33]

Dodd's effort to emphasize the effects of piracy on below-the-line workers is not a novel approach. Jack Valenti, a past head of the MPAA, made similar ominous warnings when the mass-market videocassette recorder (VCR) was first introduced in the 1980s. As Adrian Johns notes, Hollywood sought to restrict the use of such devices, surmising that the ability to copy and share videos would make people less likely to pay for movies. Further, Johns points out, the MPAA helped to reinforce crude stereotypes about Japan, the nation that prevailed in the VCR marketing wars, depicting American culture as "creative," whereas Japanese culture was imitative. As Valenti put it, "the American movie is the one thing the Japanese with all their skills cannot duplicate or clone."[34] The MPAA even produced a series of advertisements to play in theaters that were designed to "elicit pity," as John Thornton Caldwell's argues, and discourage users from pirating movies. These shorts depicted below-the-line workers directly and earnestly addressing the camera to ask audiences to stop downloading because the practice "threatens their personal and familial livelihoods as hardworking Americans."[35]

Although Dodd avoided commenting on enforcement, other than to compliment theater owners for vigilance in preventing pirates from smuggling video recorders into theaters, it is worth considering how digital delivery seems to be part of an institutional effort to combat piracy and to limit forms of sharing that were, in previous forms of media, perfectly valid. As early as 2005, J. D. Lasica, echoing arguments by Jordan B. Pollock and Lawrence Lessig, predicted that entertainment giants would become "benevolent media monarchists" seeking to control the terms and conditions under which consumers can use the media texts they have purchased in what he called a "rent-a-bit" system characterized by temporary access to music, movies, and television shows. In this sense, Lasica anticipated a version of the emerging system of digital delivery in which users are forced to exchange some of their rights to share movies for the convenience and choice that digital delivery ostensibly provides. Lasica forecast that "in such a rent-a-bit world, we will increasingly confront license agreements that grant us only temporary, day-to-day use of a product or a piece of media and that restrict our rights in other ways."[36] Thus, although digital delivery potentially made it much easier for movies and television shows to circulate, political and economic factors often created barriers that limited the circumstances in which consumers could watch movies.

In fact, these licensing agreements often led to a number of questions about how to define what actions actually constitute piracy as compared to legitimate copying and file sharing. One example of this blurry boundary involved the U.S. streaming rental service Zediva, which sought to argue that its purchase of a DVD version of a film allowed it to store the digital version of the film on its server and then rent access to customers on a pay-per-view basis. Zediva based its rental model on the principle of the first sale doctrine, which stipulates that once a media product is sold, the buyer has the right to rent or resell that media product. The doctrine served as the principle that allowed video stores to rent videocassettes and, later, DVDs to customers. As Frederick Wasser explained, the first sale doctrine was designed to balance the need to protect copyright holders' particular expressions and the right to own the physical embodiment—whether a book, cassette, or disc—in which that expression is stored. Thus users are free to do whatever they want with a particular copy once they purchase it, as long as they do not make a copy.[37]

Zediva sought to test the limits of the first sale doctrine with regard to digital copies. The company would legally purchase movies on DVD and then upload them to a server, where individual users could then pay $1.99 for a single online movie rental or $10 for a block of ten. Zediva sought to carve out a market by buying newly released DVDs as soon as they were available for purchase and distributing them via streaming video before Netflix and Redbox kiosks were allowed to rent them due to studio embargoes. Studios responded by claiming that Zedvia's actions constituted copyright infringement. Their shutdown request against the company in April 2011 was granted on August 2, 2011.[38] The conflict over Zediva illustrated the challenges raised by the materiality of digital video. While studios sought to depict Zediva's practices as a form of transmission, Zediva characterized them as similar to those of a traditional bricks-and-mortar video store renting single copies of movies. Zediva contended that it allowed only one user to download a single copy of a DVD from its servers at any given time, making its practices different from those of streaming services that paid for licenses to distribute a film to an unlimited number of customers. Zediva argued that its download model essentially created a "really long cable" between its DVD players and the individual computers where viewers would watch the movies they had rented.[39]

However, U.S. District Court Judge John Walter read the copyright law as regarding all streaming services comparable to movie theaters in that they addressed a wider public and, therefore, required permission from the copyright holder. Walter's ruling was based on a similar case from 1991, *On Command Video Corp. vs. Columbia Pictures Industries*, in which courts ruled that On Command's VOD service, which streamed movies to hotel guests from a bank of VCRs, violated copyright.[40] Thus, the arguments about the place of streaming video within the first sale doctrine seemed to be shaped by the mobility of the text itself, that is, the ability of streaming video to allow movies to migrate from one platform to another. As legal scholar Jason Schultz argued, "Zediva doesn't have control over the user and where they [sic] watch."[41] Yet, the service, as originally conceived, was contingent upon the continued existence of physical media. As Schultz went on to point out, Zediva, if it had succeeded, would likely have had to purchase hundreds, if not thousands, of copies of popular films and new releases in order to match consumer demand, a significant departure from peer-to-peer services such as Napster, where a single copy of a song could generate thousands of other copies.

Ryan Siegel pointed out that the ruling was influenced by a number of potential misconceptions about Zediva's service and played on the idea that consumers would be misled by the service. In fact, Judge Walter argued that customers may become "confused" about how competing streaming video rental services operate if they were to encounter Zediva movies that were otherwise out of stock, potentially harming Hollywood's other business models. Even more strangely, Walter argued that Zediva could confuse consumers about whether they would be required to pay for streaming movies, even though Zediva quite clearly charged for rentals.[42] Zediva eventually closed down its service; however, the rental model it proposed raised a number of questions about how a film text is perceived in the era of digital delivery.

Piracy, whether of movies, software, or any other cultural artifact, may also help to highlight the limits of distribution infrastructures. As Brian Larkin observes in his discussion of the Nigerian pirate economy, our focus on piracy's legal implications may obscure "breakdowns" in distribution models. In the case of movie distribution, discussions of infrastructure often assume "a media system that is smoothly efficient rather than acknowledging the reality of infra-structural connections that are frequently messy, discontinuous, and poor."[43] In the case of Nigerian video piracy, Larkin points out that illicit distribution developed due to a number of factors, including the oil boom of the 1970s, which actually helped to accelerate the process by which Nigerians could access inter-national films beyond outdated movies from Hollywood and Mumbai.[44] Larkin's comments help to underscore some of the ongoing challenges introduced by digital distribution in a global context. Attempts to police piracy face not only the problem of "global pricing" but also the difficulties of intervening within existing distribution infrastructures. At the same time, movie piracy, even while based in unofficial, privatized networks, speaks to a larger desire to participate in a global cultural conversation about contemporary movies and television shows.

Amid these attempts to stamp out piracy and other forms of peer-to-peer shar-ing, there is some evidence that certain media properties can benefit from the free publicity and attention made possible through file sharing. A number of technol-ogy websites have sought to argue that piracy can serve as a form of underground, or at least unofficial, marketing, allowing people to sample a film before buying it legally or paying to see it in movie theaters. Mike Masnick, writing for the blog *Tech Dirt*, pointed out that Christopher Nolan's *The Dark Knight* was both the highest-grossing film in 2008 and the most downloaded film of the same year and so argued that downloading could enable a film to achieve better box office totals.[45] Such an argument ignores the fact that *The Dark Knight's* popularity preceded both forms of access, and its popularity in pirated sites offers no guarantee that users who download a copy of the film from BitTorrent would otherwise rent, much less purchase, a copy. In many of these cases, piracy was a response to the lack of access to movies. In China, the strict quota system limited the number of American mov-ies that were legally available, prompting viewers to seek out alternatives. Similarly, the Nigerian pirate economy reflected not merely a global pricing problem but also a less efficient distribution system that made it more difficult for viewers to obtain movies through authorized channels. Even Zediva's attempt to exploit a loophole in U.S. copyright law was a response to barriers imposed by the "windows" system that governed DVD and digital distribution.

RESISTANT MOBILITIES: CUTTING THE CORD ON PAY TELEVISION

As digital delivery became a more common part of the entertainment infrastructure, a number of media consumers began to seek alternatives to cable television, an activity that became known in the industry press as "cord-cutting." The metaphor of cord-cutting builds upon the idea of liberation: users are freed from their dependence on cable television and provided new forms of mobility. Further, this decision to "cut the cord" was often depicted as a real possibility because users could access whatever television content they wished through other sources. Despite the continuing dominance of cable and satellite television, at least some evidence showed that consumers, especially younger people, were piecing together personalized viewing experiences through a combination of on-demand and digital download services. According to a Nielsen study, the number of households paying for a multichannel provider declined by 1.5 million in 2011, a 1.5 percent decrease from the previous year.[46]

However, few users seemed to base their decision to cut the cord on the perception that digital delivery offered a reasonable substitute for cable television. In fact, according to the Leichtman Research Group, only 5 percent of users who cut their cable subscriptions did so because they believed that everything they wanted to watch was easily available online, whereas 28 percent cited the cost of a monthly cable subscription as a primary factor. These concerns about the affordability of cable television during a recession led executives from Time Warner Cable, Cox Communications, and Comcast to acknowledge a "growing underclass" who might be unable to afford cable.[47] However the concept of cord-cutting did help to illustrate that digital delivery is redefining how people understand both film and television. As Henry Blodget argued in June 2012, cord-cutting, at least to some extent, made television networks appear to be "outmoded," especially as users sought out content through television show websites and subscription services such as Hulu, Netflix, and Crackle. This argument ignores the fact that consumption practices are still shaped by questions of content ownership. Still, Blodget also pointed out that cable bills represent a "wasted" expenditure, given that users often pay for channels they never watch, and he added that advertising expenditures are also ineffective because most viewers are multitasking and often pay little attention to the advertisements that typically help to subsidize television shows. These expenses led Blodget to imagine that networks will be replaced by a "library" model that allows users to purchase television shows and movies on an individual basis. Blodget also predicted that cable subscription prices will have to drop to capture decreasing demand and that distinctions between media, such as movies and television shows, will begin to fade.[48] Already, Netflix, Crackle, Hulu, and other content aggregators function much like television channels, allowing users to zap through different genres to find out what's available. Although most sites still distinguish between television and movies, in a menu-driven, on-demand culture these categories begin to lose their significance. In other cases, viewers do engage in more deliberate forms of viewing, whether that involves binge-watching a favorite television show on Netflix or Hulu or planning to watch a television show, movie, or sporting event as it is being broadcast live.

Despite the evident appeal of on-demand media consumption, users have been relatively slow to drop cable or satellite television. To some extent, this reluctance can be attributed to the habit of subscribing to cable and to familiarity with traditional television. But, as Blodget notes, one major factor preventing the widespread adoption of cord-cutting appears to be the desire to watch live sports, a preference that supports the exorbitant affiliate fees that ESPN and other sports channels demand from cable and satellite companies. In fact, while ESPN was able to charge $5.06 per month per subscriber for the right to carry the network in 2012, other channels lagged far behind; TNT, which sometimes carries NBA basketball, for example, was a distant fourth at $1.21.[49] But even the desire to watch live sports—and, in the case of shows like SportsCenter, endless replays of other games—may adapt to the logic of on-demand programming, given the availability of subscription services such as Major League Baseball's MLB.com and the National Basketball Association's League Pass, which potentially allow users more flexibility to follow their favorite teams. Despite the ongoing popularity of live sports, cord-cutting raises the specter of an increasingly on-demand video culture, one in which users will cultivate more personalized viewing experiences.

In response, cable companies and content providers have sought to give users incentives to maintain their monthly subscriptions. Cord-cutting was cited as a specific factor in the decision to create the eight-day "Hulu window," by which the Fox Network delayed the availability of its television shows for eight days after they originally aired so that users would be forced to pay for cable if they wanted to remain conversant with what was happening on popular shows. The move was designed to ensure that more viewers would watch the shows as they were broadcast in order to improve ratings, but it also contributed to increased downloads of the shows from unauthorized sites such as BitTorrent.[50] Later, a number of cable and satellite companies worked to create authentication systems that would prevent non-subscribers from accessing select content. For example, Comcast blocked non-subscribers from watching the streaming coverage of the 2012 Olympics, which was carried live by Comcast-owned NBC.[51] Similarly, Hulu moved to create an authentication system that would require users of the site to have a cable or satellite subscription to access the service.[52]

Finally, HBO required that users of its mobile service HBO Go subscribe to the premium channel, meaning that users would have to pay over $100 for a cable subscription, as well as the monthly subscription fee for HBO—usually about $12 per month—even though its shows could have generated significant interest if they were sold individually.[53] Thus, although many media consumers are experimenting with cord-cutting and other forms of on-demand viewing, content providers continue to attempt to entice viewers to consume media in real time.

CONCLUSION

The networks and methods through which movies and television shows will be distributed are far from settled. Although Netflix appeared to be a dominant player in early 2011, with its vast streaming catalog and its expansion throughout much of North and South America and Europe, there is little guarantee that it will be able to maintain this position. The studios themselves hope to create models that will allow direct distribution to consumers, and UltraViolet seemed to offer an alternative that would provide the industry with greater control over how media content circulates, although the studios were forced to retool their UltraViolet offerings just a few months after its initial public launch. At the same time, battles over digital rights have made it difficult to know whether content will be available in a specific platform or through a specific service, complicating claims about ubiquitous, enduring access to a wide range of movies and television shows. In all cases, platform mobility has reshaped the viewing experience, altering not only the locations where but also the times when viewers can watch, intensifying the practices of time-shifting that had been enabled by the VCR, the DVD, and the DVR. Digital delivery has contributed to a menu-driven viewing culture in which concepts such as channels have been rendered increasingly irrelevant, while the boundaries between film and television have been blurred.

As a result of these uncertainties, one of the greatest challenges of the early stages of digital delivery has been consumers' ability to identify and locate the movies and television shows they might want to see. In fact, complaints about Netflix and Hulu have often revolved around the instability of their streaming catalogs and the difficulty of navigating those catalogs. Further, while Netflix, Hulu, and Mubi each sought to carve out niche audiences within the globalized culture of film buffs, rights issues often made it less than clear whether users really could watch their favorite movies in a café in Tokyo. These questions are particularly relevant for the smaller global film cultures that are often forced to compete for limited theatrical space—and even more limited attention spans—with the major studios. As a result, the following chapter looks at the ways in which the media industries have sought to promote these new viewing practices, often through promotional techniques that equate platform mobility with empowerment.

3 ▶ "MAKE ANY ROOM YOUR TV ROOM"
Digital Delivery and Media Mobility

IN MARCH 2011, TIME **Warner Cable launched an iPad application that** would allow subscribers to stream some of their television content to their iPad, a total of approximately thirty cable channels, as long as they were connected to a Time Warner wireless router associated with a cable account. Like other digital delivery platforms, the app was announced as a transformative way of watching television and movies. The advertisement promoting the launch, "Make Any Room Your TV Room," consists of a series of quick cuts between various tablet computer users holding or watching the tablet at arm's length in various rooms and spaces throughout a range of middle-class, presumably suburban houses. A businessman holds it in front of his entertainment center, another man watches baseball on an iPad propped on his exercise machine, and a third follows a cooking show as he prepares a meal in the kitchen. An African-American woman watches in a clothes closet, presumably while doing housework, and another woman watches with the device propped on her bathtub, her polished toenails resting just above the water's surface. In all cases, the tablet is placed in the center of the frame, suggesting the continued presence of the screen anywhere inside or near the family home, quite literally placing the iPad at the center of our media world. At the same time, most of the scenes are shot from the user's point of view, promoting the perspective that platform mobility encourages personalized viewing, given that all of the subjects in the ad appear to be alone. The individualized viewer is in control, the advertisement suggests, able to choose when, where, and what he or she watches.

But the most suggestive shot is of a young boy, the only person fully visible on-screen. The boy has propped up his tablet on a wall and has gathered a number of toy cars in front of the device—a drive-in theater in miniature—while a child's cartoon plays on-screen, evoking nostalgia for older forms of movie watching. Although each of these figures appears on-screen for only a second or two, they tell us quite a bit about how Time Warner Cable seeks to position itself within the culture of platform mobility. Unlike the seemingly obtrusive television sets that required families to "make room," the iPad transforms any space in the house into a site for consuming entertainment and fits seamlessly into our busy lives without taking up excessive space. Further, although television watching was once seen as a communal activity that could bring parents and children together, the viewers in the Time Warner Cable advertisement all watch individually, pursuing an activity that seems visually linked to personal escape, even when older forms of communal watching are evoked, as with the small child who creates a fantasy image of a drive-in theater. In all cases, the advertisement seems to promote the app's mobility as offering the user liberation from the mundane aspects of everyday life. Although this advertisement may provide only a fleeting glimpse of viewing practices in the era of digital delivery, it is part of a larger discourse promoting a culture of media mobility. As a result, these attempts to depict formats such as the Time Warner iPad app offer a useful entry point for thinking about how the industrial discourse associated with digital delivery operates to shape the consumption practices of movie and television audiences.

This chapter seeks to map out the changing reception and distribution cultures that are forming as digital delivery—whether through streaming video, video on demand (VOD), electronic sell-through (EST), or mobile phone apps—increasingly becomes a more primary means through which audiences engage with movies and television shows. Although recent scholarship has responded to the ways in which objects such as the DVD came to produce new models of engaged spectatorship for both film and television audiences, as my previous chapters suggest, streaming and other on-demand formats now seem to be on the cusp of supplanting DVD spectatorship, with ambiguous implications for future practices of film and television consumption.[1] For example, although DVDs offered viewers the ability to engage more deeply with their favorite movies and television shows, much of the promotional discourse identified with digital delivery has tended to focus on issues of mobility, flexibility, and convenience. Further, advertising and other promotional discourse has tended to link digital delivery simultaneously to the hectic schedules of "on-the-go" workers and families, giving them the ability to watch wherever and whenever they would like, and to individualized screening experiences that cater to personal tastes and desires. These advertisements promote products and services ranging from cell phones and movie apps to cable and satellite television subscriptions, illustrating the degree to which platform mobility informs a wide range of domestic and personal screen practices. As a result, the discourses of platform mobility help to define a new mode of spectatorship, one that is associated with active and engaged, but often solitary, viewing. Although large audiences continue to watch movies in theaters, often attending opening night screenings in order to experience being part of a larger crowd, media mobility promotes a more fragmented, individualized notion of spectatorship, a situation reinforced by the diversity of platforms and delivery systems that consumers are forced to negotiate.

To make sense of these discourses, it is important to distinguish between different kinds of media mobility. First, platform mobility, as I define it, refers to the idea that movies and television shows can move seamlessly between one device and another with minimal interruption. Thus, a viewer might start a movie on her living room television set and continue it later on her iPad or mobile phone. Or using Apple TV's Air Play, a user could stream movies or television shows straight from her iPad to a connected television set. In turn, many of these devices offer varying degrees of mobility. An iPad or laptop might theoretically be used anywhere there is an internet connection and a power source, allowing audiences to carry their movie collections with them. Thus, in addition to content moving seamlessly between platforms, the platforms themselves are mobile. Of course, such connectivity is far from guaranteed, and although such services as Netflix and LoveFilm may promise unlimited access, viewers are often constrained by geo-blocking, data caps, streaming rights, and other institutional and economic factors that limit how freely content can circulate. Further, digital delivery not only opens up forms of *spatial* mobility, allowing us to watch movies wherever we happen to be, but also allows for the possibility of *temporal* mobility, expanding the time-shifting potential of television technologies such as the videocassette recorder (VCR) and the digital video recorder (DVR). This time-shifting potential has contributed to a further casualization of the practice of movie and television watching, making it possible for viewers to watch on a personal schedule rather than in the discreet time frames suggested by theater and broadcast schedules. At the same time, platform mobility also potentially enables repeat viewings, given users' ready access to collections, whether through network websites, Netflix catalogs, or their own personal archives stored on a hard drive or in the cloud.

MOBILE SPECTATORSHIP

I am interested in looking at how these promises of personal choice and media mobility shape media consumption practices. Although VOD services seem to offer further control over the viewing experience, allowing audiences to escape the demands of driving to a nearby multiplex and watching a movie according to the theater's schedule, these activities are also caught up in assumptions about the status of movies as cultural artifacts, potentially reinforcing the idea of movies as a form of fleeting entertainment rather than something meant to be collected or purchased for rewatching. Historically, media scholars have contrasted film and television spectatorship, noting that moviegoing has been associated with an immobilized spectator seated in a theater directing a fixed gaze toward a giant screen. Television, by contrast, has long been associated with a smaller screen and a viewer capable of moving around—if only within the confines of a single room—while watching.[2] However, once viewers began consuming movies at home, whether on television, videocassette, or DVD, these distinctions became blurred. More recently, the practices of on-demand viewing have contributed to new modes of spectatorship that place new emphasis on the role of mobility, making it possible for viewers to choose from vast programming menus wherever an internet connection is available.

Thus, I argue that the film and television industries are entering an era of platform mobility, one that leads to changed perceptions of film and television as media while also changing—and in some distinct ways, conflating—the social and cultural norms associated with each medium. Platform mobility involves not simply the screens and devices through which we access this content but also the ability to provide convenient and seamless access to that content even as users switch among multiple devices; however, even though the concept of platform mobility gives the appearance that video content has been rendered intangible or immaterial, it is crucial to recognize that these forms of mobility have material consequences as well. Rather than a single black box, we instead encounter a proliferation of platforms and digital delivery systems—mobile phones, laptops, tablet computers, DVD and Blu-Ray players, gaming systems, set-top boxes such as Roku players, and Internet-connected television sets—each of which will be supplanted by new devices through the processes of planned obsolescence, resulting in what Charles R. Acland calls "the outrageous environmental impact of the metals and toxins that constitute our screen world."[3]

These platforms also lead us to renegotiate the physical space of our lived environment, altering the primacy of the central television set in the family room. In fact, the introduction of platform mobility complicates traditional concepts of medium specificity, creating a situation in which many of the technological and physical properties associated with film and television as media may no longer be relevant, forcing us to rethink our understanding of media.[4] As Jonathan Sterne points out, people who watch specific programs on mobile devices can "spend many hours of their lives watching television shows and yet not think of themselves as *watching television*" (emphasis Sterne's).[5] To some extent, this form of denial is enabled by the fact that, for many people, these television shows are consumed anywhere other than on a television set, turning what was once regarded as a medium consumed passively into something watched purposefully. A similar shift affects the domestic consumption of movies. Many viewers use their Netflix menu as a kind of database of channels, flipping idly, starting a movie or television show, and then discarding it if it doesn't hold their attention. Finally, these new forms of mobility are often, though not exclusively, identified with individualized forms of media consumption, whether or not the consumption takes place on a personal mobile device. Thus, rather than the collective moviegoing experiences associated with movie theaters or even the domestic image of a family gathered around a shared television set, platform mobility engages with a seemingly empowered individual viewer who has access to a wide range of on-demand content at the click of a remote—or mouse.

These mobile technologies have the potential to disrupt traditional viewing habits and protocols, and for them to fit neatly into a domestic media environment, audiences must be presented with representations of how these new technologies can be incorporated into daily life. Advertisers have responded by creating idealized images of how consumers might take advantage of the potentials of platform mobility. These advertisements, much like the "Make Any Room Your TV Room" spot, typically depict young families or individuals in middle-class, suburban homes making use of mobile technologies in order to provide greater convenience or to resolve family conflicts. Industry attempts to introduce new media technologies into the home have a long history. In her seminal analysis of the promotion of television as a household object, *Make Room for TV: Television and the Family Ideal in Postwar America*, Lynn Spigel points out that "the media . . . published pictorial representations of domestic life that showed people how television might—or might not—fit into the dynamics of their domestic lives. Most significantly, . . . the media discourses were organized around ideas of family harmony and discord."[6] As Spigel goes on to argue, in the 1950s, an era in which family unity received special emphasis, television was depicted as promoting family harmony by bringing parents and children together to share a viewing experience at home. Further, Spigel explores the ways in which advertising discourse conveyed the idea that television consumption could help to reproduce more traditional gender roles by shaping family interactions, practices that persist in contemporary depictions of platform mobility.[7] In addition, Spigel notes the ways in which these debates about television consumption and domestic power took on specifically *spatial* configurations as a variety of women's magazines sought to determine how television sets would fit into suburban homes, with one magazine speculating that the object could replace the fireplace as the focal point of the living room, while in other cases television sets replaced pianos as a central form of entertainment.[8] Furthermore, the placement of the television set fit into cultural anxieties about gender roles. As Spigel notes, popular media in the 1950s often depicted television as turning men into "passive spectators" controlled by women.[9] By comparison, mobile devices, such as laptops or iPads, would seem to resolve the physical problem by making any space a potential site for watching movies and television shows.

However, as Spigel goes on to argue, the relationship between television and family evolved with the introduction of portable television sets in the 1960s and the roughly simultaneous shift from Eisenhower-era conformity to the Kennedy-era emphasis adventure and exploration. This shift would have profound implications not only for the characterization of gendered viewing practices but also for the perceived dynamics of the empowered media subject, turning a passive viewer into an active, mobile one.[10] In fact, portable television seemed to promise that people could escape from "their mundane domestic lives and into a world of active adventure," a theme that was reflected in television programs that depicted travel and other fantastic elements, including homes inhabited by witches, genies, and other exotic characters.[11] Spigel goes on to describe this desire for freedom as being consistent with the ideal of "mobile domesticity," pointing out that advertisements for portable television placed emphasis on individualized viewing, often by showing parents and children enjoying shows separately on personal sets.[12]

More recently, Barbara Klinger points out that in the early 2000s, home theater systems were promoted as an escape from the dangers and conflicts of public life, allowing individuals to withdraw into a technologically enhanced "Fortress of Solitude," an attractive option, especially after the events of September 11, 2001, contributed to a "stay-at-home" mentality often described as "post-9/11 cocooning."[13] Klinger goes on to argue that home theaters were explicitly tied to ideas of self-sufficiency, technological sophistication, and spectacle. Owners of home theaters could become immersed in blockbuster films without having to go to the movie theater. Klinger also points out that the popularization of home theaters was linked to the rise of DVD culture and the impulse to collect movies as a means of demonstrating technological and cinematic sophistication, especially given that DVDs provided image and sound far superior to VHS tapes.[14] Ultimately, home theaters gave rise to a much different model of television and movie consumption. As Klinger notes, "the image of the family gathered in front of the sole television set has possibly lost the currency it once had."[15] Instead, home theater systems offered the refinement and sophistication normally associated with adult tastes. In fact, Klinger notes that many home theater ads "marginalize children" in order to align this equipment with high culture and good taste. Finally, even though technologies are not innately gendered, Klinger points out that home theater systems were typically associated with masculine tastes and interests—think, for example, of the common reference to entertainment centers as "man caves"—thus reinforcing traditional gender roles and power relations within the home.[16] In this sense, Klinger documents that the promotion of home theater systems helped to usher in a new film culture and a related set of new viewing habits.

Mobile technologies complicate these viewing dynamics and practices even further. Instead of imagining the DVD as a collectible artifact, one that could be aligned with what Klinger calls "event status," platform mobility makes movie consumption a more informal and casual activity, one that can be accomplished in any location or situation. Mobile technologies also continue to be aligned with technological wizardry and self-sufficiency, a promise that is reflected in countless iPhone advertisements.[17] Many such advertisements prominently depict parents with young children; but rather than watching together, the family members are using personalized media devices to watch whatever they want on separate screens, curtailing any possible conflict over a central television set. Advertisements portraying platform mobility also tend to depict male and female users almost equally, even while prescribing uses for these technologies that may be aligned with more traditional gender roles within the family home. Thus, in much the same way that home theater systems helped to promote a new regime of watching, platform mobility helps to usher in a new film and television culture, one that is characterized by individualized, and often informal, viewing practices.

These dynamics of platform mobility were addressed in "Shining Star," a Verizon television advertisement promoting its new line of Samsung smart phones. The ad opens with a father checking sports scores on his phone while placing a star on top of the family Christmas tree, as a mashup of Earth Wind and Fire's "Shining Star" and "Santa Claus Is Coming to Town" plays. The camera then pans down to show his wife—the only family member who isn't using a mobile device—carrying a box of decorations while their daughters watch a children's holiday cartoon on a tablet computer. Finally, the camera zooms forward to show their brother playing video games on a console. The different family members are shown in the course of a single shot, uniting them physically and even emotionally, even as they are involved in separate media activities. Thus, rather than the possible distancing implied by family members distracted by their mobile devices, platform mobility, reinforced by some nifty camerawork, actually brings the family together: the entire family is in the same room, sharing in a holiday celebration without worrying about any conflicts over a central television set.

The role of entertainment in uniting families was also suggested in a 2008 advertisement for Comcast's "Triple Play" service, which bundled cable television, internet, and telephone subscriptions. The advertisement, which served as a tie-in to The Dark Knight (2008), opened with a middle-class father rushing into a shabby apartment and quickly locking the door behind him. Looking around the room at his wife and children, who are cautiously unpacking, he asks, "Hey, how was everybody's first day in Gotham City?" His wife answers that "some 'joker' blew up the minivan," and her son quickly adds, "with a rocket launcher," a reference to one of the film's more dramatic scenes. The father, still oblivious to the dangers of the city, happily touts Comcast's service, even while sirens and explosions are heard off-screen. Although the Comcast advertisement seems to mock the ideals of suburban, middle-class bliss, the parody actually serves as a reaffirmation of these values, in part by depicting urban life as undesirable and dangerous. In addition, the advertisement seems to suggest that Comcast's cable service actually has the potential to immerse viewers more deeply into the world of a movie like *The Dark Knight*.

American advertisements that place emphasis on family dynamics stand in contrast to promotions in different national contexts. In fact, they might be usefully compared to British Telecom's "Flat Six" series, which follows three flatmates attempting to negotiate the demands of college life while also juggling each other's technology needs. The advertisements show them using British Telecom's high-speed internet service to video chat, play games, and watch movies. Thus, rather than family harmony, the "Flat Six" advertisements place emphasis on hip, urban youth culture, identifying media mobility with college students who may be more likely to become early adapters of new technologies.

RETHINKING THE ACTIVE VIEWER

Although some advertisements sought to depict cable television and mobile video technologies as bringing the family back together for shared media experiences, more often than not, they showed family members engrossed in individualized screens, even if they were watching those screens in the same physical location. Further, these advertisements reflect a changed understanding of the locations and practices associated with viewing. Instead of being part of the primetime viewing audience watching at home, the mobile viewer can choose to watch during the subway ride, the exercise regimen, the coffee break, or the afternoon chores.

These images of an empowered, active viewer are consistent not only with the promotional discourse associated with digital delivery but also with the depictions of digital media users in both critical theory and cinematic narrative. For example, Kristen Daly argues that recent Hollywood filmmaking should be characterized as a "cinema of the user." Drawing from the terminology of Gilles Deleuze, she describes digital cinema as a third regime of cinematic storytelling after the movement-image and the time-image.[18] Because these films address (and sometimes depict) an active, participatory viewer or "viewser," to use Daly's term, the new technologies appear to be a form of liberation. The user is given the ability to interact with the text, altering it or at least actively engaging with it in the process of making meaning, much like Keanu Reeves's hacker hero,

Neo, is able to alter the world of *The Matrix*. Francesco Cassetti offers a similar account, arguing that traditional modes of spectatorship, based on passively watching movies on a big screen, are "no longer very relevant."[19] Instead, viewers "intervene," a process that entails everything from choosing when and where to watch a movie to what platform they will use. Cassetti concludes that spectators essentially become protagonists who actively shape their viewing experiences. His account offers a powerful overview of the diverse practices entailed under the banner of movie consumption, as users blog, tweet, and share reviews, turning movies into what Cassetti calls a "multimedia project."[20] These accounts of active viewing now find their match in advertising and promotional discourses that depict users in complete command of their media experiences, able to chose personal (pre-packaged) paths through a textual system, whether that includes DVD extras or online menus offering a seemingly unlimited choice of films and television shows.

Yet, as enticing as such models of an active, energized viewer may be, we must also acknowledge the ways in which these discourses are linked to larger cultural myths about digital capitalism. In fact, it is easy to forget that these new modes of interactivity and mobility essentially turn digital media into what Dan Schiller calls "a self-service vending machine of cultural commodities."[21] Schiller's comments emphasize the degree to which depictions of empowered viewers obscure the reality that movies and television shows are commodities. Although platform mobility undeniably allows viewers to access movies and television shows from a wider range of locations, the effect on consumer choice is a little murkier. Streaming services like Netflix promote themselves in terms of mobility, but their streaming catalogs often lack recent movies, and users renting through VOD offerings are often limited by the windows, or time frames, during which movies and television shows are available. Further, as Vincent Mosco argues, experiments with digital delivery make it possible for the film or television commodity "to be measured, monitored, and packaged" in new ways, creating what Mark Andrejevic refers to as a "monitored mobility."[22] This combined fantasy of marketing media commodities and using audience behavior to sell advertisements is powerfully illustrated by YouTube's ongoing efforts to turn itself into a centralized hub for niche entertainment ranging from buzzed-about film festival movies to serialized web videos, turning the broadcast model typically associated with television into highly individualized forms of narrowcasting and ensuring, as John Seabrook writes, that "those audiences will be even more engaged, and much more quantifiable."[23] Thus, although viewers of Hollywood films may encounter new forms of mobility, they do so at the expense of submitting to new forms of surveillance that contribute to more deeply individualized marketing.

For these reasons, it is crucial to consider the ways in which the changing processes of digital delivery have also altered the practices of doing business in the film and television industries. As digital delivery has become more commonplace, the traditional models of distribution that have existed roughly since the introduction of video and cable television in the late 1970s and early 1980s, when studios, theater owners, and distributors agreed on a theatrical window of approximately six months, have been significantly transformed, leaving the movie industry in a state of flux regarding future viewing practices.[24] Digital delivery has been promoted in terms of its utopian potential to liberate viewers from their home television screens and from programming schedules, further expanding the time-shifting potential of video.[25] This mobility can, perhaps unintentionally, contribute to what Acland describes as a "rising informality" associated with movie consumption.[26] Cassetti echoes this claim, adding that multitasking spectators treat movies as "something to pick up now and put down later." That attitude seems to apply to the bored, often multitasking Netflix subscriber who surfs through a menu of titles, perhaps using a Wii or Playstation remote, in much the same way that past audiences might have idly clicked through channels with a television remote.[27]

SELLING MOBILITY

Contemporary promotional discourse for cable companies and mobile media platforms seems to imply that digital delivery erases concerns about control over the viewing experience by allowing us to watch anywhere and on our own schedule. Advertisements for these technologies help to naturalize new viewing platforms while also showing how they will help users to transcend the limitations of current media technologies. In fact, as a 2011 Time Warner Cable advertisement sought to emphasize, viewers could move from one screen to another throughout the house, never once losing their place in a movie. "Never Lose Your Spot" depicts a young couple settling in to watch a movie on the couch. The wife is noticeably pregnant and struggles to get comfortable while her husband patiently tries to help. Unsatisfied, they climb up and down the stairs several times, trying two or three television sets and mobile devices throughout the house and a variety of increasingly absurd positions before returning to the original couch. Platform mobility has magically ensured harmony and freed them from worry about missing a single moment of the movie they were watching. Thus, there is no longer a question of where to put the television set. Instead, the whole house is transformed into a space for consuming entertainment.

Like Time Warner, DirecTV promises control over the viewing experiences through its Whole-Home DVR service. In the spring of 2011 DirecTV ran two television advertisements that touted the consumer's ability to shift between several media platforms while watching a movie. In one, "Love Match," a lone female viewer moves throughout her house while watching a Renaissance-era costume drama, complete with sword fights and eventually a love scene. As she moves from her bedroom to the kitchen and then to the living room, the action literally spills out into the spaces of her house, suggesting that the woman is immersed in the world of the movie even as she gets up for a snack or to answer a telephone call. In the other, "Robots," a male viewer enjoys a *Terminator*-style adventure featuring robots fighting each other with lasers while crashing through the walls of the rooms where he watches. Further, the viewer is able to pause the action while moving from one room to another before seamlessly restarting the movie as the action invades the next room. In both cases, the viewers are watching a movie alone, although the male viewer's wife is depicted in the background in their bedroom, reading a book while her husband watches a movie that is presumably not of interest to her. Thus, the movie choices are clearly marked by gender assumptions, with the female viewer engaged with a historical drama, albeit one with plenty of action, and the male viewer watching a futuristic science fiction film. Both advertisements also depend on the idea of a middle-class home where such technology, which allows the house to transform into a multitude of individualized viewing spaces, might appear to be a necessity. Furthermore, both advertisements conclude with the action being contained again in a traditional television set, a subtle reminder of where the satellite company would prefer that viewers watch. These advertisements—designed to domesticate and sell platform mobility—also have the effect of illustrating that movie watching is an informal activity, subject to the needs of the viewer.

This desire for immersion is often played to comic effect. In an advertisement that premiered during the 2012 Super Bowl, comic actor Ricky Gervais sits in front of a café, smugly denying a person's Facebook friend request. Gervais's refusal seems to lead to a grenade being dropped in his bread bowl, and suddenly the comedian finds himself running frantically among different movie and video game scenes, ranging from *Call of Duty* to ESPN's X Games to a romantic movie and a zombie film, until all of the worlds become blurred together, leaving the comedian—still sprinting to escape violent destruction—to accept the previously denied request. Time Warner's message here seems to be that users of its mobile service will be able to take the action wherever they wish, allowing them to "get lost" in whatever forms of entertainment they choose, possibly even to move easily between screens, interacting with social media while watching movies or playing games.

In some other cases, cable and mobile services were presented in terms of their ability to bring families together, such as in a May 2011 Time Warner Cable advertisement meant to promote its 3D service. The advertisement depicts a mother attempting to round up her children and husband for their weekly "movie night." The children are in their own rooms, playing games and chatting with friends on their laptops, while the father works in a home office. Unable to get the family to join her, the mother proceeds to pop some popcorn and put on her 3D glasses. As the smell of the popcorn attracts the family, they join Mom on the couch, settling in together to watch the movie, with the father remarking that "nobody told me it was movie night." As the four of them stare at the screen with their 3D glasses, a voice-over evokes the discourses of technology and family harmony, remarking that Time Warner Cable is "moving technology forward to bring you back to the family room." Although the advertisement fits neatly within traditional images of family harmony—with the technological twist of the 3D glasses—it is also significant for its emphasis on promoting the idea of bringing viewers back to the home's central television set.

A similar Time Warner Cable advertisement shows a father and son playing baseball on a makeshift field with golden waves of wheat in the background, evoking the nostalgic Americana of *Field of Dreams*. The father, despite promises to pitch the baseball where his son can hit it, proves unable to throw strikes, prompting his son to worry that they will miss a televised baseball game that is about to start. The father then takes out his cell phone and uses the cable company's "remote DVR management" system to ensure that the game will be recorded and that the father and son will be able to continue enjoying their moment of family bonding. The advertisement culminates with the two of them on the couch, proof that the remote DVR management service is "bringing technology forward to bring you back together." Thus, when mobility is invoked in an advertisement, it is often shown not just as a device for reinforcing family harmony but also as a means of getting families to connect in front of the main television set. A complementary advertisement targeted toward female viewers, "Sample Sale or Your Favorite Show on TV?" depicts a fashionable young woman walking down a city street and passing a store window touting a "one-day sale" on a pair of dress shoes. The woman pauses, briefly concerned about missing her favorite show, but like the baseball-hurling father, she remembers her ability to use remote DVR management, allowing her to enjoy both buying shoes and watching television. Like DirecTV's advertisements, Time Warner Cable's depictions of platform mobility reinforced relatively traditional gendered viewing practices while also implying that mobile technologies can enable families and individuals to have more control over when and where they watch.

MOBILITY AND ACCESS

These informal viewing contexts seem to stand in contrast to the concentrated viewing practices associated with DVD culture.[28] Although a number of scholars have attempted to map the role of the DVD in changing film consumption, in many ways the DVD merely served as an extension of the existing modes of distribution established with the introduction and popularization of the VCR in the 1980s. Movie theater owners were granted an exclusive "window," allowing them to show a movie without having to compete with other versions of that movie, such as pay-per-view, video, or cable. Typically, this window lasted approximately six months, although the window was gradually shortened soon after the DVD was introduced, in part because studios saw DVDs as sell-through commodities and marketed DVDs to movie collectors, whereas VHS was primarily considered to be a rental format. In fact, as Jeff Ulin observes, the average window between the theatrical premiere and the DVD release was five months and twenty-two days in 1998, but by 2008 that window had shortened to four months and ten days, a decrease that Edward Jay Epstein attributes to the desire to have the DVD releases of summer blockbusters available for purchase before Christmas.[29] Ulin adds that DVD sales have been decreasing steadily since about 2003, with a decline of 6.3 percent, for example, between 2007 and 2008.[30] However, despite these changes, the window system remained in place until recently, when the steep decline in DVD sales, one of the primary sources of profitability for studios, led studios to seek new alternatives for selling to audiences, a shift that has prompted the efforts to promote various forms of platform mobility.

On the other hand, despite depictions of an increasingly wired world, it is difficult to determine the degree to which mobile video will become a prominent mode of movie consumption. According to a 2011 Nielsen study, only 24.7 million cell phone users, out of nearly 300 million overall users in the United States, watched videos on their phones. In addition, subscribers watched roughly four hours and twenty minutes of video per month using mobile devices, a small number compared to the many hours devoted to viewing movies and television on a regular set.[31] These numbers suggest that adoption of mobile media consumption remains incomplete. In fact, as Gerard Goggin argues, adoption of mobile television has been gradual due to a range of technological, ideological, and regulatory factors. Broadband and 3G access remain far from universal, and data limits on most cell phone accounts make it more difficult or costly for users to watch unlimited content on their phones, especially in countries outside the United States, which tend to have lower broadband data caps.[32] Further, services such as Netflix must compete for streaming rights. Unlike DVD rentals, which are protected under the first sale doctrine, broadcast and streaming rights curtail this seemingly unlimited mobility, with the result that Netflix has sought to invest heavily in streaming rights. In addition, the Time Warner iPad app allows users to stream selected cable channels; however, they can do so only within reach of a Time Warner Cable wi-fi network in a home that subscribes to that cable service, limiting the physical mobility of the viewer.[33] Finally, it is important to note that regional and national contexts often shape what kinds of services and features may be available at any given time. In fact, as Niki Strange points out, the BBC iPlayer has been introduced in the midst of wider debates about the intersections between individualized consumption and public service, especially given that the broadcaster is funded by a compulsory license fee.[34] Although these factors are subject to change, as technologies improve and as demand for mobile television and film increases, it is important to be aware that these promises of platform mobility remain contingent on a wide range of social, economic, and even political factors.

ON-DEMAND DISTRIBUTION

This emphasis on platform mobility has also become a major point of experimentation for the studios themselves, especially with declining DVD sales. One recent model of digital delivery supported by the studios involves the decision by Warner to sell several of its highest profile films, *The Dark Knight* (2008) and *Inception* (2010), as well as many of the Harry Potter movies as iPhone apps. Warner's decision signaled its readiness to experiment with new models that could bypass Netflix and other similar services and sell directly to the consumer, with the hope of reviving flagging DVD sales. The basic movie apps were free and provided users with a five-minute "teaser" consisting of the opening scenes of the films and a limited number of extra features normally included on a DVD. The free *Inception* app, for example, offered a short production ("making-of") video that explained how the producers created the rainstorms while filming in Los Angeles. The user could also purchase a secondary app, priced at US $12, which included permanent access to the entire movie, as well as a number of supplemental videos about the film that might normally be found on the DVD. Warner used a similar approach with the *Dark Knight* app, although that film, which was slighlty older, was priced at $10. Unlike the iTunes versions of these films, however, the apps are limited to a single device. A consumer who purchased one or the other film on his or her iPad could watch it only there, perhaps suggesting that Warner was hoping that users would purchase these films on multiple devices or through several different platforms or that they would see them as impulse purchases that could be watched on the go. The app versions did offer more special features than are available on iTunes and also allowed Warner to sell the films through a digital platform in more than twenty countries where iTunes is unavailable, including China, the Netherlands, and Brazil, providing Warner with wider access to direct digital delivery.[35] At the same time, the apps were promoted as offering some social media features that would appeal to the fan cultures identified with both of these Christopher Nolan films by integrating the apps with a user's Twitter and Facebook accounts so that he or she could chat with other fans in real time, a supplemental feature that Warner sought to characterize as consistent with the social nature of watching movies.[36]

Despite the promotion of platform and content mobility, studios have sought to preserve a model of media collecting and ownership, rather than merely "renting" movies, whether through streaming or download, a goal manifested by the studio initiative UltraViolet. The rhetoric used to promote UltraViolet borrowed from many of the digital cinema myths and promises about interactivity, freedom, consumer choice, and even permanence, promising that users would not have to repurchase every movie they own to update their video libraries every time there is a technology upgrade.[37] UltraViolet would alleviate fears about loss of content in a hard-drive crash and obviate concerns about whether a movie might play on multiple devices. Once the account had been established, a consumer could buy a Blu-Ray DVD and, if she was separated from the physical copy of the DVD, she could watch the movie later via streaming video, digital download, or some currently unimagined future format. Theoretically, her son could watch the same movie by logging into his account while away at college, possibly even scheduling a screening for his friends in the dorm. UltraViolet is promoted through the discourses of platform mobility, selling to viewers who may be watching movies on the go as well as to viewers concerned about having to purchase multiple versions of the same film in order to keep up with format changes. In fact, UltraViolet will allow users to load any movie or television show available in its catalog onto as many as twelve devices. Further, a household account allows up to six users, a feature that could be used by families to avoid the conflicts associated with media consumption while allowing them to create a shared digital library.

At the same time, however, UltraViolet's user agreements often blur what counts as "ownership." Users could purchase a physical copy of the film and then register a "digital copy," essentially access to a streaming copy of the film stored in the cloud in a digital "locker." As many technology critics noted, UltraViolet—rather than offering users greater mobility—actually provided studios with greater control over how their content circulates. One critic sarcastically referring to the user agreement as a "kinder, gentler DRM."[38] Other critics were not so generous, pointing out that participating retailers, such as Walmart or Amazon, could dictate the conditions under which users can watch a movie, while adding that television shows were still not available through the service.[39] In this sense, digital rights management, rather than enabling content mobility, prevents consumers from sharing movies with friends who are not included on their UltraViolet account, a retreat from a practice that was commonplace when consumers could share VHS tapes or DVDs from their personal collections.

This approach challenges more traditional perceptions of television and movie consumption as a shared domestic activity, associated with a central set placed in the living room. As the UltraViolet webpage promised, there would be "no more fighting over the main TV when Dad wants to watch football at the same time the kids want to watch cartoons." This notion of platform mobility echoes the promotion of portable television sets in the 1960s, which, as Spigel noted, cast the devices "as a remedy for family fights over program choices on the living room console."[40] The UltraViolet system also promised family harmony in other ways, noting that college students would be able to engage in "rerun night" with their parents, even while living in the dorms. A closer look at these passages reveals echoes of earlier depictions of how families should watch television or movies. The father, as head of the household, controls the "main TV," while the kids obediently watch cartoons. At the same time, an UltraViolet account magically wipes away the distance between parent and child when that child goes away to college by allowing family members to continue to watch together, even in separate locations. In addition, UltraViolet promises consumer control and choice, both in terms of the range of content and in terms of the ability of families to control what content comes into the home. Like the V-Chip, filters available through UltraViolet enable parents to block content while still "allowing kids the freedom to choose." Thus, the potential risks of unlimited freedom are curtailed by giving parents more control over their children's viewing choices. In this sense, UltraViolet seems to represent the logical conclusion of on-demand viewing, selling viewers on the desire for greater control over their viewing experiences. At the same time, it brings together discourses of family harmony and platform mobility, allowing parents the ability to choose what their children will watch while also maintaining their access to that content whenever they wish. Although online and mobile viewing practices are still in the process of being developed, contemporary advertisements have sought to provide visual and narrative models for why consumers might feel compelled to use them, even when existing technologies—laptops with DVD players, for example—can perform a similar function. Ultimately, these advertisements and delivery formats promote the idea that platform mobility will enable new forms of informal and often personalized media consumption, allowing users to create what Anne Balsamo describes as a "digitally distributed self" that reflects back their interests, tastes, values, favorites, and even experiences through highly personalized advertisements and recommendations.[41] In essence, platform mobility reassures us that we will always remain connected—to the data stream, to our movie collections, to our social media profiles, and even to our friends and family.

CONCLUSION

Promises of connectivity and access hit a moment of conflict when Apple introduced Siri, a voice-activated "intelligent personal assistant" that would conduct web or map searches or perform other tasks for its user. Siri would respond in a cheerful female voice, offering—or just as often, failing to offer—the needed assistance, whether that entailed finding a nearby restaurant or movie theater or seeking out a specific bit of information available on the web. To promote Siri, Apple used a series of advertisements featuring familiar Hollywood actors and directors, including Samuel L. Jackson, Zooey Deschanel, and John Malkovich, alone in their homes but comforted by the presence of the intelligent agent that will satisfy all of their needs: a dry joke for Malkovich, a risotto recipe for Jackson's date night, and tomato soup and blues music delivered to Deschanel on a rainy afternoon. Although the ads were the object of a fair amount of ridicule online, in part because the commands used in the commercials rarely succeeded, they reinforced the idea that even Hollywood celebrities could or should have all of their needs and desires—even for companionship—satisfied through their mobile devices. Instead of encouraging a night out, as Apple's "Calamari" ad had done several years earlier, iPhones now represented the possibility that we would never have to leave our homes. In fact, Siri was simply an extension of the iPhone's existing role as what Anne Balsamo calls "the ideal techno-embodiment of the perfect mother."[42] Instead of the urban moviegoer, platform mobility now seemed to idealize the stay-at-home consumer, who could have every desire delivered.

All of these changes point to a transformation of the experiences and perceptions of movie and television viewers. The media industries now have more tools for monitoring consumers and tracking their purchases and surfing habits, rendering active users even more visible to advertisers. In his discussion of digital television distribution, William Boddy argues that the media industry will know a viewer "by the decisions he has made about how to spend his time, each and every moment of which is recorded by his black box."[43] To be sure, digital delivery enables much more concentrated forms of monitoring, as well as targeted advertising to the individualized and fragmented audiences who watch on personal devices, using personalized media accounts. But the more crucial shift entails a more generalized transformation of spectatorship, one that is consistent with the mobile viewer who is ostensibly empowered to watch movies and television shows whenever or wherever. This temporal and spatial mobility produces a number of shifts in the cultures and business of movie consumption.

Discourses of platform mobility tap into larger desires for community, in part through depictions of how these new technologies can be incorporated seamlessly into the suburban, middle-class home, especially in the United States. Much like the popular discourses surrounding television in the 1950s, advertising for cell phones, portable media players, and other forms of platform mobility all help to define the ways in which these media technologies are understood. Personal technologies, it is suggested, can help to reduce family conflict over entertainment, in most cases by offering individualized viewing experiences. And yet, this shift should not imply that these discourses of platform mobility are determinative. As Francesco Cassetti points out, these new devices can, in some cases, become embedded in a socially networked and engaged film culture, one in which users share, blog, tweet, and even remix films, a potential made possible by the logic of platform mobility. Further, micro-ethnographic examinations of local uses of media technologies often reveal how users resist and reshape these media discourses to their own purposes in their everyday practices of movie and television viewing. We must, as Shaun Moores suggests, remain attentive to media users' "practical consciousness . . . of media environments," even as those platforms evolve and become imbued with new meanings and uses.[44] Thus, even while we recognize the role of industry discourse—in all of its different and sometimes contradictory forms—on media consumption, we must also attend to the ways in which platform mobility offers a powerful expression of the cultural desire for a greater autonomy over when, where, how, and what we watch.

The previous three chapters have examined platform mobility and its implications for consuming movies in the home or on mobile devices. Chapter 4 looks at the implications of digital delivery for movie theaters, specifically by focusing on the role of 3D movies in helping to usher in the use of digital projectors in theaters. Although the theatrical experience may seem to be distinct from the practices associated with platform mobility, I argue that its changing nature illustrates the ongoing reinterpretations that shape how we perceive movies and the activity of moviegoing. Though initially marketed as a special event, 3D has become a relatively standard practice for major studio films. More crucially, the technology reinforces the perception that films have become files, capable of circulating easily among devices and available for periodic upgrades (from DVD to Blu-Ray; from 3D to IMAX 3D). Again, as we will see, consumers are depicted as having new choices and new viewing experiences.

4 ▶ BREAKING THROUGH THE SCREEN

3D, *Avatar*, and the Future of Moviegoing

AT SHOWEST 2005, one of the pre-eminent trade conventions for the motion picture industry, *Avatar* and *Titanic* director James Cameron, in cooperation with Texas Instruments, sought to promote the emerging format of digital projection in theaters. At the time, theater owners were reluctant to change over, given that conversion costs were estimated at $100,000 per screen. However, Cameron argued that digital projection could help to launch a transformation in film spectacle through the use of digital 3D, which would, in turn, bring audiences back to movie theaters by providing them with an unprecedented visual experience. In his typical visionary language, Cameron promised that

> with digital 3D projection, we will be entering a new age of cinema. Audiences will be seeing something which was never technically possible before the age of digital cinema—a stunning visual experience which "turbocharges" the viewing of the biggest, must-see movies. The biggest action, visual effects and fantasy movies will soon be shot in 3D. And all-CG animated films can easily be converted to 3D, without additional cost if it is done as they are made. Soon audiences will associate 3D with the highest level of visual content in the market, and seek out that premium experience.[1]

Cameron's comments place emphasis almost exclusively on Hollywood's role in producing blockbuster spectacles, the kind of "big" films that are promoted as being most enjoyable on the big screen. In fact, his metaphor of "turbocharged" entertainment treats moviegoing as a kind of thrill ride, a notion not inconsistent with Cameron's reputation as a risk taker. This attempt to promote 3D positioned the format as an innovation on a par with the introduction of color and sound, making it appear to be a revolutionary change for audiences.

Significantly, press releases at the time did not mention Cameron's work on *Titanic* or *The Terminator*, but focused on an underwater documentary, *Aliens of the Deep*, which had required Cameron to develop new cameras capable of filming deep below the ocean's surface. Although it would be easy to dismiss Cameron's comments as mere hype, they offer a useful introduction toward thinking about how cinema has been redefined in the era of digital projection and provide a way in which to see Cameron as a kind of "technological auteur," someone who not only makes movies with a distinct artistic signature but also builds the tools and technologies that shape future motion picture production. Cameron's public comments, along with those of Martin Scorsese, Steven Spielberg, and Robert Zemeckis, helped to confer legitimacy on 3D, reframing it as consistent with Hollywood artistry. Further, Cameron, like other technological auteurs, presents a visionary discourse that attempts to define how audiences will watch movies, centered on the idea that 3D will offer an upgraded experience. Such imaginative language arguably has implications for the social role of movies and television shows within a wider media culture. Even as 3D was promoted as a technology that would provide audiences with new forms of visual pleasure, it also functioned as a kind of "Trojan horse" for digital delivery, providing theater owners, who were reluctant to invest in expensive new equipment, with an additional incentive to switch over from film projection.[2]

This chapter explores the marketing and promotion of 3D film exhibition, particularly through the lens of James Cameron's *Avatar*, which was billed by studio marketing executives and entertainment journalists as a "reinvention of how movies are made."[3] These debates about the re-introduction of 3D revived questions not only about cinematic realism but also about the very nature of film as a medium and about audience expectations for the moviegoing experience. 3D productions also inspired new approaches to distribution that were designed to revive theatrical attendance, especially during the era of digital transition. These questions about digital delivery have the potential to lead to a radical transformation in how movies are distributed, providing studios with much greater control over how theaters are programmed. As David Bordwell notes, "the projector-as-computer inserts cinema into what has become an on-demand popular culture."[4] However, although 3D initially served as a means of increasing lagging theatrical revenue, it subsequently became a normal distribution practice rather than a novelty; many audiences in fact chose to watch films in 2D, suggesting that viewers were inclined to weigh factors other than image quality, such as screening times and locations, when making choices about what movies to attend. Or, just as often, they concluded that seeing a movie in 3D simply wasn't worth the additional surcharge.

Although debates about the potential for digital 3D surfaced in 2007 with the release of Robert Zemeckis's 2007 adaptation of *Beowulf*, public interest in 3D's uses as a storytelling tool deepened with the promotion and release of James Cameron's *Avatar*. The film shattered both North American and worldwide box office records, earning a reported $760 million domestically and a total of $2.7 billion worldwide. Even if these numbers appear somewhat more modest when adjusted for inflation, Cameron's film is still the fourteenth highest-grossing film in Hollywood history.[5] The box office success of *Avatar* prompted the hasty reworking of a number of movies in post-production to take advantage of moviegoers' apparent interest in 3D, most notably Tim Burton's adaptation of *Alice in Wonderland* (2009). The box office numbers for these films—and several other 3D movies—seemed to confirm an argument frequently expressed by Cameron in interviews and lectures: 3D represents the future of film and media. These arguments promoted digital 3D in language that evoked ideas of scientific progress and technological inevitability, even while audiences, whether ticket buyers or film critics, began to raise questions about the format.

AVATAR AND IMMERSIVE NARRATIVES

Few filmmakers have been more explicitly associated with the promotion of 3D than James Cameron, who developed a reputation as a technological auteur not only through his films but also through his role in developing the cameras and other equipment used in many of them. This image of the technological auteur is reinforced through a wide variety of promotional materials, including production ("making-of") documentaries, public lectures, and interviews, as well as the theatrical trailers used to introduce viewers to his films and their visual style and narrative. Thus, even before *Avatar*'s premiere, audiences were primed to anticipate a groundbreaking film. *Avatar* also represented a unique marketing challenge, given that it was not based on a familiar character or story world. All movie trailers must persuade viewers to pay for something they have not seen, to speculate about whether they will enjoy the experience. As Lisa Kernan reminds us, trailers are "quintessentially persuasive cinematic texts" that serve a variety of purposes beyond simply convincing viewers to see a specific movie, turning audiences into "shoppers" engaged in the practices of speculative consumption. They also promote preferred interpretations and, in some cases, even instruct viewers on how to understand themselves as spectators.[6] In this respect, the publicity for *Avatar* helped to set the stage for its eventual interpretation and for the renewed emphasis on 3D spectacle as a crucial aspect of the moviegoing experience.

Thus, although it is tempting to focus on *Avatar*'s breathtaking visual imagery, the film's significance was cultivated through a carefully crafted marketing campaign, one that helped to establish how audiences should interpret the film. As Jonathan Gray points out, "films and television programs often begin long before we actively seek them out."[7] In the case of *Avatar*, Cameron's public appearances, movie trailers, and even making-of documentaries that showed on television before the movie was released all contributed to the reception culture that developed around the film. Gray goes on to cite John Ellis's argument that trailers, rather than simply promoting a movie, are actually part of the narrative.[8] The *Avatar* trailer helps to establish several of the major plot and thematic elements of the movie. First, the trailer sets up the visual design through sweeping shots of military aircraft flying over the planet Pandora, the film's primary setting. As the camera glides over one of Pandora's many tree-covered valleys, we hear Marine pilot Trudy Chacon (Michelle Rodriguez) telling Jake Sully and other new arrivals to Pandora, "you should see your faces." By extension, Chacon also seems to be describing the expected response to the film by the theatrical audience. In addition, the trailer prepares viewers for the key plot device, in which a wounded Marine, Jake Sully, takes over the body of a one of the planet's natives. The trailer not only includes the scene where military doctors instruct Sully on how to operate his "new" body but also briefly shows the actor who plays him, Sam Worthington, explaining the plot device. Although this form of metacommentary in trailers is relatively rare, here it helped to establish the idea that the film would be intellectually challenging as well as visually stimulating.

This hype was interconnected with the technologies used to produce and exhibit the film, and the success of *Avatar* became linked not only to Cameron himself but also to a whole range of digital technologies that could, in turn, transform the ways in which movies are made. Cameron's speech at Comic Con was just one example of how *Avatar* was linked to the idea of technological revolution in the way that films are produced and exhibited. As Charles R. Acland observed before the film was released, "few media products have such elevated expectations as *Avatar*. And these expectations are not only for its own success, but for a number of other products and technologies it has bundled to share its revenue-generating glory."[9] Eventually, these discussions of immersive realism would find their way into the promotional discourse associated with the planned *Avatar* theme park at Disney's Animal Kingdom, as Cameron sought to expand ever further the perception of the film as something to be actively experienced rather than passively consumed. Thus, in addition to selling a film, *Avatar*'s promotional discourses became tied to a new way of thinking about movies.

PLOTTING THE FUTURE OF MOVIES

Perhaps not surprisingly, concerns about technological change are directly addressed in *Avatar's* narrative. Although *Avatar* is most noted for its environmental allegory, it also engages with questions about spectatorship and ways of seeing. As the trailer implies, the film itself is about the very processes of immersion and identification that structure debates about moviegoing. A wounded Marine and paraplegic named Jake Sully is commissioned to take control over the body of a Na'vi, one of the blue-skinned and highly agile natives of the planet Pandora, where the U.S. military is involved in protecting corporations that are seeking to extract "unobtainium," a precious resource that could replace fossil fuels and other lost energy sources. Jake is placed in a tank that allows him to control the body of one of the Na'vi. Initially the soldier struggles to control this new body, but Jake quickly embraces this new, physically active self, even as his human body deteriorates from more and more time in the tank. His interactions with the Na'vi gradually lead him to identify with the natives and against the rapacious military-backed capitalists who seek to mine unobtainium. Thus, on an obvious level, *Avatar* seems to offer a superficial parable about the dangers of overreliance on fossil fuels. A second reading, one based in an overt anti-colonialist perspective, seeks to engage with the treatment of Native Americans by the U.S. government and operates alongside the environmental storyline, comparing the Americans' arrival on Pandora to the colonization of North America. In addition, Cameron makes topical references to the war in Iraq, leading some conservative reviewers to mock the film as "*Dances with Wolves* Meets *Ferngully.*"[10]

However, as Jeffrey Sconce argues, the film offers a secondary allegory, one that focuses on the transition from film to digital media, with Jake's journey into Pandora seen as a means of playing out "the warring production paradigms the film so conveniently spatializes within its diegesis."[11] In other words, the film stages a conflict between photographic and digital realism, one that is mapped onto the conflict between the human and Na'vi worlds. In fact, it seems to be no accident that one character describes the entrance to Pandora in words that echo Dorothy's dramatic arrival in the world of Technicolor in *The Wizard of Oz*: "We're not in Kansas anymore." Although it is a throwaway remark, the comment underscores the idea that *Avatar's* use of digital tools is even more revolutionary than past technological advancements. In short, we are told that Cameron is transforming cinema, and we, the audience, are simply along for the ride. The old, decaying medium of film has been supplanted by the potential of digital perfectionism, the possibility that digital tools can create a fully immersive narrative world. And much like the brightly colored world of Oz, Pandora offers a visually stimulating world that opens up the immersive potential of 3D filmmaking.

AVATAR AND DISCOURSES OF 3D REALISM

The promotion of *Avatar* and much of the subsequent debate over it centered on the film's engagement with realism. The publicity and promotion campaign for the film initially sought to link the film's use of 3D technology to Cameron's commitment to creating a fully immersive motion picture. Promotional articles emphasized Cameron's attention to detail in creating Pandora. For example, in the *Los Angeles Times*'s "Hero Complex" blog, Geoff Boucher reported on Paul R. Frommer, a professor of linguistics at the University of Southern California, who spent several years creating the language spoken by the Na'vi. In the interview, we learn that Frommer focused not only on devising a vocabulary of over 1,000 words but also on creating a syntax to make the language sound more believable.[12] Other articles, including one in *Wired*, highlighted Cameron's commitment to revolutionizing cinema through technological innovation, including his dedication to inventing what he called "'the holy grail of cameras,' one that could render feature-film quality images in both 3D and 2D," with the hope of creating a film that would allow viewers to experience life on Pandora "viscerally."[13] Finally, many promotional articles also mentioned Cameron's Pandorapedia, an interactive companion to the film that explains its history, flora, fauna, and language. Twentieth Century Fox also released a glossy book, *Avatar: A Confidential Report on the Biological and Social History of Pandora*,[14] which purported to be a research document produced by the "Resources Development Administration," the agency that oversees the colonization of Pandora in the film. The book is divided into sections that survey the astronomy and geology of Pandora, explain the physiology of the Na'vi, and provide a Na'vi-English dictionary.[15] Whether or not fans and critics consulted the Pandorapedia, discussion of the project helped to promote the idea that Cameron was committed to producing a fully immersive 3D experience, one that would create a thoroughly believable world.

Further, the emphasis on *Avatar*'s realism was grounded in Cameron's status as the film's "author." The concept of authorship has a long, highly contested history within film and media studies, a conflict that has become exacerbated in the era of transmedia storytelling, in which audiences are frequently involved in the production of texts. However, as Jonathan Gray notes, the concept of authorship has been transformed within popular culture, and authors now serve to instill or promote preferred meanings. As Gray describes the phenomenon, drawing on Michel Foucault, an author is "a discursive entity used by the industry to communicate messages about its text to audiences."[16]

Thus, although the concept of the auteur has been challenged from a number of different angles, publicity for *Avatar* often sought to guarantee the film's immersive realism through references to Cameron's status as a technological auteur, someone who is deeply committed to producing innovative entertainment not only through effective cinematic storytelling but also through the creation of technologies that can be used by other filmmakers. This depiction of Cameron appears not only in media interviews and DVD extras but also in biographies of the director. In *The Futurist: The Life and Times of James Cameron*, Rebecca Keegan offers an enthusiastic depiction of the director as someone who is pushing boundaries technologically and aesthetically: "He's a tinkerer and a dreamer who pioneered tools that revolutionized the way stories are told, technologies that a generation of filmmakers now rely upon as surely as they do sound or color. . . . More than anything else, Cameron has muscled movies into the digital age, freeing filmmakers to tell stories that had once been possible only in their imaginations."[17] Cameron is then credited with a number of "advancements" in digital effects: the water tentacle in *The Abyss*, the liquid-metal cyborg in *Terminator 2*, and the sinking of the *Titanic*.

The perception of *Avatar* as a form of immersive entertainment was further advanced in the promotional hype surrounding the announcement of an *Avatar*-themed attraction at Disney World's Animal Kingdom. Although movie-themed attractions are nothing new—Cameron also participated in the creation of a *Terminator* ride film produced for Universal Studios—Cameron used the publicity for the *Avatar* ride to defend and promote 3D and his idea of narrative immersion:

> It's also not just a single ride attraction—it's an environment. So you leave an attraction and come out and it's a themed experience. So you go buy food and somehow the food is themed to that world of Pandora or of the Na'vi culture. And so, you'll have a number of attractions and spaces within this 12-acre land that all are constantly reinforcing to your mind and to your imagination that you're on Pandora. And I think that's great. I think that people want that kind of immersion.[18]

Thus, rather than merely seeing Pandora, visitors to the park would feel as if they were actually on the lush planet depicted in the film.

However, Cameron's efforts at creating a visually rich and narratively engaging story world were far less significant than the role that *Avatar* played in reinforcing the blockbuster economy of digital distribution. *Avatar* not only offered justification for producing more 3D films but also reinforced the idea that 3D projection provided added value for moviegoers, which translated into the surcharges imposed on every ticket sale. In fact, Cameron frequently promoted the idea that viewers were returning to theaters to "upgrade" their experience, seeing the film in the best possible viewing conditions, providing further incentive for theaters to convert to digital projection. As David Bordwell has noted, the financial success of *Avatar* provided reluctant theater owners with the incentive to convert, in part because they could charge an additional \$3–4 per ticket, a significant cost for a family of four paying for a night at the movies.[19]

AVATAR GOES HOME

The theatrical release of *Avatar* was just one piece of a larger entertainment franchise. The film was part of a larger project to promote a utopian technological narrative, in which the experience of watching movies would be forever transformed, whether the viewer watched on a giant screen at her local IMAX theater or in the comfort of her home. In this sense, *Avatar* was more than an expansive textual commodity: it was also caught up in the discourses of revolutionizing movie watching. However, whatever else it might be doing, *Avatar* was primarily a valued entertainment commodity, one that could be marketed on the strength of its relationship to Cameron as a technological auteur capable of crafting the ideal conditions under which a movie could be watched. These questions about ideal viewing conditions even came to shape the promotion of the different DVD versions of the movie when they were released over the course of several months.

The first version, available in the standard DVD format as well as a two-disc DVD and Blu-Ray package, was sold as a means to give fans, who presumably couldn't wait to see the movie again, early access after it left theaters. The hope was that fans and collectors would be impatient enough to purchase the basic DVD and still buy the loaded versions when they came out a few months later.[20] Notably, this initial DVD release was timed to annual Earth Day events, highlighting the film's pro-environment narratives and providing yet another way of expanding its appeal. However, the absence of special features was seen as a cynical ploy designed to encourage not just multiple viewings but also multiple purchases. In fact, the absence of extras led Richard Corliss to complain that the slim DVD was released so that buyers "could leave space for the *real* editions coming later."[21] Corliss also noted the disjunction between the theatrical marketing of *Avatar* and the promotion of the DVD, observing that theatrical screenings of the film were sold as "an experience that couldn't be duplicated at home." This "no frills" DVD was followed by a "Collector's Edition," a three-disc set available in both Blu-Ray and DVD formats, which featured three different versions of the film, including an "extended cut," as well as three hours of special features, such as documentaries and deleted scenes. The Blu-Ray edition also boasted extra-textual materials, including the Pandorapedia, as well as an "interactive scene deconstruction" feature. This second DVD was meant to encourage sustained engagement with the film, allowing audiences to immerse themselves in production details and the narrative choices made by the director.

But each of these versions seemed to anticipate the planned 3D home version of the film, the release of which was delayed as distributors waited for consumers to purchase Blu-Ray players in sufficient quantity. As Charles Acland notes, the multiple versions of the *Avatar* DVD reinforced the perception that "the movie itself is elastic, a mutable and varying entity, a work-in-progress."[22] Acland goes on to argue that the documentaries, deleted scenes, and other special features on the DVD combine to promote the new technologies of production, creating what he calls "a romance with a particular mode of cultural production defined by an engagement with new technological materials and processes."[23] The practice of releasing multiple DVDs of a popular film was not new to *Avatar*. Movies such as Ridley Scott's *Blade Runner* have been revisited multiple times in different versions, allowing the film to be reinterpreted and resold, but Acland's comments underscore the extent to which *Avatar* was specifically identified with a new regime of digital delivery in which movies can be endlessly reworked, upgraded, and re-circulated as technologies improve. Thus, although the original advertising for *Avatar* sold it as something that should be experienced theatrically, promotional materials were revised to sell the idea that *Avatar* was, in fact, a pioneer on a more general technological cutting edge, one that would revolutionize motion picture entertainment through the magic of new technologies, a shift that would even alter how we watch movies at home.

Cameron's status as a technological auteur was used to market and promote home video technologies. These advertisements built upon his ostensible role in creating a new technological experience, one that surpassed traditional cinema. One advertisement for Panasonic's 3D Blu-Ray Disc Player announced boldly, "Experience Avatar in 3D at Home," next to a flat-screen television set in which a Na'vi warrior riding an "ikran," the flying mountain banshees, appears to be soaring out of the frame, in much the same way that 3D images in theaters appear to break free from the plane of the movie screen. The ikran had provided some of the film's more breathtaking visual set pieces, allowing the camera to glide effortlessly through space as it captured the Pandora landscape from a completely mobile point of view. At the bottom corner of the advertisement a text claimed that the player was using "James Cameron's *ideal settings* to watch Avatar" (emphasis in the original). Thus, even while *Avatar* sought to entice audiences back into theaters and advertisements encouraged repeat viewings in order to see the film in the best format possible, the movie was also used to promote the struggling Blu-Ray format and to generate interest in the idea of 3D television. Further, as Acland notes, *Avatar*'s ancillary products were directly tied to the promotion of 3D television sets. In fact, Ubisoft's *Avatar: The Game*, which was released just days before the movie hit theaters, works best on 3D-enabled television sets or computer monitors, thus using technological settings to entice game players to upgrade their home entertainment devices.[24] This use of technological auteurs to sell home theater equipment is far from new. As Barbara Klinger notes, advertisements for home theater systems in the early 2000s "subtly create a pantheon of directors in their promotions," including Cameron and Steven Spielberg, filmmakers known for their spectacle-driven blockbusters.[25]

Consistent with his role as a technological auteur, James Cameron led the charge for 3D television, joining *Avatar* camera operator Vincent Pace to promote the use of 3D for television broadcasting. In particular, Cameron envisioned that 3D could be used to enhance everything from live sporting events and television series to advertising.[26] These attempts to sell 3D television were caught up in the discourses of technological innovation and enhanced realism that had been used to sell 3D in movie theaters. Echoing Cameron's assertion that 3D could help television broadcasting to realize its "full potential as a creative and powerful storytelling and live broadcast medium," advertisements for 3D television sought to depict it as opening up new ways of seeing that were unavailable through traditional broadcasting. In one British Samsung television advertisement, 3D blurs the boundaries between the "actual" and the "televisual" worlds by having animals and plants seem to cross over from the other side of the screen: a whale dives into a tiny pond, a lion overlooks a city street from the top of a building, a butterfly flutters toward a small child. The images suggest the ways in which viewers can potentially become more immersed in the world of entertainment.

Attempts to market 3D involved the collaboration of broadcasters, such as ESPN, and television manufacturers, including Samsung, Sony, and Panasonic. Like the use of 3D in theaters, 3D television was sold in terms of its immersive potential, especially when it was launched during the 2010 World Cup, which was held in South Africa. ESPN's 3D broadcasts of several of the key matches were described in terms of their ability to transport viewers to remote locations, with *USA Today*'s Mike Snider, in a typical conversion narrative from skeptic to supporter, reporting that "3D adds depth to the field, increasing the illusion that you are watching the event in person." Snider's account of watching the World Cup on a 3D television screen underscores the complex interplay between immersion and spectacle that 3D broadcasters face. Snider suggests that 3D broadcasts of the World Cup are capable of placing us at the scene in South Africa, both in terms of visual point of view and in terms of the capturing the excitement of being there, albeit with a shifting point of view. Whereas wide-angle shots provide us with the perspective of being a "fan in the stands," the mobile camerawork almost seems to transcend actually being there, making the experience of watching at home potentially more exciting than being there in person. As Snider describes it, "the 3D effects almost put you in the action. The post-goal close-ups of celebrations of fans in the stands and players on the field brought home the energy of the event." Thus, despite the clunky machinery required to watch 3D television at home—expensive glasses, in particular—the liveness and excitement of a sporting event such as the World Cup helped to reinforce the emotional and immersive realism promised by 3D television advocates.[27] Although television has long been associated with this promise of liveness, with the ability to transport viewers to distant locations in real time, 3D seemed to offer, for some critics at least, an even deeper immersive potential, one that could provide an even better experience than sitting in the stands.

However, despite the attempts to promote 3D television, it remained unclear whether viewers would convert, especially given that many had recently purchased expensive LCD and plasma sets. With 3D sets retailing at $2,000 or more in 2011, 3D often appeared to be a luxury rather than a necessity.[28] In fact, the set itself represented only one piece of the overall expense associated with bringing 3D home. Glasses for home sets cost $150 for a single pair with regular batteries and $200 for a pair with rechargeable batteries, a significant expense for families or groups expecting collective viewing experiences. More crucially, early efforts at creating 3D television broadcasts required that viewers sit approximately five to seven feet from the standard set in order to get the full effect of the visual image, essentially reducing their mobility.[29] Finally, although sales of 3D television sets increased from 600,000 in 2009 to 1.91 million in 2011, adoption of 3D television still seems destined to be a gradual process.[30]

THE 3D THEATRICAL GOLD RUSH

Because of *Avatar*'s box office success, a number of Hollywood studios immediately began to convert their films to 3D to capitalize on the "premium" ticket prices that theaters could impose because of the perceived popularity of the format. Several films, including Tim Burton's *Alice in Wonderland* and Louis Leterrier's remake of *Clash of the Titans* (2010), were initially filmed with plans for projecting them in both 2D and 3D and were converted in post-production; many other movies were imagined and carried through as 3D films. Many of these 3D productions were marketed via the idea of textual novelty, aligning them with Cameron's rhetoric of technological innovation. However, as Kristin Thompson noted, the newness of 3D quickly wore off, even if the practice of charging anywhere from $3–5 extra per ticket did not.[31] The films that were converted in post-production were often criticized for their boxy images and their sloppy use of 3D. In fact, a number of websites were created to document whether a film was made in "real" or "fake" (that is, post-production) 3D. However, Cameron was able to turn even these complaints into a tacit support for the role of the auteur in making effective use of 3D technology. As Thompson pointed out, "for Cameron, conversion is a problem when it is done hastily and carelessly." Cameron singled out *Clash of the Titans* as an example of a situation where 3D was applied needlessly, "like a layer, purely for the profit motive."[32] Despite Cameron's claims about the potential artistry of 3D, his complaints about its supposed misuse, and his implicit disavowal of his own economic incentives, 3D has become a crucial part of what Edward Jay Epstein refers to as the "blockbuster economy."[33]

As 3D became a significant industrial strategy, a number of trends emerged, with all of the major studios and some independent studios taking on 3D projects. By the summer of 2011, 3D had become standard for superhero films: Warner's *The Green Lantern* (2011), Columbia's *The Green Hornet* (2011), and Paramount's (in collaboration with Marvel Comics) *Thor* (2011), *Captain America* (2011), and *The Avengers* (2012). One of the few superhero films not made in 3D was Christopher Nolan's *The Dark Knight Rises* (2012), the final film in his Batman trilogy, for which he was able to negotiate the right to shoot exclusively in 2D.[34] Given that superhero films are often associated with actions that defy the laws of physics, they provided ample opportunity for filmmakers to create visually compelling narratives that could attract audiences into theaters. Other modes that were heavily identified with 3D included animated films, which were typically easier to convert and had the added bonus of attracting family audiences.

One of the other significant genres that took advantage of 3D was the concert film. Several musical artists and ensemble groups became the subject of concert films, including U2, Hanna Montana (Miley Cyrus), Justin Bieber, Michael Jackson, the Jonas Brothers, the Foo Fighters, Katy Perry, and the cast of the Fox television series *Glee*. In most cases, these productions seemed targeted toward youth audiences, and in virtually all cases, the concert films were tied to other media properties, whether an album or a television show. Like *Avatar*, 3D concert films were promoted in terms of their ability to provide audiences with an experience that could not be duplicated in the home. Many were billed as exclusive engagements that would play in theaters for only a few days in order to build up additional demand. Furthermore, they helped to reinforce a promotional strategy that emphasized the experience of live attendance at the concert. In particular, *Glee: The 3D Concert Movie* took this approach by creating advance screenings designed to attract more enthusiastic fans of the show and its musical performances. These ticket packages cost $30 for a single ticket and included a number of *Glee* collectibles, such as a hat, a pin, a backpack, and a bracelet; an additional shipping charge of $5.95 brought the total cost to more than triple the price of a normal movie ticket.[35] The movie also retained its event status by placing more emphasis on the performances, many of which were recorded during a forty-city concert tour, than on the narratives associated with the television show, while also keeping sustained attention on the show as audiences waited for a new season to start.

REIMAGINING THEATERS

The popularity of 3D concert films is consistent with an ongoing trend toward trans-forming theaters into sites for consuming a wide range of entertainment. Digital projection gives theaters increased programming flexibility, allowing them to show not just movies but also concerts, ballets, sporting events, and, in rare cases, fina-les of television series, as happened when the executive producers of *Lost* hosted a live question-and-answer session broadcast via satellite to theaters across the coun-try along with the final episode of the show. In the case of *Lost,* such an event could speak to the intense fandom sparked by the show's puzzling narrative.[36] Like the *Lost* finale and the *Glee* concert tour, this alternative content is often associated with live or special event status. This alternative content potentially allows theater owners to fill seats on weekdays when, by some estimates, only 5 percent of the available tickets in a given theater would be sold. In fact, this content accounted for approximately $112 million in ticket sales in 2010, usually for events held on weekday mornings or evenings when theaters would normally sit empty.[37] It's worth emphasizing that these special events do more than simply provide theater owners with an additional rev-enue stream. In many ways they change our perception of moviegoing as an activity, turning it into something closer to the practices associated with television broadcast-ing. As Charles Acland observes, these events produce a "sense of immediacy and 'liveness'" normally associated with television in ways that potentially expand our expectations about the social role of movie theaters.[38]

Significantly, a small number of independent filmmakers and studios sought to enter the 3D marketplace, although many of their films fit into more tradi-tional genre categories, such as the Screen Gems horror film *Priest* (2011) and Summit's action film *Drive Angry* (2011), which starred Nicolas Cage and fea-tured extensive car chases that could take advantage of the extra dimension. Perhaps the most compelling independent project was Werner Herzog's *Cave of Forgotten Dreams,* a documentary in which Herzog visited the Chauvet caves in southern France, site of the earliest known human-produced pictorial creations. Finally, the Christian-oriented Animated Family Films produced the feature film *Lion of Judah,* a retelling of the Easter story in which a lamb named Judah attempts to avoid being sacrificed on an altar in the days leading up to the cruci-fixion of Jesus, providing religious audiences with what the trailer referred to as "an extraordinary salvation parable." Although *Lion of Judah* was produced on an estimated $15 million budget, it is more difficult to judge the film's financial success, given that it was distributed in part through churches and other reli-gious organizations in addition to movie theaters. However, the film's produc-tion ran into problems, and its 3D animation was not fully ready for the film's June 2011 release, forcing it into a limited 2D release followed by a subsequent 3D roll-out.[39] Thus, although 3D is typically associated with expensive blockbusters, it has been used to limited effect by low-budget and documentary filmmakers.

TABLE 2.   Partial List of 3D Films, 2007–2012

Disney:	Warner:	Paramount:
Alice in Wonderland	Clash of the Titans	Beowulf
The Avengers	Wrath of the Titans	Hugo
Piranha 3D (Weinstein)	The Great Gatsby	The Last Airbender
Piranha 3DD (Dimension)	Dolphin Tale	Madagascar 3
G-Force (Bruckheimer)	Hubble 3D (IMAX)	Jackass 3D
Step Up 3D (Touchstone)	Happy Feet 2	Justin Bieber: Never Say Never
Toy Story 3	Harry Potter and the Half Blood Prince	Katy Perry: Part of Me
Spy Kids 4		Thor
Jonas Brothers 3D	Harry Potter and the Deathly Hallows, Part 2	Captain America
Pirates of the Caribbean 4: On Stranger Tides (Bruckheimer)	Yogi Bear	Transformers: Dark of the Moon
	Green Lantern	
Up	The Hobbit	Titanic (re-release, with Fox)
Bolt		
	Columbia:	Puss in Boots (Dreamworks)
Brave	Green Hornet	
Tangled	Tintin (Paramount)	**Dreamworks:**
Cars 2	The Smurfs (Sony)	Shrek Forever After (Universal)
Tron: Legacy		
Gnomeo and Juliet	**Screen Gems:**	Monsters vs. Aliens
Toy Story 1 and 2 (re-releases)	Priest	How to Train Your Dragon
	Summit:	Megamind
Animated Family Films:	Drive Angry	Kung Fu Panda 2
Lion of Judah	Step Up Revolution	**Twentieth Century Fox:**
Creative Differences:	**Lionsgate:**	Ice Age: Dawn of the Dinosaurs 3D
Cave of Forgotten Dreams	Saw 3D	Avatar
3ality Digital Entertainment:	Final Destination 5 (Warner)	Prometheus
U2 3D (National Geographic)	Journey to the Center of the Earth	Gulliver's Travels
		Rio
Universal:	Texas Chainsaw Massacre	Life of Pi
Sanctum	Dredd	Glee: The 3D Concert Movie
Coraline (Focus)	Battle for Terra	Star Wars 1: The Phantom Menace (re-release, with Lucasfilm)
Despicable Me	**Sony:**	
Dr. Seuss's The Lorax	Monster House	
	The Amazing Spider-Man	
	Men in Black 3	

NOTE: Co-production companies in parentheses.

CINEMA OF THE UPGRADE: REBOOTING AND REVIVING

The most common use of 3D projection was to expand existing media franchises and to provide new forms of technological and textual novelty that could
be used to entice audiences back into theaters. These goals can be achieved in
two ways: through the production of sequels to existing franchises or through
the re-release of older films to theaters in a 3D format. A quick glance at table 2
will show that 3D has been used to bring novelty to existing franchises. This
process was explicitly addressed by Michael Bay in a discussion of why he chose
to make *Transformers: Dark of the Moon*, the third film in the series, in 3D. As
Anthony D'Alessandro remarked, "for a sequel to succeed at the box office, its
stakes, in some form, always need to trump its predecessor. In the case of *Dark
of the Moon*, the mindblowing 3D should satisfy those audiences emptying their
wallets for the ride."[40] 3D was also used to expand or reboot animated franchises,
including *Toy Story*, *Happy Feet*, and *Cars*, as well as a number of horror films
series, such as the *Texas Chainsaw Massacre* and *Saw* films. In this sense, the 3D
format contributed to the practice of rebooting Hollywood franchises, providing
audiences with new motivations to revisit familiar characters and story worlds.

Rebooting entails a somewhat more specific practice than merely adapting or remaking an existing media text. As Anne Friedberg notes, movies may
be remade to alter historical details or respond to technological change. This
practice is hardly new, of course. When sound became *de rigueur*, for example,
a number of silent films were remade to take advantage of the new storytelling
tool.[41] The reboot, on the other hand, is a special form of remake, one that takes
an existing character or story world and re-imagines it. The idea of the reboot
comes from the term for restarting a running but failing computer system. In
film or television, the term refers to the idea of taking an existing media franchise
and starting anew. Quite often, this practice involves returning to the origin
story of a character such as Batman or Spider-Man and retelling, for example, the
traumatic night when Bruce Wayne's parents were killed or the moment when
Peter Parker was bit by a radioactive spider. Usually, reboots introduce a new
director and new stars as a means of reimagining or reinterpreting these characters, providing the spark to extend the commercial lifespan of an intellectual
property.[42] Thus, director Christopher Nolan and actor Christian Bale were able
to reboot the Batman franchise after the critical failure of the Joel Schumacher
films. These retellings allow the new creative personnel to re-imagine the story,
often in ways that build upon the aesthetic inclinations of the director, the social
or political concerns of the moment, and the technological innovations in the
movie industry. As William Proctor observes, reboots entail "a removal or nul-
lification of history in order to 'begin again' from 'year one' without any require-
ment of canonical knowledge of previous incarnations (which is, of course, an
implausible conceit as the audience cannot be rendered amnesiac at the whim

of a corporate monolith)."[43] To be sure, most viewers of a reboot are well aware of the past versions of the story; however, rebooting can allow a filmmaker to retain essential elements of a story while discarding aspects of the franchise that are no longer functioning properly. Although the mania for rebooting has been crucial to the film industry for some time, 3D provides an additional motivation for revisiting existing franchises, further entrenching the idea that films have become data that can be upgraded or rebooted.

The innovation of 3D was also involved in attempts to revitalize dormant franchises through sequels. Perhaps the most notable example was Disney's decision to go ahead with *Tron: Legacy* (2010) nearly thirty years after the original *Tron* debuted in 1982. Although the visual special effects of the first film were influential for a whole generation of filmmakers, the film itself had limited success theatrically because it was released against Steven Spielberg's *E.T.: The Extra-Terrestrial* (1982). Like the original *Tron*, the sequel was created at a moment of significant turmoil in the film production process. As Anne Thompson noted, the 1982 film helped to pave the way for the use of computer graphics. *Tron: Legacy* emerged at a moment when the use of a range of new production technologies, including digital performance capture and advanced 3D cameras, was becoming more commonplace.[44] Thus, like other 3D films, *Tron: Legacy* quickly became identified with a technological cutting edge.

However, *Tron: Legacy* is also significant for its role in reviving the long-dormant *Tron* franchise. Even though the film had achieved cult status for fans of special effects films, it was most visible within popular culture as the object of parody, most notably in an episode of *The Simpsons* in which Homer enters a geometric world similar to the Grid, the computer world depicted in the film. Disney sought to counter that impression by using the sequel to revive interest in the 1982 film, in part by creating demand for the DVD through artificial scarcity. As Jason Sperb observes, Disney held back a DVD release of the original *Tron* until after the sequel left theaters. He speculates that this ploy was part of a carefully orchestrated strategy to restrict access to the original film in order to build demand for it, a model that Disney has used for decades.[45]

In addition, digital effects have been used to update older films, a technique used by Steven Spielberg for the twentieth anniversary re-release of *E.T.* As Dan North points out, many of the changes to the original *E.T.* were cosmetic, such as altering the alien's lip movements to sync better with his dialogue and adding footage of the bath scene that had been removed because the animatronic E.T. malfunctioned in the water.[46] The more controversial digital alterations concerned Spielberg's decision to remove the guns held by the federal agents in the film's final chase scene and replace them with walkie-talkies, which, as North correctly stated, changed the original meaning of the film.[47] Although directors have commonly engaged in revisions of their earlier work—think of all the different edits of Ridley Scott's 1982 film *Blade Runner*—this alteration led to complaints that Spielberg had diminished the drama of the original film.

Similarly, 3D has been used as a means to re-circulate older films in theaters, allowing studios yet another window through which they can pull in audiences willing to pay to see a film in theaters. Thus far, several major films, including *Titanic, Toy Story, The Lion King,* and *Star Wars I: The Phantom Menace,* have been re-released in 3D. Disney has frequently re-released older animated classics theatrically in order to draw new generations of children (and their parents) back into theaters, but these conversions have come with some financial risk, in that it costs approximately $100,000 to convert a single minute of film from 2D to 3D, meaning that full conversion of a feature-length movie could cost from $10–20 million.[48] Once again, James Cameron was at the forefront of this textual recycling. He produced a digital 3D version of *Titanic* for a worldwide release on April 6, 2012, the one-hundredth anniversary of the sailing of the ship.[49] In interviews, Cameron spoke of the theatrical release as a generational event—something that everyone should have a chance to experience. More crucially, he pointed out that viewers would finally have a chance to see *Titanic* "as it was meant to be seen, on the big screen."[50] Thus, Cameron was promoting theaters as the primary site for viewing movies; but what seems more significant about his remarks is the idea that the 3D version is superior to the 1997 original, suggesting that for Cameron and other technological auteurs the ideal viewing conditions for movies evolve as new technologies are introduced.

Revisions to beloved films are not always greeted with enthusiasm, however. George Lucas's announcement that he planned to re-release the original *Star Wars* films was met with a great deal of opposition by a fan base that is not shy about expressing its ambivalence about Lucas's ability to protect the legacy of the films he created. As Will Brooker noted, many *Star Wars* fans began sounding their concern about Lucas's role as a creator soon after the release of *Star Wars: The Phantom Menace* in 1998, in part due to the polarizing Jar Jar Binks character. They sometimes expressed these sentiments by creating their own re-edited versions of *The Phantom Menace,* which they regarded as more faithful to Lucas's original vision and which they distributed at fan conventions and, eventually, online.[51] The announcement that Lucas was again planning to tinker with his films not only fed into a passion to "protect" these films but also contributed to a growing backlash against 3D itself, one that was based in audience perceptions of being manipulated.[52]

3D BACKLASH

While 3D was promoted as an idealized viewing experience, one that could revolutionize both theatrical and home entertainment, a growing backlash developed among movie fans and film critics, who offered a range of explanations for why 3D was inferior to earlier modes of producing and exhibiting movies. For the most part, these complaints were based in aesthetic distaste for the appearance of 3D images on-screen. The most common complaint was that 3D movies often failed in their quest to make audiences feel as if they were immersed in the world of the movie. Film critic Stephen Kelly insisted that the format actually had the effect of reminding viewers that that they were "sitting in a room gawping at a screen"; he also described it as "a vandalism of vibrant imagery" disconnected from any specific narrative significance.[53] A similar complaint, popularized by Roger Ebert, was that 3D images were too murky, due in part to the darkened lenses on 3D glasses, as well as the lenses inserted into the projectors. This resistance to 3D projection boiled over when the *Boston Globe* published an article by longtime film critic Ty Burr that detailed his opposition to the format. Like many other critics, Burr had complained that 3D images were darker and murkier than their 2D counterparts, but Burr also pointed out that many 2D films were being projected with the polarizing 3D lens still in place, meaning that even 2D films were likely to be shown significantly darker than the director intended.[54] Ebert's follow-up blog post seemed to portend the end of movies themselves: "I despair. This is a case of Hollywood selling its birthright for a mess of pottage. If as much attention were paid to exhibition as to marketing, that would be an investment in the future. People would fall back in love with the movies. Short-sighted, technically illiterate penny-pinchers are wounding a great art form."[55]

Although such criticisms might seem to be reserved for cinephiles, they eventually began to resonate with more mainstream moviegoers. As Kristin Thompson points out, Paramount quietly worked to distribute a number of prints of Michael Bay's *Transformers: Dark of the Moon* (2011) in a special digital 3D format that was ostensibly twice as bright as a normal 3D movie. However, Paramount's strategy risked alienating audiences for other 3D movies by tacitly admitting that prior 3D films had not been projected properly.[56] Although 3D screenings of *Transformers: Dark of the Moon* performed relatively well, it is difficult to determine whether the availability of brightened prints made a difference. Audiences for other films released at around the same time, including *Captain America*, *Cars 2*, and *Green Lantern*, were increasingly choosing to see them in 2D when possible.[57]

Despite ongoing efforts to market 3D as an event, by summer 2011 entertainment pundits were beginning to speculate that North American audiences, in particular, were rebelling against the increased ticket prices for 3D films. This skepticism emerged relatively early in the 3D revival, but it became much more explicit in the summer of 2011, when a number of aging movie franchises, including the *Pirates of the Caribbean* series, began to make use of the format. As David Poland put it, the box office performance of *Pirates of the Caribbean 4* "will be the poster child for the next era of 3D, which is to say, it's now just another price point and combined with studio efforts to disincentivize the theatrical window, one has to conclude that 3D pricing is now pushing away ticket buyers in some cases."[58] Although Poland's comments ignored the international box office totals for the film, which were far more substantial, they reflected a wider sentiment that 3D was just another "price point," one that was more costly for many people, especially families with multiple children. The attitude toward the format underscored the perception that with digital delivery, films were simply files that could be "upgraded" for audiences who were willing to pay more.

Despite early optimism that 3D would help to revive the activity of moviegoing, the overall impact of 3D was somewhat ambiguous. Worldwide box office totals continued to increase steadily, if not dramatically, from 2008 (the year before *Avatar* was released theatrically) onward, but the number of admissions in the United States and Canada actually dropped after peaking briefly in 2009 while *Avatar* and other early 3D films were in theaters. Thus, although studios experienced a slight increase in box office totals in the United States, the total number of ticket sales suggests that this increase was due primarily to price increases commonly associated with the 3D surcharge. In fact, the box office numbers illustrate the ongoing emphasis on consumers overseas, where viewers were slower to reject 3D films, and especially in China, where a growing middle class became one of the largest audiences for Hollywood films.[59]

CONCLUSION

By the middle of 2012, it seemed clear that digital delivery would fully supplant film projection. At CinemaCon in April 2012, John Fithian, president and CEO of the National Association of Theater Owners, announced that Twentieth Century Fox would stop producing film prints within the next couple of years. The announcement was greeted with little surprise, given that the studio had already stopped distributing film prints in China on January 1. Fithian speculated that the use of "the format of celluloid film could cease by the end of 2013."[60] Thus, despite the mixed reception of 3D, the format had successfully served to usher in the transition to digital delivery. But even as theaters were in the process of converting, a number of directors, including Peter Jackson and James Cameron, were already calling for upgrades to digital projection. At the same CinemaCon where Fithian announced the end of celluloid, Cameron argued that projectors needed to show movies at 48–60 frames per second (fps) rather than the standard 24 fps, and he stated that he planned to film the two *Avatar* sequels at one of the higher frame rates.[61] Similarly, Peter Jackson screened ten minutes of material from his upcoming *Hobbit* adaptation at 48 fps to demonstrate the value of the format. However, while many viewers praised the depth and detail,

TABLE 3   Worldwide Box Office, 2006–2010 (in billions)

Year	U.S./Canada	International	Total
2006	$9.2	$16.3	$25.5
2007	$9.6	$16.6	$26.3
2008	$9.6	$18.1	$27.7
2009	$10.6	$18.8	$29.4
2010	$10.6	$21.2	$31.8
2011	$10.2	$22.4	$32.6

SOURCE: Motion Picture Association of America, "2011 Theatrical Market Statistics," http://www.mpaa.org/Policy/Industry.

TABLE 4   Total Admissions, U.S. and Canada, 2006–2010

Year	Total
2006	1.40 billion
2007	1.40 billion
2008	1.34 billion
2009	1.42 billion
2010	1.34 billion
2011	1.28 billion

SOURCE: Motion Picture Association of America, "2011 Theatrical Market Statistics," http://www.mpaa.org/Policy/Industry.

others complained that the images appeared almost too sharp, making *The Hobbit* seem less "cinematic" than other movies. Jackson defended the technique by claiming that viewers needed more than ten minutes to adjust to it; once familiar with it, he promised, they would find it to be more "immersive" than past formats. Jackson saw the use of higher frame rates as a response to an industry in crisis, given that many younger viewers were willing to watch movies on mobile devices, and implied that the sense of immersion would add value to the theatrical experience.[62] Although the higher frame rate seemed to resolve the dimness problem, it also illustrated the degree to which cinema now followed the logic of the "platform," in which exhibition technologies are constantly subject to revision, innovation, and rapid obsolescence. Thus, as David Bordwell observes, "Film exhibition, once a stable technology undergoing only mild alterations, will henceforth suffer change that is fast, radical, unpredictable, and perpetual."[63] As a result, he adds, theater owners will incur significant costs to upgrade and replace obsolete equipment, while the manufacturers of digital equipment will benefit from selling ever newer devices.[64]

Although users complained about the limitations of 3D, as well as the increased ticket prices, the format served a number of industry aims, especially by providing theater owners with greater incentive to convert from film to digital projectors. At the same time, digital 3D prompted new questions for consumers, studios, and theater owners about the value of the moviegoing experience. While an on-demand culture seemed to contribute to a diminished desire to own copies of movies or television shows, 3D was promoted, with some success, as adding value. In addition, the marketing of 3D was caught up in the discourses of technological advancement, with James Cameron, in particular, selling *Avatar* on the basis that it would transform the activity of moviegoing, providing viewers with a far more immersive experience, one that was caught up in the logic of the "upgrade." Cameron was positioned in a variety of media contexts as a technological auteur, someone who could not only tell powerful stories but also, primarily through sheer strength of character, remake the very technologies of filmmaking. Promotional discourse, such as profiles in publications like *Wired*, emphasized Cameron's (often collaborative) role in developing new cameras that could render 3D more effectively, while also portraying him as a risk taker. The success of *Avatar* helped to usher in a new era of 3D storytelling, one that was caught up in the expansion of Hollywood's blockbuster economy. And even though a backlash against 3D began almost immediately after *Avatar* was released, the format helped to gain greater acceptance of digital projection.

At the same time, the marketing of *Avatar* was used to promote new technologies for consuming entertainment at home, including 3D. This promotion of *Avatar* ultimately led to several contradictions, given that Cameron frequently seemed to imply that 3D films were meant to be viewed on the big screen, even while suggesting that television sets by Panasonic provided the "ideal settings" for watching *Avatar*. In all cases, these debates centered on questions of value, that is, what users might be willing to pay to be entertained. Despite the numerous attempts to market 3D technology both in theaters and in homes, many consumers opted instead for the cheapest alternative possible, leading to the popularization of low-budget formats such as the Redbox kiosk service. Thus, while theaters faced a future of perpetual upgrades, watching movies at home, an activity typically associated with informality and convenience, often involved seeking out the best possible value.

5 ► REDBOX VS. RED ENVELOPE, OR CLOSING THE WINDOW ON THE BRICKS-AND-MORTAR VIDEO STORE

THE DIGITAL DELIVERY of movies seems to democratize access to a wide array of movies, but it also threatens to disrupt some of the traditional ways in which studios have been able to produce revenue, especially after a film leaves movie theaters. Specifically, the persistent availability of movies in streaming catalogs lessens consumers' need to buy a copy of a film and, in turn, decreases the value of that title. The popularity of Netflix—U.S. subscribers watched an average of eighty minutes per night, far more than even the most popular cable network—showed that users had embraced the convenience of video on demand (VOD).¹ The growth of digital delivery means that audiences seeking a night's entertainment often have a variety of choices, both in terms of the sheer number of films available from "long tail" services such as Netflix and iTunes and in terms of the variety of formats available to screen those films. Meanwhile, television audiences are now increasingly able to time-shift through online aggregators such as Hulu and iTunes or through their digital video recorders (DVRs), deepening a process established by videocassette recorders (VCRs) and extended by box sets of television shows.²

In this context, digital distribution has become identified not only with ubiquitous access to movies and television shows but also with unprecedented choice in terms of content and platform. Enthusiastic accounts of platform mobility tout Netflix and similar services as providing anytime, anywhere access to a wide range of movie choices. However, despite these seemingly unlimited options, one of the most popular tools for accessing movies, Redbox, offers a much narrower selection of movies and requires users to visit one of the company's kiosks in order to rent a physical DVD in twenty-four-hour increments. These changing rental practices bring into relief some of the challenges associated with digital distribution, specifically the attempt by distributors to control the consumption of movies and television shows in order to protect the enduring value of their titles.[3] Thus, rather than focusing on the rhetoric of consumer choice, this chapter seeks to make sense of how Redbox upset a number of assumptions about how audiences wished to rent movies. Underlying these changes is a transformation of the value of the film text itself. The cheap rentals offered by Redbox and the apparently inexpensive access to movies and television shows promoted by VOD services have affected the expected cost of watching movies, especially ones that may be viewed only once or twice. This change has contributed to a significant decline in DVD sales, even while the DVD as a format remains a viable alternative for many media consumers. In fact, despite some of the utopian promises associated with digital delivery, entertainment industry estimates suggest that physical media, such as DVDs and Blu-Ray discs, will remain the dominant form until 2015.[4]

Thus, although digital delivery seems to represent a technological cutting edge, one that feeds into desires for mobility and connectivity, families and individuals seeking convenience and inexpensive entertainment instead are making use of kiosk services such as Redbox. Even though renting physical DVDs from a kiosk may seem incompatible with the shift toward on-demand culture, Redbox contributes to the desire for informality and convenience associated with platform mobility. Both streaming video and kiosks are part of an emerging "everyday film culture" that encompasses a range of activities, values, beliefs, and perceptions about the role of entertainment in everyday life and its relationship to personal finances. In response to the potential for ubiquitous and inexpensive access to motion picture entertainment, movie studios have sought to regulate how, when, and where audiences can consume movies. These changes are consistent with what Ted Striphas has described, following Henri Lefebvre, as a "society of controlled consumption," in which consumer behavior is directed and regulated by media industry forces seeking to protect the profitability of their movie franchises with mechanisms ranging from copyright law to distribution windows.[5] As Striphas notes, the processes of controlled consumption are constantly being renegotiated within the media industries, as trade organizations such as the recording industry and the television industry have sought to shape consumption practices. Thus, although this chapter focuses primarily on the movie industry, these shifts are symptomatic of wider changes in media distribution in general. Instead of unlimited, universal access, media conglomerates have sought to create a carefully calibrated distribution system that offers multiple access points (theaters, DVDs, cable, video-on-demand, digital down-loads, streaming video) and a variety of price options.

Therefore, when Redbox's cheap rentals contributed to a changing video rental system, questions about when and where audiences watch movies came to the forefront and highlighted some of the media consumption practices that often go ignored in utopian accounts of digital delivery. In order to make sense of these changes, this chapter examines, first, the depiction of Netflix and Red-box within entertainment discourse. Although digital delivery systems are often understood as technologies, it is crucial to recognize that these tools are shaped by an assemblage of promotional, marketing, and legal discourses that condition their use. As a result, this chapter places emphasis on the ways in which Redbox meets a need that was not initially addressed by VOD. After discussing how Redbox was promoted, I then consider the legal cases and negotiations that took place between the studios and Redbox over the course of several months in 2009 and 2010. These negotiations illustrate quite clearly the industrial stakes associated with the rental and sale of videos, especially in the United States, although these changes have begun shaping distribu-tion practices in other countries as well. Finally, Redbox's distribution model, which emphasizes select new releases, primarily from major studios, rather than many "long tail" titles with small viewership, raises questions about the role of the DVD in promoting deeper engagements with film culture. Further, the delays in adapting streaming and kiosk services outside the United States point to some of the challenges associated with the shift to new forms of digi-tal delivery of movies.

DIGITAL CINEMA AND CONTROLLED CONSUMPTION

As former Lucasfilm, Paramount, and Universal executive Jeff Ulin reminds us, "Studios are financing and distribution machines."[6] Although many studios may arrange for films to be produced, they are defined primarily by their capacity to market and distribute movies with an eye toward generating the maximum pos-sible profit. Ulin adds that successful distribution requires studios to maintain control over their various intellectual properties and to divide up a movie's rights as carefully as possible as it circulates through a variety of channels and screens across the globe. Thus, distributors will carefully delineate the windows or time segments when a movie might be available in a given format.[7] Prior to the pop-ularization of Netflix and Redbox, this cycle typically consisted of a theatrical release followed by pay-per-view (PPV) access at hotels, home video (rental or purchase), domestic video-on-demand (VOD), and eventually premium cable and broadcast television access. Each window was carefully timed to ensure that studios would be able to maximize profitability. Theatrical screenings typically generate more revenue than the delivery options that follow, for example, a screening on a premium cable channel such as HBO or Showtime. In addition, theaters can serve as a means of marketing and promoting DVD sales. Even if a film does not recover its full budget during its theatrical window, the advertising for and word-of-mouth about the movie help to generate interest that could encourage DVD sales. More recently, however, inexpensive streaming video and digital downloads of movies—the ubiquitous access provided by long tail distribution—have clashed with attempts to preserve the periods of exclusivity associated with each window, a process that has been complicated even further by the cheap DVD rentals available at Redbox kiosks.

Thus, one of the biggest changes accompanying the popularization of Redbox and Netflix is the transformation of the window structure that shapes the current theatrical and DVD distribution system. As Ulin observes, "distribution is all about maximizing discrete periods of exclusivity."[8] When VHS first emerged as a movie rental platform, studios and theater owners worried that it would cannibalize box office receipts, with customers choosing to stay at home and rent videos rather than going to theaters. Film distributors addressed this problem by creating a window between theatrical and video release dates, eventually arriving at a six-month time frame in the early 1980s as an ideal after experimenting with windows ranging from several weeks to several years. Twentieth Century Fox, for example, refused to distribute films on VHS that were less than two years old, but in 1981 it abruptly announced that the Dolly Parton vehicle *Nine to Five* would go to video just ten weeks after its theatrical premiere, arguing that theater and home audiences were different.[9] The six-month window eventually became the norm, allowing studios to provide theaters with a period of exclusive distribution while attempting to capitalize on their initial marketing push to support video rentals and sales. However, as Edward Jay Epstein carefully documents, with the introduction of the DVD in the 1990s and the related emphasis on sales rather than rental, the six-month window began to narrow, in part because media conglomerates wanted the summer blockbusters they released to theaters in June and July to be on the shelves in DVD format in time for Christmas. The result was the establishment of what amounts to a four-month window.[10] Recognizing the opportunity to profit from their film libraries, including older classics, media conglomerates focused on a sell-through strategy rather than on rentals, as they had with VHS. The practice of using a low retail price to promote purchasing was reinforced when retailers like Walmart sold DVDs at low prices in order to draw customers into their stores to purchase more expensive—and profitable—items.[11] DVDs, much more than videotapes, were marketed as collectibles, thanks in part to the added commentary tracks and making-of documentaries that helped to position movie audiences as film buffs, unofficial film students learning from Hollywood masters.

These changes in the window system have attracted attention from a range of media and entertainment journalists. For example, Edward Jay Epstein, noting the continued trend toward shortening the DVD window, wonders, "Does any barrier, no less a fragile window, make sense in the quest for the couch potato in an increasingly digital age?"[12] By the same logic, industry observers such as Chris Anderson have discussed the "long tail," the almost mythological premise that the "future" of media distribution lies not in selling (or renting) massive quantities of a few centralized "hits" but in the margins, that is, in selling small numbers of texts to increasingly fragmented and specialized niche markets.[13] Anderson's arguments quickly took on the appearance of common sense. With the rise of Netflix and the decline of bricks-and-mortar video stores such as Blockbuster, not to mention the success of online retailers like Amazon and iTunes, viewers seemed much more prepared to seek out content online. Rental services such as Netflix provide film buffs with a seemingly unlimited array of movie choices, which were initially dutifully sent through the mail in square red envelopes that helped to establish the company's brand. More recently, Netflix has placed emphasis on digital delivery through its Watch Now Player for laptops and set-box connectivity that allows viewers to stream movies on their computers or directly to their television sets, while also enabling them to stream movies through their Wii and Playstation gaming systems. It is worth noting that the company anticipated that DVD-by-mail shipments would continue to grow before peaking in 2013, followed by a gradual decline over the next two decades as Netflix presumably secures rights to more streaming content or as consumers see VOD subscriptions as a convenient and viable option for informal entertainment.[14] However, in August 2011 Netflix's contract with the cable channel Starz, one of its most significant sources of online content, was not renewed. Although the deal could have earned Starz over $300 million, it chose not to renew in order to give consumers an additional incentive to subscribe to the cable channel rather than pay for a streaming Netflix subscription.[15] Netflix eventually obtained rights to more streaming content, but the end of the deal with Starz illustrated one of the limitations of digital delivery. Even though consumers have been conditioned to expect content to be readily available online, streaming rights, unlike the right to rent a DVD once it has been purchased by a retailer, often expire, making it difficult to ensure that specific titles will always be available.

Further, Netflix gradually began to create pricing incentives that would encourage users to select either streaming video or DVDs by mail, further altering the place of the DVD in the current on-demand media culture. Customers would pay $7.99 a month to have one DVD per month and/or $7.99 per month for an unlimited streaming package, although those prices gradually increased. In effect, as David Poland observes, Netflix was asking users to choose between streaming or DVD-by-mail. Although Netflix claimed that it was offering consumers more options for watching movies, Poland was quick to point out that such an approach actually decreased the choices available to consumers, given that the service had streaming rights to only a small percentage of its full DVD catalog: "the new reality that filling the streaming gap with discs is now relatively expensive makes Netflix a Somethings Sometimes business."[16] Poland's comments underscore the ways in which Netflix's original model of unlimited DVD-by-mail selection was gradually transformed into a more piecemeal mixture of streaming and DVD options. The pricing change provoked some resistance. When Netflix's CEO, Reed Hastings, announced that the company would split its streaming service and its DVD-by-mail service, which would be called Qwikster, the move provided a more specific target for consumer complaints. Although the price change had taken effect months earlier, the launch of Qwikster contributed to the service's loss of nearly one million subscribers. The public relations problem was exacerbated when it was revealed that Netflix had neglected to secure the rights to the Qwikster Twitter handle, which belonged to a twenty-something college student who frequently bragged about his marijuana use. Ultimately, Netflix withdrew plans to separate DVD and streaming, but the conflict illustrated the extent to which Netflix users were still in the process of negotiating how to take advantage of digital delivery formats.[17]

Thus, although Netflix built its reputation on the strength of its deep catalog of movie titles, it has evolved into a much more complicated distributor of film and television content. The somewhat more limited choices available for streaming compelled consumers to make more deliberate choices about how, when, and where they would consume Netflix content. In fact, even as Netflix began marketing its streaming video service in 2009, CEO Reed Hastings acknowledged that DVD rentals would continue to grow for anywhere from five to ten years, notably because a large number of Netflix users do not have broadband access, but also because Netflix did not have streaming rights to a large collection of titles.[18] The streaming service was further limited by bandwidth caps that implicitly regulate how many movies viewers can watch in a given month, especially over mobile devices. This problem has been especially acute in Canada, where Netflix operates a streaming-only service. In fact, Netflix was forced to implement lower-quality streaming versions of its movies in order to help customers avoid costly fees for exceeding bandwidth caps. Although the Canadian internet service provider Shaw Cable eventually agreed to increase bandwidth caps, a move that was seen as an attempt to accommodate Netflix customers, these limitations on use continue to challenge the perception of ubiquitous and inexpensive access to motion picture entertainment.[19]

By comparison, Redbox complicated the prevailing logic that consumers are seeking unlimited choice. Its emphasis on a small number of best-selling titles offered an important limit case for discussions of the long tail as a model for video rental. In addition, its success served as a challenge to some traditional assumptions about the place of the DVD in film culture, as more home video consumers seem content to rent movies as cheaply and conveniently as possible, rather than purchasing them for personal collections or making use of digital downloads or streaming video. Within the larger industry context, the conflicts over Redbox and Netflix are two of the more visible expressions of the shifting value of the film object and of the attempts to control how, when, and where content will be distributed, what David Poland bluntly refers to as "the battle . . . about who owns the rights to deliver what content via what delivery systems."[20]

These changes in DVD culture may also be caught up in some of the more prosaic uses of DVDs and other forms of movie consumption in the home. The large body of scholarship focused on the relationship between cinephilia, fandom, and DVD special features often neglects other uses of DVDs as a form of casual entertainment.[21] For example, Barbara Klinger has traced the role of DVD supplemental features in producing what she calls a "rhetoric of intimacy" between the makers of a movie and the implied viewer for most special features.[22] Klinger argues that these extras contribute to "the sense of owning a personalized product," feeding into the promotion of the DVD as a collectible artifact.[23] In addition, as Catherine Grant observes, DVD extras help to foster auteurist readings of films that emphasize the work of individual artists rather than the creation of a commercial product.[24] Although these aspects of DVD consumption are significant, the focus on supplemental features often overlooks some of the more common uses of DVDs, especially their role as a form of inexpensive entertainment, often for parents seeking the kind of "electronic babysitter" that television has been since the 1950s.[25] In fact, as Jeff Ulin observes, the rise of the sell-through DVD market in the 1990s was fueled by videos geared toward children, and industry observer Edward Jay Epstein confirms that child- and youth-oriented films are an essential part of Hollywood's "Midas formula."[26]

This emphasis on children's content was a crucial strategy for both Netflix and Redbox. In July 2010 Netflix invested heavily to purchase streaming rights to a number of children's television shows and developed contracts with the cable channel Nickelodeon, which specializes in shows for children and "tweens," and with PBS, which sold rights to *Barney*, *Kipper*, and *Thomas & Friends*, as well as older episodes of the children's classic *Sesame Street*.[27] Netflix later expanded its children's content by acquiring streaming rights to a number of shows owned by the media conglomerate Viacom, including additional shows from Nickelodeon, such as *Yo Gabba Gabba*, *iCarly*, *Dora the Explorer*, and *SpongeBob SquarePants*.[28] Thus, we should consider DVDs not just in terms of the supplemental features found on the disc itself but also in terms of how the disc circulates. In fact, both Netflix and Redbox made extensive use of "stripped" DVDs that were devoid of the extra features that had originally been central to definitions of domestic movie watching. By focusing on the ascent of Redbox and Netflix, we can address not only the transformed stature of the video store and the apparent decline in DVD retail, but also the changing habits, values, and beliefs that accompany these shifts and their implications for a distribution system in which the value of the movie and television text has been redefined.

CLOSING THE WINDOW ON THE BRICKS-AND-MORTAR VIDEO STORE

Redbox is a service that rents movies, originally for one dollar per day, from kiosks prominently situated in grocery stores, gas stations, airports, and other convenient locations. Because it offered perceived accessibility and low prices at a time of declining DVD sales, the service has contributed to a changing distribution culture, one that has Hollywood studios, big-box retailers, and bricks-and-mortar video stores scrambling to adjust. In addition to offering inexpensive nightly rentals, Redbox has built up its popularity through the use of promotional codes that allow customers a free one-day rental of the movie of their choice, a practice that contributes to the perception that viewing DVDs at home should be relatively cheap. This approach threatens to shut down traditional bricks-and-mortar video store chains—Blockbuster, Movie Gallery, Hollywood Video—that must typically pay for large amounts of retail space and has unsettled the revenue streams that have become crucial to major studios.

The growth of Redbox became one of the biggest stories in the entertainment press in 2009 and 2010. By August 2010, there were approximately 25,000 Redbox kiosks offering customers access to a comparatively small selections of films, especially when contrasted against the offerings at a bricks-and-mortar video store or the much deeper catalogs associated with online retailers. By April 2011, there were 36,000 kiosks, with each kiosk estimated to draw in approximately $40,000 annually.[29] Most kiosks carry approximately 200 titles and hold a total of about 700 DVDs, a far smaller selection than at a bricks-and-mortar store or an online rental service. The vast majority of these films are relatively new releases from major studios rather than the "long tail" titles that are typically associated with digital distribution, with many of them focusing on youth- and family-oriented content.

Although Redbox is a place-based service with physical media, it has been promoted in terms of its convenience and its ability to provide users with greater personal flexibility and mobility. For example, Redbox customers are able to return their movies to the kiosk of their choice. Moreover, Redbox's prices and convenience placed many of its rivals at a huge competitive disadvantage. Blockbuster Video, for example, made plans in early 2010 to close up to 1,300 stores and twice announced plans to file for bankruptcy, first in March 2010 and again

FIGURE 1. A typical Redbox kiosk in the lobby of a Holly Springs, North Carolina, grocery store. (Photograph courtesy of Yasmine Haddad.)

in August 2010.[30] This dramatic decline would have been almost unimaginable in 2001, when Blockbuster had more than 8,000 stores and when it could boast that it had collected $5.4 billion in revenue from approximately three million annual customers.[31] In February 2010 Movie Gallery, the second-largest video chain and owner of Hollywood Video, declared Chapter 11 bankruptcy. Cited in the filing was a statement that Redbox was "cannibalizing" business from traditional video stores. In May 2010 Movie Gallery announced that it would close its remaining 2,415 stores.[32] Likewise, Blockbuster Canada, citing a lack of interest among potential buyers, announced in September 2011 that it would cease operations.[33] With Redbox kiosks accounting for 30 percent of all U.S. rentals by August 2010, up from 19 percent the year before, the service presented a significant challenge to traditional rental practices.

Despite the widely reported struggles of bricks-and-mortar video stores, DVD rentals rose 8.3 percent during the first six months of 2009, while sales dropped 13 percent, numbers that industry observers attributed to saturated film libraries—most collectors already owned an average of seventy DVDs—and to a struggling economy.[34] The Los Angeles County Economic Development Corporation speculated that Redbox had cost the movie industry as much as $1 billion, both from "lost" DVD sales and from producers' decisions to forgo making some movies based on their assessments of profitability, leading to less work for the Hollywood region's below-the-line workers.[35] Whether or not such "ripple effects" can be proved and whether or not Redbox can be identified as a primary factor, the study itself illustrates the degree to which Redbox may be contributing to the ongoing industry crisis over declining DVD revenues and to the ongoing attempts to control the distribution process.

REFRAMING DVD AUDIENCES

DVD-by-mail and streaming services have become a relatively common feature on the entertainment landscape. Netflix, with its ubiquitous red envelopes, originally made its reputation by promising nearly unlimited consumer choice. Redbox, however, has complicated the "long tail" hypothesis and similar claims about the preference for unlimited choice by offering only a limited selection of movies and television shows, but with convenient access and inexpensive prices. In an interview with *Home Media Magazine* in July 2009, Redbox's president at the time, Mitch Lowe, described the typical Redbox customer as "a family with small children who's renting a film for the parents and a film or two for the kids. They are typically both working in the household and the kids are high school age or younger."[36] Thus, instead of offering the deep catalog of titles that might satisfy the urbane, globalized moviegoer associated with Mubi or even Netflix, Redbox addresses the needs of working parents seeking inexpensive entertainment for their families, a crucial audience that often goes unnoticed in utopian discussions of the long tail. According to Redbox's calculations, the most frequently rented movies in 2011 were *Just Go with It*, *No Strings Attached*, *Rango*, *The Dilemma*, and *Due Date*, and the top rentals for 2010 were *Shutter Island*, *The Bounty Hunter*, *Grown-Ups*, *The Karate Kid* (2010), and *The Blind Side*.[37] For 2009, the most often rented films included *Paul Blart: Mall Cop, The Proposal, Taken, Grand Torino,* and *Knowing,* illustrating that the service consistently targets youth and family audiences.[38]

Although the logic behind Redbox seems straightforward, with much of its technological infrastructure relatively invisible to consumers, it is worth noting that the company's business model is based upon a combination of technological advances and social protocols, suggesting that new media distribution practices may become viable only when a "need" emerges. As Brian Winston has observed, citing examples ranging from the telegraph to cable television, widespread adoption of new media technologies often lags far behind the initial development of those communication tools.[39] As Winston goes on to point out, cultural acceptance of new technologies

> is never straightforward, however "needed" the technology. As a society we are schizophrenic about machines. On the one hand, although perhaps with an increasingly jaundiced eye, we still believe in the inevitability of progress. On the other hand we control every advance by conforming it so that it "fits" to pre-existing social patterns.[40]

Thus, new technologies may not be accepted initially because they do not fit recognizable practices for consuming movies. In this case, Redbox fit neatly into the ongoing introduction of automated transactions that had become familiar in grocery store checkout lines and gas station pumps, making it appear more convenient than stopping off at a video store.

The idea of familiarity is further underscored by Lowe's prior, failed attempts to launch a vending machine–based video rental service in the 1980s, when widespread adoption of VCRs was first taking place.[41] In terms of technological change, Redbox benefits from improvements in the ability to process credit card transactions quickly and securely, given that in August 2009 the company was handling close to eighty transactions per second at peak times on Friday nights, far more than online retailers such as Amazon, even during the winter holidays.[42] Furthermore, the Redbox ninjas, the workers who stock and maintain kiosks, often perform maintenance work on them remotely through wireless internet connections, using faster broadband speeds to supplement the rental process; compared with the clerks who operated cash registers and made movie suggestions at the counter of the bricks-and-mortar stores, these workers are virtually invisible. Finally, in addition to walk-up transactions, users can reserve a copy of a DVD from the Redbox website and find out which nearby kiosks have a desired movie by using a Google Maps mashup. This simplicity and convenience allowed Redbox to meet what Diane Garrett refers to as an "untapped need" that is not addressed solely by "technological innovations" such as Blu Ray, high definition, or the deep catalogs made possible by unlimited server space. Instead, Garrett argues, Redbox is an example of what Clayton Christensen describes as a "disruptive innovation," one that fulfilled the rudimentary needs of a movie-watching consumer base that was interested in inexpensive and convenient access to a moderate selection of movies.[43]

But the perception that Redbox provided a convenient way to rent movies quickly was negated somewhat when kiosk users encountered long lines as other consumers were slow to return movies and select new ones. The term "Redbox rage" came to describe patrons who were unable to hide their impatience with the people in front of them in line. Complaints about Redbox users who were unable to pick a movie even inspired a number of bloggers to promote codes of "etiquette" to reduce tension at kiosks. Suggested behaviors included allowing users who were simply returning a title to use the kiosk first and planning ahead to decide what movie to watch while standing in line.[44] In response to these complaints, Redbox introduced a tool that would allow people who were simply returning movies to do so while others were searching for, selecting, and renting DVDs. As a result of these technological fixes, Redbox has taken a relatively simple strategy—movie kiosks have been around for some time in Europe and in rural areas in the United States—and made them into powerful and popular tools.[45]

This emphasis on convenience plays a defining role in shaping perceptions of kiosks and other services, often leading to dismissive depictions of Redbox as catering to a cultural shallowness. For example, Wheeler Winston Dixon argues that the relationship between McDonalds restaurants and Redbox kiosks brings together "fast food and fast food movies, all under the same roof,"[46] a description that carries with it a set of assumptions about Redbox users, as well as their motivations for renting and even their taste in movies. Dixon claims that users of kiosks are likely to have no knowledge of film beyond the entertainment sections of non-specialist publications, such as USA Today or Cosmopolitan. However, given Redbox's low barriers to rental—there are no monthly membership fees or other forms of commitment—it is equally likely that Redbox potentially allows casual users entry into wider cultural conversations. In fact, given that no single platform—whether Netflix's streaming archives or Apple's iTunes or Hulu—can offer access to every single film or television show, Redbox and similar kiosk services, may in some cases serve as a supplement to other forms of media consumption that are more readily associated with technological trendiness or highbrow cinephilia. Even if Redbox is regarded as "fast food" entertainment, there is no reason that a kiosk user cannot also enjoy cinematic haute cuisine on occasion.

In addition to Redbox's success with a DVD rental model, there have been experiments with storing movies on other portable storage devices. A couple of companies have considered the possibility of renting movies on flash drives, but critics pointed out that flash memory chips cost about $2.50 for a gigabyte (GB) of storage versus 50 cents for a DVD. Another possibility, to allow consumers to download movies to reusable flash drives while standing at the kiosk, was deemed too inconvenient, given a download time in 2008 of about one hour for a single movie on a standard USB drive.[47] But in 2008 PortoMedia, a Galway-based company backed by IBM, developed a kiosk technology that used 2 GB flash drives, cutting the download time to less than two minutes for its Movie Keys, which were designed to expire after twenty-four to forty-eight hours. Like other kiosk services, PortoMedia was promoted as a kind of ATM for movies.[48] The company also planned to use digital rights management software to allow the Movie Key to play only on a select number of devices, preventing people from sharing the movie with others, and the movie could not be copied onto a disc that would play in a conventional DVD player, making the content far less mobile than it might have initially appeared.[49] The company was eventually dissolved in May 2010.

More recently, the start-up Digiboo sought to use flash drives to offer inexpensive movie downloads to air travelers. The service would provide rentals for $3.99, and consumers could purchase movies for $14.99. Digiboo launched in March 2012, placing kiosks in airports in Seattle, Minneapolis, and Portland. The focus on airports was deliberate because patrons would typically have time to upload a movie while waiting to board and because most airlines do not allow passengers to access wireless internet while in flight. The user would have access to rentals for thirty days, a significant window. To play a movie, users would have to download the Digiboo Player to their portable device, which they could do the first time they rented or purchased a title, and they would have to provide a credit card as a form of personal identification to reduce the risk of piracy. Digiboo developed the service in part because the optical drives used to play DVDs were becoming less common in portable media players, but initially the player did not work on Android or Apple devices.[50] Given these technological barriers, it was less than clear that a flash drive model would satisfy the needs already addressed by Redbox. While the flash drive companies were promoted as a convenient alternative to Redbox—one executive for Digiboo likened renting a movie to buying a bag of M&Ms from a snack machine—they sometimes faltered when it came to providing true platform mobility.

MOVIE KIOSKS ON THE GLOBAL SCENE

The idea of using kiosks to rent movies has a long history in Europe. The company Video System Italia (VSI) was marketing video rental kiosks as early as 1991, and by 2004 the service had more than 10,000 kiosks in locations all over Europe.[51] Most kiosks were installed in the front window of video stores and were promoted primarily in terms of their ability to allow existing video stores to provide twenty-four-hour service. Patrons could rent movies through pre-paid membership cards, in part because of restrictions on using credit cards in kiosks. According to one estimate, over 90 percent of video stores in Spain and Italy had kiosks.[52]

In some places kiosks have not fit neatly into the emerging on-demand culture associated with platform mobility. For example, Play! Entertainment, launched in Singapore in 2004, several years before Redbox, used a membership system: a user would scan her identification card at the kiosk, which would store information such as the user's date of birth and, most intriguingly, her thumbprint. The user could then rent movies simply by scanning her thumbprint. This technology was also used to ensure that underage customers could not rent NC16 and M18 titles (essentially the equivalent of R and NC17 movies in the United States). Members would buy a $2 stored-value card that originally would hold up to $30 in credits that could be applied to the rentals, which initially cost $4.50 for the first twenty-four hours and 50 cents for every hour thereafter, much like the membership blocks used at a number of independent video stores.[53] Although the kiosks placed emphasis on convenience, the value to customers was less than clear. Play! shut down service in 2011, citing rampant movie piracy and internet downloads, as well as discomfort with vending machines, as contributing factors. A competing service in Singapore, CineNow, also faced struggles, closing seven of its eleven DVD kiosks. Although internet downloads were no doubt a factor, local observers suggested that the kiosks did not fulfill the same needs as in the United States or Japan, given the city's relatively dense shopping and residential areas. As Innoform Media president Angeline Ang acknowledged, in Singapore "we can walk everywhere and shops close late. There is no need to rent a DVD at kiosks."[54]

Beginning in May 2011, Playdium installed a limited number of "Movie Magic" kiosks in convenience stores, Walmarts, and other retailers in the Toronto area, charging $2 per night and offering a selection of recent films similar to that in a Redbox kiosk.[55] Just over a year later, electronics retailer Best Buy announced that it would launch a combined streaming video and kiosk service in Canada, an approach that would combine Netflix's streaming model with the apparent convenience and simplicity of a service such as Redbox. However, once again, the challenge was to acquire the streaming rights to content.[56] Netflix had been criticized for failing to offer an adequate selection of Canadian content, a situation that Best Buy claimed it would avoid. In this sense, the promises of unlimited content choice and convenience made by kiosk and streaming services must be carefully interrogated, especially when it comes to providing access to local media. Eventually, Redbox announced plans to expand into at least 2,500 locations in Canada, specifically at Walmarts and Couche-Tard convenience stores. But the slow adoption of Redbox kiosks in Canada provided further evidence of the legal, cultural, and economic obstacles that limited the growth of kiosks or shaped their use.

THE OPENING OF THE RETAIL WINDOW

Changes in DVD distribution affect not only the consumption of movies at home but also the entire system of windows, including the duration of theaters' exclusive right to show a movie. Due to declining DVD sales, studios continue to consider shorter windows between theatrical and DVD release, even when that reduction threatens to undercut theatrical box office. The structure was severly tested by the box office success of Tim Burton's adaptation of *Alice in Wonderland*, which Disney released on DVD just three months after the film opened in theaters despite opposition from theater owners. Threats of boycotts came from the three major cinema chains in the United Kingdom (Odeon, Vue, and Cineworld), as well as from the Kansas City–based AMC theater chain.[57] The conflict over *Alice in Wonderland* echoed an earlier struggle over the Ben Stiller film *Night at the Museum*; several British theater chains pulled the film when Fox scheduled the DVD release just twelve weeks after its opening in theaters.[58] Both of these situations illustrate the degree to which the interests of distributors, theater owners, and DVD retailers may come into conflict and point to the challenges studios face in rethinking the distribution window structure in the era of digital delivery.

Redbox's biggest challenge to the film industry, therefore, has been its role in reshaping how and when DVDs are distributed. Because Redbox threatens traditional revenue streams, studios have sought to regain control over the DVD distribution process. The attempt to limit the effect of Redbox on DVD sales was met with a series of fascinating, if contradictory, responses by the movie conglomerates and big-box retailers like Walmart and Target. Many of these changes took place over the course of a few months in late 2009 and early 2010, as it became clear that Redbox was both contributing to and symptomatic of changing DVD rental and purchase habits. These changes are worth examining, in part because they illustrate the extent to which the interests of home video distributors and rental services may not be fully aligned. The conflict between the studios and Redbox began to heat up when several studios, including Twentieth Century Fox, Warner Brothers, and Universal, all refused to sell DVDs directly to the kiosk service until they had been available for purchase via retail outlets for several weeks. Redbox responded with a series of lawsuits, first against Universal in October 2008, alleging, according to Ryan Paul, that the studio was "engaging in anticompetitive behavior and . . . abusing copyright law."[59] In addition, Redbox claimed that Universal sought to limit the selection of titles available for rental in the kiosks. Specifically, Redbox complained that Universal had violated antitrust law by threatening to cut off DVD wholesalers Ingram and VPD unless Redbox agreed to Universal's demands that it wait forty-five days after a DVD was released before renting it in kiosks. Two of Redbox's suits against Universal were dismissed; however, the judge supported the company's complaint on antitrust grounds. Later, in August 2009, Redbox filed suit against Warner Home Video in Delaware Federal Court in response to Warner's attempt to block Redbox from distributing Warner titles. Given that Redbox kiosks are stocked primarily with new releases, any imposed delay was seen as a potential threat to the company's ability to compete with Netflix and other rivals in the movie rental business.[60]

As Redbox continued to emerge as a key player, video wholesalers were discouraged from selling directly to Redbox, forcing the service to buy copies of movies directly from retailers such as Walmart and Target. In January 2010, however, Walmart took the unusual step of limiting consumers to a maximum of five copies of a DVD at a given time, mirroring a policy already in place at Target stores. Although Walmart stated publicly that the policy was designed to ensure that its stores would have copies of popular films in stock throughout each day, there was speculation that the retailer was attempting to prevent Redbox employees from buying as many as twenty copies of a newly released DVD and then promptly stocking the kiosk at the front of the store.[61]

This Walmart policy served as a temporary fix while studios negotiated with Redbox. Sony, for example, crafted a $460 million, five-year deal that gave it a guaranteed 19.9 percent share in Redbox kiosks. Paramount initially reached a probationary deal in exchange for rental data before later agreeing to a revenue-sharing pact in July 2010, having concluded that the kiosks had little impact on DVD sales.[62] Lionsgate and Disney had also agreed to contracts with Redbox, while Warner Bros., Universal, and Twentieth Century Fox sought Redbox's agreement to wait for one month after a DVD had been available for purchase in stores before making it available to rent in kiosks. Warner and Redbox eventually settled on a twenty-eight-day "retail window." This retail window proved to be one of the more enduring changes introduced as a result of the negotiations between studios and Redbox, with studios seeking to continue to maintain some control over their fragile window system. In addition, the Warner agreement stipulated that once Redbox is finished with a DVD, it is legally obligated to destroy it, rather than reselling it. In late February 2010 Warner negotiated a similar deal with Netflix, stipulating a twenty-eight-day window in exchange for cheaper DVD prices and assistance in providing more streaming titles from the Warner catalog.

Because of Redbox's success, Blockbuster began investing in rental kiosks, with a plan to have 3,000 kiosks by the end of 2009 and as many as 10,000 by December 2010, many of them at Publix grocery stores. The Blockbuster kiosks would hold up to 1,000 films, offering slightly more choice than their rivals, while

FIGURE 2. A typical Blockbuster Express kiosk outside a Holly Springs, North Carolina, grocery store. (Photograph courtesy of Yasmine Haddad.)

also having earlier access to newly released DVDs than either Netflix or Red-box, thanks to the chain's contracts with studios. However, given Blockbuster's primary identity as a bricks-and-mortar store, as well as Redbox's early lead in placing kiosks, it is less than clear whether the company can serve as a viable alternative to Redbox or Netflix. The main point is that studios, in cooperation with Netflix and Redbox, have created a retail window that will temporarily limit access to renting new releases in the hope that retail DVD sales will grow.

Despite earlier negotiations, the conflict between the studios and the rental companies continued into 2012. Warner announced in March 2012 that it would not sell DVDs directly to Redbox for fifty-six days after a film was available for retail purchase. As a result, Redbox continued its practice of purchasing Warner movies from store shelves—usually at a higher cost than it would pay through wholesalers—and putting them in kiosks, often less than a week after they were available to consumers. Universal also expressed a preference for a longer retail window but declined to join forces with Warner, choosing instead to renew its current deal through 2014.[63]

These industrial changes raise important questions about movie consumption practices. Accompanying the red box and the red envelope is a changed perception of the "value" of a film text, a shift that reflects the increased mobility of the film text and the fluidity of the window system, in which movies and television shows circulate in a wide variety of platforms and can be packaged in a wide variety of formats. Perhaps the biggest impact will be on DVD sales. Although some studies, including Paramount's market research, have suggested that Redbox's effect on DVD sales is negligible, research cited by the *Wall Street Journal* claims that 25 percent of renters indicated that they would buy fewer DVDs because of their availability in kiosks.[64] Although such self-reporting may not be consistent with actual practice, the decline of DVD sales seems tied to changing perceptions of access. The logic of the retail window rests in part on the recognition that 90 percent of all DVD sales take place during the first month that a film is available for sale, but it is less clear that audience enthusiasm for specific films will translate into increased sales. More crucially, however, competition from Redbox kiosks could lead to lower prices not only for rentals but also for digital downloads, shaping future expectations about the value of renting and owning copies of movies in whatever format. In fact, even with the twenty-eight-day retail window in place, industry observers continued to detect a preference for renting videos rather than purchasing DVDs, marking a continued shift away from the practices of collecting in favor of paying a lower price for temporary access.[65]

Although Redbox grew at the expense of video store chains such as Blockbuster, Movie Gallery, and Hollywood Video, some studios have argued that "mom-and-pop" stores have been the most directly affected.[66] However, there is evidence, some of it admittedly anecdotal, that independent video stores have actually gained traffic thanks to the closure of the chain stores. Independent video stores might also benefit from the twenty-eight-day retail window imposed upon Netflix and Redbox, because they operate under the first sale doctrine, which allows a purchaser to sell, rent, or give away a lawfully made copy of a copyrighted work once it has been purchased. Thus, bricks-and-mortar video stores would be one of the few rental services to have new releases on the date they become available for purchase, a considerable advantage when consumers are seeking a night's entertainment and are uninterested in purchasing a DVD.[67] In fact, many video stores, both independent "mom and pop" stores and chains such as Blockbuster, have explicitly marketed themselves in terms of the ability to rent videos before Redbox and Netflix. For example, Blockbuster's advertisement for the Sandra Bullock film *The Blind Side* placed specific emphasis on the customer's ability to "get it today at Blockbuster," in stores, on demand, or by mail.

Blockbuster's role in the rental marketplace changed again when it was purchased by the satellite television service Dish TV, which paid $320 million to pull the chain out of bankruptcy proceedings. Dish then offered a free three-month subscription to Blockbuster's DVD-by-mail service to attract new customers.[68] Like many other media transactions, Dish's Blockbuster offer built upon the "free" model described by Chris Anderson, in which retailers offer a basic service for free in order to get customers to pay for a more expensive service.[69] Notably, the deal did not include access to Blockbuster's streaming service. Further, Blockbuster adopted a pricing model similar to that used by Redbox, in which new releases cost $2.99 for the first day and $1.00 for each additional day, while older films cost $1.99 for the first day and $1.00 thereafter. Although renting a movie at Blockbuster continued to be more expensive than getting the same movie from Redbox, the new pricing scheme showed a recognition that the company would have to adapt to the lower prices set by kiosks. At the same time, the slightly higher price allowed Blockbuster to maintain its contracts with the studios to obtain newly released films twenty-eight days before its competitors.[70]

CONCLUSION

The place of Redbox within the business of movie rentals can tell us quite a bit about everyday film culture. Although Netflix, Mubi, and other long tail distributors continue to promote themselves in terms of their deep catalogs and their ability to give customers more meaningful engagement with film culture, rental kiosks have become a crucial site through which home audiences rent and watch movies. The popularity of Redbox's kiosks unsettled traditional DVD distribution patterns. As a result, studios worked to negotiate a retail window of twenty-eight days between the "street" date when new DVDs would be available for purchase and the date when they would be available for rental via Netflix and Redbox. This attempt to regulate when and where movies become available for consumption at home challenges prevailing wisdom about the web supporting ubiquitous access to content, while also highlighting the ways in which studios and retailers continue to negotiate the rights to control which content will be available on which delivery systems. Thus, the negotiations between the studios and Redbox served as a means for studios to regulate and police the distribution of DVDs in ways consistent with the logic of controlled consumption postulated by Henri Lefebvre and described in detail by Ted Striphas in his discussion of the book industry.

Moreover, rental kiosks help to challenge the idea that consumers are necessarily interested in access to the deeper catalogs celebrated by digital utopians such as Chris Anderson. Instead, kiosks might be productively read as a "disruptive innovation," one that meets the unrecognized needs of a group of consumers, especially parents seeking to use a DVD as an "electronic babysitter." Finally, Redbox reminds us that, as media scholars, we must engage not only with the textual artifacts of a media-saturated culture but also with the distribution cultures in which these texts circulate. Ultimately, Redbox and Netflix remind us that in thinking about everyday film culture, we should consider not only the shiny object of the DVD itself but also the locations where it is rented or sold.

6 ► THE TWITTER EFFECT
Social Media and Digital Delivery

Even as digital delivery made it possible to access movies on demand, movie fans faced the challenge of navigating the different platforms where content was available. At the same time, consumers were introduced to the notion of more personalized and fragmentary media experiences. Rather than promoting the idea of watching collectively, platform mobility seemed to offer the ability to identify and watch movies and television shows that fit an individual's singular interests. However, movie and television watching continue to be defined as social activities to be shared with friends and family or, in the case of movie theaters, a wider public. As Charles Acland has noted, discourses on moviegoing have long emphasized "the material and sensory experience of commune," and opening weekends are particularly identified with the pleasurable opportunity "to be with strangers and to be part of the crowd."[1] Similarly, television watching has long been identified with a wide range of social activities, such as watching with family or friends and discussing the shows afterward. In this regard, social media tools have begun to play a vital role in promoting collective viewing activities that allow viewers to identify movies and television shows they might want to see and to discuss those texts with others. At the same time, social media can be used to promote movies and even to structure the cultures of anticipation associated with films and television shows.

The changing status of social media within the film industry seemed to be affirmed at the Academy Awards ceremony in February 2011, when co-host James Franco posted several tweets to his Twitter account during the broadcast, including pictures of himself with co-host Anne Hathaway and Oscar presenter Oprah Winfrey. The show also continued practices from prior broadcasts, including a backstage camera where winners could complete the speeches that had been cut short on the live broadcast. But the most significant social media experience was the apparently spontaneous practice of "live-tweeting" by viewers who were watching the show from the comfort of home or checking for updates while working on their computers. Over the course of the ceremony, hundreds of thousands, if not millions, of tweets were posted, remarking on literally every aspect of the broadcast event. Similar estimates suggested that the show was mentioned nearly one million times on Facebook by U.S. users and almost two million times worldwide.[2] The sheer flood of commentary seemed to imply that social media were helping to facilitate new collective forms of shared television consumption, giving movie fans the opportunity to participate in a broader conversation about entertainment culture. This activity on Twitter is an extension of the informal practices of film criticism that have taken place in blogs and YouTube videos, where individual audience members began to supplant the role more traditionally occupied by professional film critics.

In addition to measuring the number of tweets about the Oscars, tracking services were also able to compile lists of the most frequently mentioned moments during the broadcast, including Melissa Leo's profanity-laden acceptance speech for Best Supporting Actress for her performance in *The Fighter* and Oprah Winfrey's presentation of the Best Documentary Oscar to Charles Ferguson for *Inside Job*. Finally, the services could also determine which individuals and titles were most frequently named in posts to Twitter, providing interested people with an informal and unofficial guide to the celebrities and movies that were attracting the most attention.[3]

Looking beyond all of the enthusiastic rhetoric about fan activity, the role of Twitter, Facebook, and other social media sites in shaping a broader film culture must be examined more carefully. Most importantly, we must remain attentive to the ways in which social media have become a powerful new means of promoting Hollywood films. In addition to their role in facilitating fan activity, Twitter and Facebook, like other social media tools, are crucial sites where studios seek to generate publicity for upcoming films and television shows. Thus, platform mobility not only serves as a delivery system for movies and television shows but also facilitates more traditional media consumption activities, such as watching broadcast television and seeing movies in theaters. In fact, social media technologies and mobile apps have come to play a vital role in disseminating information about upcoming movies and even in selling movie tickets. In addition, social media tools provide studios with vast amounts of data that can be used to help them market and promote new movies and television shows. However, as the live-tweeting at the Oscars illustrates, this form of fan activity often exceeds the control of movie studios, leading to situations in which movies and television shows receive unwanted or undesirable forms of publicity, including negative reviews.

THE TWITTER EFFECT

There continues to be some debate about the role of social media in shaping the reception of newly released Hollywood films. Although a number of Hollywood marketing experts have emphasized that moviegoers are much more likely to see movies based on friends' recommendations than on critical reviews, the relationship between social media and movie attendance remains unclear. These debates about the role of social media came to the surface in the summer of 2009, when entertainment industry journalists sought to make sense of the inconsistent box office performance of several major summer releases. This discussion centered around the mockumentary *Brüno*, Sasha Baron Cohen's follow-up to his previous film, *Borat: Cultural Learnings of America for Make Benefit Glorious Nation of Kazakhstan* (2006), which had also featured Cohen playing a naïve character who pushes social boundaries in order to get unsuspecting participants to react in inappropriate, if ostensibly humorous, ways. *Borat*, which served as a form of criticism against post-9/11 racism, had been an unexpected box office success, grossing over $260 million worldwide on an estimated $18 million budget, setting expectations high for the next film.

However, after a strong opening weekend in which *Brüno* made $30 million, attendance dropped precipitously, with the film earning only $12 million in its second week. Even more puzzling, the film had a 39 percent decrease in box office from Friday to Saturday during its first weekend in theaters, a decline that corresponded to a high volume of negative postings about the movie on Twitter.[4] The box office performance of *Brüno* became the most commonly cited example of the "Twitter effect," the perception that the accumulation of positive or negative social media postings could have an impact on the financial fortunes of a film. Arguably, *Brüno*'s failure could be attributed to the polarizing nature of Cohen's brand of humor. More specifically, *Brüno* depicted an aspiring and flamboyantly gay fashion model, oblivious to social mores, especially when it came to personal sexual boundaries, leading to some controversy over whether the movie was homophobic or whether it was too provocative for mainstream audiences.[5] Thus, although social media commentary may have been a contributing factor in the film's steep box office decline, *Brüno* already faced a number of marketing challenges.

Because of its early positioning within the discourses of media mobility and its status as a more "public" venue for commentary, Twitter, perhaps more than Facebook, came to be associated with an energetic, empowered, and responsive moviegoing audience. In fact, Twitter's initial utility came from the fact that users could link the service to their text messaging service on their cell phones, allowing them to send and receive tweets via their cell phones as text messages in an era before smart phones became more commonplace. Twitter gained its initial popularity in part as a result of the publicity associated with it at the 2007

South by Southwest Film Festival, where the number of messages sent via the site exploded from 20,000 per day to well over 60,000 and where Twitter won the festival's Web Award.[6] Twitter use has increased exponentially since then, and the tool has become associated with platform mobility, serving as a kind of public water cooler where participants could follow the latest trends in political, consumer, and entertainment cultures. This water-cooler effect became known within social media circles as a form of "continuous partial presence," whereby members of a social circle could follow a stream of messages answering the question, "What are you doing?"[7] Quite often, the answer involved watching a television show or movie. In fact, social media play a vital role in how audiences consume movies and television shows, with 79 percent of young adult users reporting that they "always" or "sometimes" browse Facebook while watching television; 41 percent stated that they post on Twitter about whatever they are watching.[8]

Twitter's constraints—users are limited to 140 characters—helped to establish the idea that participants were posting their most banal, unreflective thoughts, a perception reinforced by media reports that imagined millions of Twitter users broadcasting to the world what they had for lunch.[9] However, this sense of continuous partial presence allowed users to remain in contact and to develop a more detailed awareness of what their friends, colleagues, and contacts were thinking, while active hyperlinks allowed some Twitter users to post links to videos, blog posts, and other material. In addition, Twitter's use as a site where celebrities—most famously Ashton Kutcher, Shaquille O'Neal, and Lady Gaga—could broadcast directly to fans helped to foster the idea that users could be discovered or could contribute to ongoing public conversations. As a result Twitter has evolved into a space where a number of complex rhetorical practices have developed, many of them generated by users themselves. Thus, there is little question that Twitter has become a powerful communication tool, one that embraces loose ties as ideas, thoughts, and conversations circulate, often well beyond the associational boundaries of the original user.

The potential power of social media quickly became a subject of conversations about how these tools might affect the marketing and reception of movies and television shows. The earliest use of the term "Twitter effect" in newspapers appeared in a *St. Petersburg Times* article warning potential job candidates not to disclose too much personal information on social media sites such as Facebook and Twitter.[10] Soon after, the term began to gain currency in the entertainment press, starting with an article in which entertainment journalist Sharon Waxman quoted Dick Cook, chairman of Walt Disney Studios, using the term to describe the unusually effective word of mouth enjoyed by Disney's animated film *Up*.[11] Waxman's piece reinforced the assumptions made by most articles about social media: word of mouth, good or bad, is instantaneous, and these pronouncements will have an effect on the youthful audiences who go to the local multiplex on a Saturday night. Waxman even predicted, correctly, that *Brüno* would become an important test case for measuring the potential effect of social media on box office performance. Implied in Waxman's article is the perception that fans were becoming more empowered, thanks to the ability to share their immediate reactions to films, that audiences, rather than critics and advertisers, were becoming the new gatekeepers, determining which films will be successful.

However, even while marketers continue to account for the role of social media in shaping audience behavior, it is less than clear whether social media actually affect box office totals.[12] Measuring the collective reach of a number of tweets is far from a simple task. Richard Corliss imagined a world in which "early moviegoers tweet their opinions on a film to millions of 'followers,'" but most Twitter users actually have only a few dozen followers.[13] In fact, as of early 2012, the average Twitter user had 115 followers, and 40 percent of all Twitter users never tweet, instead using the site to follow others.[14] Expectations of empowerment also grew out of the perception that media commodities are inherently democratic, that the potential availability of television shows and movies, whether at the local multiplex or on cable television, means that these choices are equally accessible. Intel futurist Brian David Johnson articulates a version of this argument when he states that "the shows that get the highest audiences, the ones that get the highest ratings make the most money. It's pretty simple and very democratic. People vote by what they watch."[15] Johnson's comments ignore the fact that a variety of gatekeepers often work to determine which content is available at any given time. Further, even on Twitter, popularity can be shaped by "promoted tweets" and other features, whereby media companies pay to ensure that attention is directed toward upcoming television shows and movies. Thus, although Twitter often served as a convenient scapegoat for poorly performing television shows and movies, most conversations on the site were meant to provoke discussion, turning the site into a virtual water cooler, albeit one that rewarded users who were in the know about a new movie or television show.

TWITTER AS LIVE WATER COOLER

Although Twitter and Facebook have been discussed in terms of their potential for movie marketing, Twitter has often served as a means of shaping new forms of collective, distributed television and movie watching, a cultural phenomenon that has only widened with the rise of social media software that allows users to "check in" at various locations, whether bars and cafés or "at" television shows they happen to be watching. Twitter often functions as a means of remaining aware, with many users keeping the program open in the background while they pursue other activities. This practice of keeping Twitter open and allowing the stream of tweets to flow produces what Jean Burgess and Axel Bruns refer to as a form of "ambient" awareness: Twitter users can calibrate their levels of attention. Further, with the ability to tune in when something important is happening, Twitter users can participate more fully in what Burgess and Bruns describe as the process of "instant evaluation," by which participants develop reactions to major news stories quickly.[16] Stories such as the crash-landing of an airplane on the Hudson River immediately become international news, with users adding details and speculating about what was happening. Thus, although James Franco's tweets during the Academy Awards received quite a bit of attention, it was the collective production of millions of tweets during the broadcast that was more significant. With its emphasis on synchronous conversation, Twitter has become associated with the idea of a live water cooler, where a global collective of viewers can interpret, discuss, and even mock television broadcasts together. Twitter has even been seen as a means of reinforcing live television watching, given that 76 percent of those who tweet about shows do so while the program is being broadcast.[17]

This form of global participation is an extension of what Charles R. Acland has described as the "felt internationalism" of contemporary media culture.[18] In *Screen Traffic*, Acland addresses the ways in which the timing of theatrical distribution contributes to a global sense of connectedness. As movie studios continue to emphasize simultaneous global release dates, audiences can imagine themselves as part of an internationalized moviegoing public. To be sure, these opening weekends are often the subject of massive marketing and promotional campaigns; however, Acland also emphasizes the ways in which such openings can contribute to a cosmopolitanism in which people welcome the opportunity "to be with strangers and to be part of the crowd."[19] Twitter builds upon this desire for inclusion, inviting users to comment on and share their reactions to popular culture events, whether global movie premieres, film festival screenings, or weekly episodes of popular television shows. Attending a film on the opening weekend or keeping up with popular television shows also helps to reinforce the sensibility of "being in the know," and tweeting about popular culture allows users to demonstrate this sense of cultural cosmopolitanism not only to their followers but also, potentially, to a much wider audience of Twitter users who might see their comments re-circulated when others respond to or repost them.

Twitter has actively embraced the idea that its messaging service can be used as a form of collective entertainment consumption. As users began experimenting with different ways of organizing conversations, Twitter responded by editing the code to reinforce these organic developments. For example, Twitter users began using hashtags, words or phrases preceded by the pound sign, in order to make the site more searchable and to make it easier to track and follow conversations as they evolved over time. Eventually, Twitter responded by installing code that would turn all hashtags into hyperlinks so that users could click on the link to see other users who had discussed the same topic. In addition, Twitter has sought to produce community by listing trending topics—often associated with hashtags—in the sidebar of the main Twitter page so that users can get a quick read of the most popular topics of the day, listings that are often organized by region, so that a user in Raleigh, North Carolina, could check to see what was happening nearby.

To be sure, these uses of Twitter eventually became a means of generating publicity, not only for Twitter but also for the networks and studios themselves. The emphasis on trending topics soon became a way for television shows and movies to direct attention to themselves, especially through "promoted tweets," whereby companies could pay to have a phrase listed as a popular topic. In addition, Twitter encouraged the notion that incorporating references to Twitter into a show would create more engaged viewers who would be more likely to watch live and (presumably) to become more involved in the show: "when TV shows bring Twitter elements into the broadcast, there's a direct and immediate increase in engagement on Twitter: anywhere from two to ten times more Tweets created while the shows air."[20] Such claims about "engagement" are complicated, given that it would be impossible to measure the engagement levels of people who are not tweeting; however, live-tweeting can make visible some of the ways in which viewers do engage with each other in relationship to the broadcasts they are consuming.

Given this sense of a global, simultaneous community, Twitter use seems distinctly tied to live programming, to live television's potential for producing the unexpected and unpredictable, as audiences share in the sense of anticipation. As Graeme Turner notes, the pleasure of watching television collectively is "about sharing an experience that is unpredictable and continually immanent."[21] For the broadcast networks, a more crucial aspect of the liveness of Twitter is that it potentially helps to deliver an audience watching the show in real time, often on a television screen, making it more likely that the users will watch commercials rather than skipping through them, as they might if they were watching on a DVR or online. In fact, the FX show *It's Always Sunny in Philadelphia* provided users with incentives to tweet during the live broadcast of the show, such as a T-shirt that would be available only for a limited time.[22] Given that network and cable television still depends on generating large audiences watching shows during the regular broadcast schedule, these forms of live participation may help generate incentives that will encourage users to seek out these forms of community.

This relationship between liveness and moviegoing is more complicated, given that the use of cell phones in theaters is generally discouraged, if not overtly prohibited. Cinephiles, in particular, frequently complain about texting as a distraction from the movie. These anti-texting sentiments were reinforced through a viral video circulated by the popular Texas indie movie chain the Alamo Drafthouse. The video begins with a series of titles stating that "at the Alamo Drafthouse, we have a simple rule: If you talk or text during a movie, we kick you out." We then hear a recording of a voicemail the theater received. A young, female customer who was kicked out for using her cell phone complains that the theater was "too fucking dark" and that she was using her phone as a flashlight so that she could find her seat. Later in the message, which ran several minutes, she appeals to the discourses of freedom, arguing that she should not have been prevented from using her phone "in the U.S.A., where you are free to text in a theater."[23] The video was seen nearly three million times, suggesting that it was widely shared on Twitter and Facebook, whether out of solidarity with the anti-texting message or because of the humor of hearing a caller humiliated for leaving such a message. But the underlying sentiment is that sites such as movie theaters come with a set of social norms that include sitting quietly and avoiding unnecessary disruptions.

But despite complaints about texting, Regal CEO Amy Miles acknowledged during the 2012 CinemaCon that the chain was considering the idea of allowing patrons to text during some movies. As Miles explained, teens are "accustomed to controlling their own existence," including the ability to communicate with friends via social media during a movie.[24] Regal's proposal seemed to reflect the interest of the chain in appealing to teens and young adults. In fact, a *Hollywood Reporter* survey in 2012 concluded that a slight majority of young adults had texted during a movie and that nearly half claimed they would seek out theaters that allowed them to use phones during a movie, even if 75 percent admitted that people using smart phones during a movie would make the experience less satisfying.[25] As a result, movie theaters appear to be taking on some of the attributes of home screenings, as users increasingly seek to reproduce the viewing experiences they have at home.

TWITTER AND THE CULTURES OF ANTICIPATION

Although Twitter is typically associated with liveness, it can also be used to create cultures of anticipation around an upcoming film. In this situation, studios can generate excitement by encouraging different forms of participation, whether that involves a scavenger hunt, an alternate-reality game (ARG), or some other activity that will tap into what Pierre Lévy refers to as the "collective intelligence" of online groups, by which internet users pool their resources to work together to solve a puzzle or find a solution to a problem.[26] For Lévy, these new forms of collective intelligence have the potential to create new forms of political power, which may be able to threaten traditional powers such as the nation-state and corporations. Henry Jenkins has adapted Lévy's concept to describe the collective behaviors of movie and television audiences when they combine their skills to solve or make sense of a complex narrative. Jenkins points to the fans of the television show *Survivor* who sought to "spoil" the show by using clues compiled online to predict what would happen months before it was broadcast.[27] Simiarly, Jason Mittell discusses how *Lost* fans attempted to make sense of clues that might explain the show's increasingly complex narrative, a process that involved the creation of a wiki, the Lostpedia, to compile details about the show.[28] As Jenkins points out, the practices of "spoiling," in particular, were linked to a sense of anticipation regarding a television show or movie that had not aired. *Survivor* fans who were collecting clues about an upcoming season were doing so because of their excitement about the show, playing against the immediacy and sense of liveness fabricated by the show's editors.[29]

As studios and broadcasters began to recognize the power of this sense of anticipation, they increasingly incorporated activities, such as ARGs and scavenger hunts, to cultivate more engaged audiences. For example, to promote the release of *The Hunger Games*, Lionsgate created a scavenger hunt that was organized and launched on Twitter. To be sure, Lionsgate used many of the traditional marketing techniques associated with promoting a Hollywood blockbuster based on a hugely popular novel—the studio gave away 80,000 posters and advertised on 3,000 billboards to create awareness of the film—but as Brooks Barnes noted, the "centerpiece" of its effort to reach younger audiences took place online.[30] The online game smoothly incorporated elements from the narrative to provide participants with a more immersive experience that invited a sense of involvement in the film. In one activity, more than 800,000 fans took advantage of the opportunity to create digital identification cards as if they were living in Panem, the futuristic society depicted in the novels and films. Later, fans with ID cards could compete on Twitter to be elected "mayor" of one of the twenty-four districts in the books. Finally, Lionsgate launched a puzzle on Twitter: digital pieces of the puzzle went to a hundred separate websites, and users were asked to post their pieces simultaneously to reveal a new poster.[31]

Warner Brothers used similar tactics to promote both *The Dark Knight* and *The Dark Knight Rises*. Capitalizing on the intense fan support for Christopher Nolan's first film, *Batman Begins*, Warner used a creative approach to reveal more information about the second film's chief villain, the Joker, played by Heath Ledger. As Kimberly Owczarski explains, Warner placed Joker cards, similar to those that appeared at the end of *Batman Begins*, in comic book shops with a web address on the back. When users went to the address, they were prompted to submit their email address and, in turn, were given a location on the screen where they could "remove" one pixel from a campaign poster of Harvey Dent, the politician turned villain, Two-Face. As more pixels were removed, a new poster featuring the image of the Joker was revealed.[32] Bane, the villain for *The Dark Knight Rises,* was introduced in a similar fashion. Fans were directed to the film's website, where they encountered an all-black screen and an audio file of people chanting. One fan managed to capture an image of the visual spectrum of the audio file and discovered that it contained the hashtag, #thefirerises. As more people tweeted with that hashtag, their Twitter avatars were used to fill in pixels of an image, which gradually revealed a poster of Bane.[33] This revelation occurred a full year before the film was scheduled to be released, suggesting that Warner Brothers hoped to maintain a sustained sense of anticipation for the film. In all cases, Twitter was tied not merely to a sense of liveness but also to a desire to orchestrate the temporality of anticipation.

CURATING AUDIENCES

In addition to the more public attempts to use social media to promote and market films and television shows, there have been a number of experiments that harnessed the communal and cosmopolitan aspects of social media to promote, market, and even distribute movies. These experiments often fit neatly into the social aspects of movie consumption, but they also build upon and attempt to address the challenges faced by independent filmmakers, who find it difficult to compete for attention. In a number of discussions of digital delivery, media industry observers have noted the difficulty of "curating" the wide selection of movies and television shows available at any given time and on such a wide range of platforms. In an era beyond the networks, cable television, and the video store, identifying and tracking down movies and television shows presents a new challenge. Social media tools, databases, recommendation engines, and other sources are often cited as useful tools that might help users find entertainment they would enjoy; however, this argument may actually be wrong. In fact, it would be more precise to argue that audiences are being organized into recognizable demographic and taste groups that can be reached more effectively through targeted advertising campaigns, a process that Intel futurist Brian David Johnson refers to as "addressability." As Johnson points out, this identification "could be as simple as a zip code for local advertisers or as complicated as a robust user profile."[34]

In some cases, social media offer a relatively straightforward marketing tool, one that incorporates populist activities such as voting for a favorite movie in a menu of new releases. For example, Vudu, Walmart's digital movie delivery service, offered a promotion for users voting on Facebook for their favorite new release of the week. The movie that received the most votes would then be available for a discount rental price of ninety-nine cents that Friday.[35] But other forms of participation often entailed more focused forms of surveillance. To be sure, users who contribute to social networks are mostly aware that much of the information they generate can be used by other parties. Participation in these networks is voluntary, expressive, social, and often banal. Users of sites like Netflix may rate films with the hope of becoming more informed movie and television consumers, or they may do so while passing time on a rainy afternoon. Or they might simply respond to a friend's tweet that happens to mention a movie or television show.

In addition, social media check-in services helped to negotiate the relationship between mobility and media consumption. Sites such as Foursquare launched with the promise that people could locate others, including strangers, who shared similar interests. These services allowed people to identify and meet others or to broadcast their activities to friends who might also be on the service. Often, these practices were associated with young, mobile users who could check in from trendy bars or other locations. Social media check-ins can also serve as a form of self-expression. Checking in, using the social media service Foursquare, at the local art-house theater or the hip new bar would likely cultivate more cultural capital than checking in from a local laundromat or gas station.

These sites built upon a transformation in viewing practices in the age of digital delivery, where viewers were likely to be surfing the internet while watching television, a practice that came to be known as "second screen" viewing. In fact, according to a Nielsen study, three out of four adults used a second screen, most often their mobile phone, while watching television. The study also found that, contrary to popular wisdom, women were slightly more likely to multitask while watching television than men. More crucially, multitasking viewers reported that the internet drew more of their attention than the television show that was playing. Finally, Nielsen found that only 7 percent of multitaskers were searching for websites related to the television shows or advertisements they were watching.[36] In this sense, social check-in apps, such as GetGlue and Miso, could serve as a means of encouraging not only live television viewing but also deeper engagement with the shows as they were broadcast. These social check-in apps complicate what Lynn Spigel has referred to, building upon arguments by Raymond Williams, as television's "privatized mobility."[37] For Williams, television, along with suburbanization, helped to promote forms of isolated individualism. Spigel argues that the marketing rhetoric associated with the rise of portable television built upon what Lisa Parks refers to as a "distinct culture organized around middle-class fantasies of transport, personal freedom, and citizenship."[38] But with the emergence of social media as a technology of media consumption, we are now approaching something closer to a more communal form of mobility, in which media taste is shared and publicized by television and movie viewers, often with those users voluntarily submitting to forms of surveillance that make them more visible as targets for advertising and other forms of promotion.

Building upon social media services like Foursquare, GetGlue allows people to "check in" to their favorite television shows, movies, books, and music in order to see and share media preferences.[39] The tool taps into the impulse to make media consumption a social activity, encouraging users to imagine themselves as participants in a wider community built around shared interests. In addition, users can get other kinds of rewards, such as points or badges for every time they check in. The service grew rapidly, from 500,000 users in July 2010 to over 1.3 million in July 2011, when the service expanded into the United Kingdom. As the service widened its reach, GetGlue was able to collect vast amounts of demographic data about users who checked in to their favorite television shows, movies, music, and books. Time Warner served as a sponsor for the company, and a number of television channels, including Discovery, HBO, and the USA Network, paid to gain access to the information and to what GetGlue described as a "self-service marketing dashboard," through which the networks could distribute stickers and other rewards, including discounts on merchandise, while also determining the "social media reach" of their shows.[40]

Users who enroll in GetGlue are immediately asked to identify ten current television shows they "like," allowing the site to build a taste profile. Participants can obtain their first "Bootcamp" sticker by checking in, following other users, and downloading the GetGlue app to their telephone. In addition, when I used the site, I was automatically followed by a dozen Facebook friends who were also GetGlue users. Because check-ins typically appeared in a user's Twitter and Facebook feeds, users were rewarded for watching television shows when they were first broadcast, allowing them to demonstrate engagement with their favorite shows and to communicate interest in watching collectively, albeit virtually. GetGlue rewards participants for checking in frequently, leveraging their desire for participation in order to obtain information about them. Significantly, although GetGlue was primarily associated with fictional entertainment, it also was used by a number of sports broadcasters as a means of tapping into elements of sports fandom. The Turner network partnered with the mobile app to promote the National Collegiate Athletic Association (NCAA) basketball tournament, and the National Hockey League and the San Antonio Spurs basketball team also signed deals.[41]

Similarly, Miso pitched itself as a social network for television lovers that would encourage collective forms of watching while also allowing users to accumulate points and badges that rewarded their enthusiasm for specific shows. Like GetGlue, Miso was depicted as a place where users could demonstrate their cosmopolitanism not through the discourses of mobility but through expressions of cultural taste. Thus, as CNN's Doug Gross implied, rather than touting one's presence at a popular bar or coffeehouse, Miso allows "couch potatoes" to publicize their tastes in media, essentially turning the practice of posting a status update into a form of cultural mobility.[42] Miso further sought to integrate the two screens in September 2011 with the launch of a deal with DirecTV, which allowed Miso's iPhone app to synchronize with the television delivery service's set-top boxes: when a user downloads the Miso iPhone app and tunes into a television show on a DirecTV set, the app will automatically call up the webpage associated with that show. The app works whether the program is watched live or consumed later using a DVR and was promoted as a means to allow users to learn more about their favorite shows. Thus, a fan of *Glee* could be directed to information about a song performed on the show, to background on characters and plots, or even to gossip about the actors.[43] Although these forms of interactivity were promoted as a means of keeping fans engaged, they also offered new opportunities for advertisers to create content that might be pertinent to the users who checked in.

MOBILITY, SOCIAL MEDIA, AND COSMOPOLITANISM

These varying forms of media mobility have inevitably shaped the promotion of movies, offering new sites for filmmakers to reach audiences and to build anticipation for upcoming films. Although digital delivery has often been accused of complicity in the decline of moviegoing, two U.S.-based services, Gathr and Tugg.com, sought to use social media tools to promote theatrical screenings. Both were billed as empowering audiences to control what comes to local theaters. These services were not unlike the Rain Network's cinema-on-demand service in Brazil, which allowed participants to request films for a network of 149 art-house screens in that country.[44] Both services relied upon the greater programming flexibility of movie theaters equipped to handle digital delivery. By demonstrating large demand for a specific film, fans could advocate for the screening of films that normally might not receive a theatrical run or for the revival of popular older movies. As David Bordwell notes, the use of social media to program local movie theaters builds upon the fact that these theaters are now part of a wider on-demand culture.[45]

Tugg,com worked with a number of chains, including AMC Theatres, Alamo Drafthouse, Cinemark Theaters, Goodrich Quality Cinemas, and Regal Cinemas, to allow users to schedule screenings of movies during times when their theaters are less crowded. Once a minimum number of users have committed to buying tickets, Tugg automatically reserves the theater, manages ticketing, and ensures that the theater has access to the film. Notably, the service arranged to work with three of the largest chains, AMC, Cinemark, and Regal, illustrating that the service could be a useful way to fill empty theaters during the week. Other enthusiasts hoped that Tugg could bring independent films to communities that otherwise might have to wait for them to appear on DVD or

VOD.[46] In fact, Tugg was instrumental in helping to schedule several screenings of Matthew Lillard's crowdfunded directorial debut, *Fat Kid Rules the World*.[47] Although Tugg was most commonly associated with independent movies—and the related practice of crowdsourcing—it also offered users a chance to see older movies on the big screen in much the same way that film clubs and repertory theaters might advertise and promote special screenings and could be used both by filmmakers and theater owners, as well as film buffs, to schedule events. One theater owner in Chattanooga, Tennessee, was able to offer a program of Oscar-nominated animated short films, as well as other independent and documentary films that might not play in a smaller city.[48] Similarly, Gathr offered a cinema-on-demand model that was marketed to independent filmmakers and theater owners who could promote and schedule screenings. Gathr's model was similar to Tugg's in that if enough users committed to seeing a movie, reservations would be collected, a screening scheduled, and viewers' credit cards charged. Like Tugg, Gathr allowed promoters—whether theater owners or filmmakers—to use Facebook or Twitter to disseminate information about a potential screening. Gathr founder Scott Glosserman emphasized that the service could operate on a much smaller scale than most theatrical releases, suggesting that a screening could be scheduled for an audience as small as fifty people. Citing the increased popularity of film festivals, Glosserman went on to assert that audiences are seeking alternative content.[49] Ultimately, services like Tugg.com and Gathr coincide with a longer history of do-it-yourself and independent cinema while at the same time promoting the idea of a mobile, engaged moviegoing audience.

This relationship between mobility and cosmopolitanism was also at the center of Shawn Bercuson's short-lived start-up Prescreen, which sought to update the traditional test-screening model by linking it to the marketing potential associated with social media sites such as Facebook and Twitter. Prescreen was promoted as a service that would be of particular interest to independent filmmakers in an era of digital plenitude, in which movie fans were confronted with too many options for their limited attention. Subscribers to Prescreen received daily emails alerting them to a new unreleased movie available for a "test screening." The email took users to the movie's trailer and gave them an opportunity to purchase a digital download to view within a sixty-day window, at which point the movie was rotated out. Movies were sold for $4 on the first day they were available and $8 afterward. The stated goal of Prescreen was to appeal to the desire of movie fans to be in the know about critically acclaimed movies and to be able to share that knowledge with their peers across their social media networks. As Bercuson succinctly put it, "movies are inherently social."[50] In addition, the mobile test screenings allowed users who lived outside of urban centers to participate in this form of online cosmopolitanism. Because many of these films were likely to play only at film festivals or in art-house theaters in large cities and college towns, audiences with less access to these sites could partake in the experience of being ahead of the curve when it came to the latest independent film or documentary. These forms of access even led Bercuson to claim that his service could reduce piracy by allowing more people to be involved in the launch of new independent films.[51]

The service's debut film, *How to Start Your Own Country*, Jody Shapiro's documentary about six unrecognized and self-declared micro-nations, was promoted for raising questions about the relationship between nationhood and identity while also exploring concepts such as national sovereignty, topics that could easily provoke conversations on social media sites. In addition, Prescreen sought to align the documentary with the discourses of cinematic cosmopolitanism by emphasizing the festivals where it played, including the Toronto International Film Festival, the Amsterdam International Documentary Film Festival, and Michael Moore's Traverse City Film Festival, among others. Within twelve hours of its release, the documentary's trailer had received 820 views, and the film had been purchased forty-one times; by day three, a few more than two thousand people had viewed it, and seventy-one had purchased it. Other early releases followed a similar trajectory, potentially adding modestly to both the word of mouth and the revenues for these films. Once a film's two-month run on the site ends, Prescreen provides the filmmaker with a 50 percent split of any revenues and a detailed "performance report" to help in marketing the movie effectively.

Prescreen would use the demographic data of the audience that watched—and enjoyed—a film to construct a more carefully targeted marketing campaign for its filmmaker, while also creating good word of mouth in advance of its potential release. Like other digital delivery services, Prescreen was wrapped up in the rhetoric of digital plenitude, promising "exclusive access to watch free previews, discover new movies, and stream from anywhere." Prescreen also billed itself as reinforcing the practices of shared moviegoing that are so crucial to cultural definitions of the cinema. Within just a few months, however, Prescreen was forced to suspend service, in part due to the difficulty of attracting attention in a competitive distribution ecosystem. Though it could list more than 100,000 email subscribers, the service had only about 10,000 rentals of 168 films. Prescreen likely faltered because it was competing with a number of other digital delivery systems in what amounted to a "zero-sum game" for the attention of movie fans who were seeking content.[52]

At the same time, Facebook and other social media sites have become more crucial as marketing tools for both Hollywood and independent films. In a talk at the 2011 Cannes Film Festival, Facebook executive Jon Fougner argued that social media tools could be used not only to create positive word of mouth for a film but also to generate demographic data on the audiences for specific films.

Fougner went on to speculate that Facebook marketing campaigns had added millions of dollars to the box office totals of films like *The Dark Knight*.[53] Fougner further argued that movie theaters should become much more savvy in using social media tools, such as the Netflix map feature that tracks the popularity of specific Netflix films by zip code, to create targeted marketing plans for a local community. He also suggested that online ticket sellers should integrate with Facebook Connect because "implementing Facebook Connect could make it easier for a customer to broadcast his ticket purchase to all his friends, at no cost to the ticketing site. Better yet, when he arrived on the site, he could see which friends were going to see which screenings of which movies. Moviegoing, after all, is social."[54] Similarly, the movie ticket website Fandango, which is owned by the cable company Comcast, sought to integrate more deeply with Facebook by encouraging users to share information with friends about when and where they planned to see a movie. Fandango became a key site for streamlining mobile ticket sales, with 25 percent of the company's sales in early 2012 coming from its cell phone app, and most being sold two to four hours before the movie started. Eventually, the company plans to implement paperless tickets that can be scanned directly from a person's smart phone.[55] Fougner's comments take the social aspects of moviegoing and translate them into forms of advertising, where friends can influence their peers by "broadcasting" their movie plans. In all cases, platform mobility plays an important role in encouraging users to share their movie tastes with friends through social media tools.

Further questions about the role of social media in promoting theatrical moviegoing arose when Warner Brothers purchased the online movie hub Flixster at an estimated cost of $60–90 million.[56] In addition to its social media site, which allowed Facebook users to rate movies and share those ratings with their friends, Flixster also owned the movie review aggregator Rotten Tomatoes, which compiles the reviews of a number of published film critics. Although many observers pointed out the implications of Warner's control of a major source for moviegoers to find reviews, the purchase of Flixster more crucially served as an attempt by the studio to alter its approach to digital delivery. Eventually Warner moved to leverage Flixster as a portal to encourage users to sample its digital locker service UltraViolet. At the same time, Warner could employ the massive amount of data generated by Flixster to present consumers with more directly focused marketing efforts. As Sharon Waxman, an unapologetic champion of these direct marketing efforts, put it, "with its recent purchase of Flixster and its 30-million strong consumer base, the studio has bought direct access to people who watch movies, rate them, read about them, and want to share that information with their friends."[57] Nick DeMartino, a retired senior vice president of media and technology at the American Film Institute, echoed Waxman's claims, arguing that data are "the secret sauce of social media that will empower Hollywood to take control of its own business."[58] Like Fandango, Flixster provided a smart phone app that would allow users to purchase tickets to movies before arriving in theaters. Thus, in much the same way that social check-in services such as Miso and GetGlue allowed television broadcasters to develop detailed accounts of their audiences, online movie portals such as Flixster, Facebook, and Prescreen were creating reports about moviegoers.

SOCIAL MEDIA, FRICTIONLESS SHARING, AND ROBERT BORK

In the midst of attempts to merge social media and movie consumption, some legal and ideological limits inhibited a fuller integration. Perhaps the most notable example was the attempt by Netflix to create an app that would join its service with individualized Facebook accounts. Users could set up an account so that when they watched a movie, notice would automatically be sent to their news feed. This idea was described as "frictionless sharing," and it was based upon the notion that users wanted to share their tastes in movies with others. To some extent, this goal was an extension of Netflix's ongoing efforts to individualize their marketing by encouraging households to create "family" accounts, by which multiple individuals would be registered simultaneously. This service was sold as a means for users to get more accurate personal recommendations, thus allowing parents to separate children's programming from their preferences for adult dramas or indie films. But when Netflix was preparing to launch the app on Facebook, it announced that the service would be available only in the emerging Netflix markets in Canada and Latin America. The reluctance to open a Facebook app in the United States was attributed in part to the Video Privacy Protection Act (VPPA), a 1988 law that addresses how and when a user's video rental history can be shared.

The law is known as "Bork's Law," after Supreme Court nominee Robert Bork. During Bork's highly contentious nomination hearings in 1987, the *Washington City Paper*, an independent weekly, managed to obtain his video rental records. Although Bork's taste in movies was relatively banal—he showed a strong preference for Alfred Hitchcock, Cary Grant, and John Ford films—Congress correctly regarded the publication of these records to be an invasion of the nominee's privacy and therefore passed the VPPA.[59] Thus, video rental records are considered confidential, unless the user consents to have them made available publicly. These privacy laws were of special concern to Netflix, because the company had been sued in 2009, when it made rental records available during a contest in which it invited participants to improve its recommendation algorithm.[60] A closet lesbian alleged that Netflix had made it possible for her to be identified and outed when it made demographic data available to participants in the contest. The suit also sought to prevent Netflix from launching a second contest in which users' zip codes, age, gender, and movie ratings would be provided to participants. As a *Wired* article about the lawsuit argued, there is an 87 percent likelihood that a user could be positively identified if gender, zip code, and birth date were provided.[61] Thus, although Netflix hoped to sharpen its recommendation algorithms, many users expressed serious concern about having private information revealed to others. In fact, according to a survey conducted by Citi analyst Mark Mahaney, most Netflix users expressed little interest in knowing what movies their Facebook friends were watching and were similarly reluctant to reveal what they were watching.[62]

In order to get around these privacy concerns and to allow the creation of a Netflix Facebook app, the company lobbied for the passage of H.R. 2471, legislation that would enable people to give their consent for their video rental records to be shared on the internet.[63] However, the bill received additional scrutiny, in part because its sponsor, Bob Goodlatte, a Virginia Republican, had received a significant number of donations from internet companies, including eBay, Google, Yahoo, and Comcast.[64] The bill illustrated some of the challenges associated with digital delivery, social media, and mobility and did not clarify how Netflix would reconcile viewers' expectations of privacy with the company's desire to use Facebook as yet another hub for the digital delivery of movies. Unlike Netflix, Hulu appeared to be unconstrained by VPPA. Although the legal issues are murky, some observers speculated that Hulu might be immune because it does not rent discs, instead offering only a subscription-based streaming service. In fact, Hulu launched an app in 2011 that allowed users to share automatically what they watch, a move that prompted widespread complaints from users who believed they were losing their privacy.[65]

CONCLUSION

For the most part, social media have been promoted as a means of providing users with a more interactive and collective media experience. Audiences could cultivate collective, simultaneous viewing experiences through practices such as live-tweeting and social check-in services. In turn, these tools could provide users with richer media experiences, allowing them to identify the content they want to see and to demonstrate their knowledge of popular culture. Thus, even though users might be far removed from the cultural centers associated with film festivals and art-house theaters, they could join larger cultural conversations about film and television. However, these social media tools also helped to generate detailed information about the people who watch and discuss movies and television shows, raising important questions about personal privacy.

In the best cases, filmmakers and theater owners could use social media tools to build a community that could help them to promote interest in specific movies or even in special screenings. Tools such as Tugg and Gathr were part of an emerging culture of do-it-yourself filmmakers who built audiences online. In fact, social media tools became a powerful component of what independent filmmaker Kevin Smith referred to as "Indie 2.0," a new model of distribution based upon leveraging the participation and, in some cases, the financial contributions of audiences who might be interested in supporting a film. In both cases, social media and digital delivery technologies contribute to a transformation in the value of a media property. Thus, the following two chapters examine two key aspects of this phenomenon. First, I look at practices such as crowdsourcing and crowdfunding to examine the ways in which social media have been used to cultivate new models of indie film production, distribution, and exhibition. Then I survey film festivals, sites that have historically helped to generate cultural capital for movies, directors, and stars. Festivals, which are typically associated with quality cinema, allow films to compete for awards and to receive promotion in the entertainment press that can then be used to sell them during their theatrical run. Festivals have also typically been associated with the production of exclusivity by providing limited access to movies that haven't yet been released to theaters or in other delivery formats. More recently, however, festivals have been reinvented, becoming sites of distribution where fans can access selected movies online during the festival itself. In both cases, social media provide the word of mouth that makes these new forms of promotion and exhibition possible.

7 ▸ INDIE 2.0
Digital Delivery, Crowdsourcing, and Social Media

AT THE 2011 Sundance Film Festival, prolific indie filmmaker Kevin Smith announced that he would be holding an "auction" for his latest movie, *Red State*, a low-budget horror film that satirized the homophobic and publicity-hungry Westboro Baptist Church, survivalist groups, and media sensationalism, among other targets. Eager for a scoop, members of the entertainment press packed into the theater, awaiting the kind of bidding war that had been commonplace at past festivals. However, rather than holding the promised auction, Smith immediately "sold" the film to himself for $20 before proceeding to offer an elaborate lecture on the ways in which expensive distribution and marketing plans made it difficult for indie films to make a profit. Smith's auction served as a commentary on the distribution cultures that had formed around Sundance during the 1990s, when his 1994 film *Clerks*, which he had financed using credit cards and filmed in the convenience store where he worked, became an unexpected hit after it was purchased at the festival by Miramax. Thus, the auction of *Red State* allowed Smith to underscore the ways in which the Miramax-Sundance model was broken beyond repair.

Smith's performance helped to illustrate the role of festivals in generating hype for new and innovative filmmakers, or at least those who can easily be marketed to art-house audiences. Smith, in his typical profane fashion, described the making of *Red State* as a labor of love, one in which cast and crew members worked for lower salaries in order to see the film get made, depicting the experience as "the same old independent story that you've heard a zillion fucking times." Thus, even while embracing the dedication and passion that goes into the production of an independent film, Smith also argued that the festival narrative reinforced an exhausted depiction of indie success, one in which an underdog auteur makes a movie, gains acceptance to Sundance, and then sells that movie to the highest studio bidder. However, as he opened the mock auction, Smith reminded his audience that studios typically spend millions—Smith estimates that many studios spend over $20 million to sell even a low-budget independent film—to market new movies, often with the goal of building a solid opening weekend. Given the high-risk stakes associated with this approach, Smith argued that this practice does not serve the interests of independent filmmakers, who would then be alienated from the film they have produced.

Instead, Smith urged the cultivation of new models of self-distribution, ones that built upon Smith's savvy use of social media and on his highly popular podcast series, which he refers to as "smodcasts." Smith then announced that he would tour with the film, visiting twenty cities across the United States, where he would show the film and then hold question-and-answer sessions. After the tour, *Red State* would be distributed to theaters and through video-on-demand before being sold on DVD. Thus, rather than selling his film at Sundance, Smith argued that keeping the film would allow him to connect with audiences, and he hoped to forge a new narrative, one that would emphasize the idea that "anybody can make a movie, but we want to prove that anyone can distribute a movie." Ultimately, Smith referred to his intentions as "Indie 2.0," a reinventing or rebooting of independent filmmaking in the age of digital delivery and social media. Implied in Smith's comments is a distinct pedagogical purpose. Rather than merely seeking to entertain and profit from fans, Smith views his experiment as a potential model for other aspiring moviemakers. Of course, it is important to acknowledge that Smith is better positioned to take advantage of digital distribution networks than most indie filmmakers. *Red State* was his tenth film, and he had built a massive fan empire through his films, his comics, and his podcast series. However, Smith's arguments also echoed an ongoing trend within indie film culture toward do-it-yourself (DIY) filmmaking.

Smith's tirade clearly unsettled the power players and executives working in the industry. *Los Angeles Times* entertainment journalist Patrick Goldstein reported that industry executives described the affair as a "bitter joke" and characterized Smith as a "boorish boob" who had exploited media attention at the festival to promote his movie, a move that "left a bad taste in everyone's mouth."[1] However, Smith's remarks also reflected an ongoing dialogue about the opportunities available for independent filmmakers in the age of digital delivery. The self-distribution of *Red State* attracted significant press attention, but Smith is just one of many independent filmmakers who have experimented with alternative distribution models. Thus, in much the same way that film festivals adopted new distribution models to create new forms of visibility online, independent filmmakers sought to assume control over the marketing of their movies. Further, Smith's emphasis on self-distribution offered a reminder that the past approach—a brief theatrical run, followed months later by DVD and televi-sion distribution—no longer worked in a way that benefited most filmmakers. Instead, Smith's comments seem to point to the possibility that talented artists, using savvy business techniques, could potentially break through when they dis-tribute their films outside of a major studio. As Karina Longworth argued in her analysis of the *Red State* phenomenon, "we're moving from a top-down culture in which media companies dictate where the eyeballs will be directed to one in which each of us curates our own personal 'main stream' from a variety of niche content streams."[2] Longworth's comments echo a longstanding assumption about digital media, namely, that access to unlimited storage space would allow users to sample a wide range of content and that artists would be free to distrib-ute their work without the constraints of traditional media gatekeepers, such as major studios and theater chains. However, it is less than clear whether indepen-dent filmmakers will be able to benefit from this form of open access, especially given the large number of independent films that are produced annually.[3] Thus, rather than considering whether digital delivery is benefiting independent film, I am interested in making sense of how indie has been redefined.

This chapter focuses on a number of independent and DIY projects that have tapped the powers of the internet. Although these projects account for only a very small percentage of the overall box office and rental market, they have a much more significant impact on how concepts of film community and film pro-duction are formed. Further, as the example of Kevin Smith's *Red State* implies, DIY filmmakers often appeal to the language of empowerment and choice in order to forge alternative models to traditional distribution. DIY distribution points to the challenges that independent filmmakers face in sustaining an audi-ence. As Lucas Hilderbrand notes, these changes are taking place in a world in which "feature-length independent and art films have become almost impossible to finance."[4] Further, given the marketing costs required to support even a mod-est theatrical run, a number of observers have speculated that traditional distri-bution models for independent films are in the process of being transformed. However, even though independent film is frequently defined economically, it is also important to recognize, as Michael Z. Newman reminds us, that con-cepts such as art and indie are socially and culturally constructed.[5] Instead, as Geoff King argues, independent and "Indiewood" films are defined in relation-ship to other categories, most often mainstream Hollywood films, a practice that allows audiences to perceive themselves as consuming something "differ-ent" than the norm.[6] This concept of independence is the product not merely of a specific aesthetic foregrounding quirky characters, realistic storylines, indie rock soundtracks, or even casting choices but also of paratextual features such as trailers, posters, festival awards, DVD extras, and reviews.[7] To accompany the release of Wes Anderson's *Moonrise Kingdom* (2012), for example, Focus Features used not only a traditional theatrical trailer but also an online video in which Bill Murray, an actor often associated with indie film, provided viewers with a "tour" of the film set. While taking us "behind the scenes," Murray pretends to be drunk and engages in moments of self-deprecating humor that undermine the "all-knowing" production documentaries typically encountered as DVD extras or online publicity. Anderson's self-conscious promotion of an indie sensibility is consistent with his ongoing efforts to fabricate a "star" image for himself as someone who is engaged with the ideas of creativity as they are manifested through techniques such as whimsical set design and handcrafted props to create the illusion of authenticity.[8]

Thus, rather than treating indie film merely as an economic category shaped by DIY practices, we must also understand it as one that is produced discursively. In fact, despite celebratory accounts of digital delivery opening new distribution outlets, these independent productions almost invariably depend upon resources owned by major media conglomerates. As Yannis Tziomakis points out, these ownership models are part of a larger process of "creating even larger super-powers that own, control, or have significant stakes in every conceivable distribution outlet possible due to digital technology allowing the compression and transmission of huge volumes of data whether through satellite, cable, or DVDs."[9] Thus, even films that are self-distributed may get into homes via on-demand platforms such as the partnership between the cable company Comcast and the Tribeca Film Festival or through cable channels such as the Independent Film Channel. In some cases web retailers, mostly notably Amazon. com, have begun optioning screenplays for development in an effort to obtain inexpensive content that could then be marketed using their video on demand (VOD) player.

In this sense, Smith's promotion of *Red State* opened up a number of questions about the role of self-distribution in redefining media production. Self-distribution demands new roles for filmmakers and transforms the nature of the film text, while also using paratextual features to establish new ways of thinking about independence. In some cases, filmmakers have sought to create expanded transmedia worlds or textual universes that can attract new audiences, a practice that Henry Jenkins has referred to as "transmedia storytelling."[10] In the case of *Red State*, Kevin Smith's efforts to court publicity through podcasts and tours may help to expand the "View Askew" textual universe associated with his films, but they also open up the possibility, as Longworth points out, that everything he does, including his promise to retire from filmmaking, may be nothing more than a "publicity stunt." Longworth goes on to add that these forms of publicity contribute to a situation in which "a product and its promotion are virtually indistinguishable—it's all entertainment."[11] These new models of self-distribution often rely upon what Daren Brabham refers to as a "new iteration of the same old American myth of the self-made man."[12] As Brabham argues, narratives about self-distribution success have the potential to exaggerate the degree to which digital delivery democratizes access. However, despite these concerns, the culture of self-distribution potentially opens up new avenues for creative productivity, allowing us to rethink and potentially transform how media texts are promoted, distributed, exhibited, and perceived. These collaborative projects—and the culture of self-distribution in general—promote what might be called a "pedagogy of self-distribution," in which media makers teach others how to use digital delivery and social media tools to promote and distribute their films, allowing filmmakers and audiences to develop new categories for distinguishing their films from both independent and mainstream movies. These pedagogical and productive activities fall into two commonly cited practices: crowdfunding and crowdsourcing. Crowdfunding is the process of soliciting financial contributions from supporters of a project, while crowdsourcing involves the use of collective labor—from fans, supporters, and other participants—to produce and distribute a text. Finally, I will use DIY filmmaking to refer broadly to the processes of self-distribution, by which artists choose not to sell their movies to established distributors, opting instead to undertake promotion and marketing themselves, often through social media and other low-cost tools.

CULTIVATING INDEPENDENCE

As recently as 2005, Chris Holmlund, writing in a popular anthology of academic essays on independent cinema, could look at the popularity of and critical acclaim for a range of films, including *Gangs of New York* (2002), *Far from Heaven* (2002), *My Big Fat Greek Wedding* (2002), and *Bowling for Columbine* (2002), and proclaim that "independent films would seem to have moved squarely into the mainstream."[13] And yet, within a few short years, the perception is that quality independent cinema is endangered, threatened on one end by an increasing focus on blockbuster franchises and on the other by an exponential growth in content, in which thousands of independent and DIY films and web series compete for people's attention. The year 2003 marked a moment when all of the major studios had a division for distributing independent movies, but by 2008 most of the major studios had shut down their specialty divisions; others were buying far fewer movies, in part due to the banking crisis, which made many of the financing models for independent films unsustainable. As Edward Jay Epstein has documented, foreign pre-sales, the technique used to finance independent film budgets in the Sundance-Miramax era, evaporated with the banking collapse in 2008 and with the decline in DVD sales starting in the mid-2000s. Finally, Epstein pointed out that increased competition, due to digital delivery, dramatically decreased the potential value of broadcast rights to an independent film, especially when that film would likely be available on a streaming site within a few short weeks.[14] To be fair, Holmlund acknowledged that the outlook for indie films wasn't quite as rosy as she originally suggested. By the mid-2000s, it was clear that many indie filmmakers operating on the margins would struggle to get distribution.[15]

One of the concepts that helped to define some of the changes associated with independent filmmaking was the contested idea of the "long tail," a concept used by Chris Anderson as a means of explaining the explosion of content made possible by what he described as the "unlimited 'shelf space' of the Internet."[16] Anderson famously argued that digital distribution made it possible for websites such as Amazon, iTunes, Rhapsody.com, and Netflix to make vast sums of money from selling not only the mainstream hits but also niche items. This approach has been embraced by a wide variety of filmmakers who emerged from the 1990s independent boom, a group that has been labeled as the "Sundance-Miramax" generation (Michael Z. Newman) and "The Harvey Boys" (Kevin Smith).[17] One of the more noteworthy figures, Edward Burns, eventually became an advocate of digital delivery, championing VOD and online models as an alternative to theatrical distribution. Accordingly, he released his 2010 feature *Nice Guy Johnny* on a wide variety of platforms, including iTunes, DVD, and Comcast's VOD service. In fact, Burns remarked that he had "completely fallen out of love with the idea of a theatrical release" and instead embraced the creative freedom that online distribution offered him.[18] Because storing songs and movies online is relatively inexpensive, selling or renting a song or a movie just once every few weeks would still be profitable. Anderson used this observation to make the argument that the internet had given rise to a diverse culture, one that would speak to the interests of a wider listening or viewing public; however, the effects of the long tail haven't been entirely clear. Although digital enthusiasts such as Longworth might envision a "personal 'main stream,'" long tail models proved far more lucrative for aggregators such as Amazon, Apple, and Netflix than for the actual producers of media content, who might generate only a few sales per month, given the intense competition for people's attention spans. As *Bomb It* (2007) director and DIY filmmaker Jon Reiss acknowledged, "the long tail is very long."[19]

PARTICIPATORY PRODUCTIONS

Crowdsourcing is typically described as a process by which media producers seek assistance from others whose talents and abilities might be incorporated into a project, and it encompasses a wide range of practices. The term "crowdsourcing" can be traced to a 2006 *Wired* article in which Jeff Howe made the argument that content creators could tap into the skills and labor of others

online. Howe cited the example of iStockphoto, a website where amateur pho-
tographers could post pictures that could be licensed cheaply for use by others.
As a result, distribution models based on scarcity—a professional photogra-
pher licensing her photographs for use in a museum exhibit, for example—were
being undercut. Howe went on to link the crowdsourcing phenomenon to other
activities, such as the use of "solvers" by corporations such as Eli Lilly and Proctor & Gamble to tackle scientific problems. Similarly, Netflix famously tapped
into the research skills of the wider public in order to strengthen its recommendation algorithm.[20] Building upon the wisdom of crowds allows these companies
to find creative solutions to problems. Even though solvers may be compensated
for their work, in amounts up to $100,000, Howe surmised that crowdsourced
research is likely cheaper than maintaining a company's research and development staff. He concluded that crowdsourced "labor isn't always free, but it costs a
lot less than paying traditional employees."[21] Thus, in some sense, crowdsourcing
allowed corporations to make use of outside, often voluntary, labor for significant financial gain. However, filmmakers have adapted the idea of crowdsourcing to cultivate new tools that could be shared in order to complete tasks that
might require additional expertise that would be too costly for a smaller budget.
In other cases, crowdsourcing was used to describe the process of compiling a
mosaic of video clips that were produced in separate locations in order to tell a
larger story.

In the case of *Life in a Day* (2011), Ridley Scott and Kevin Macdonald invited
YouTube users to produce short clips that could be incorporated into a planned
documentary. Similarly, the web developer Casey Pugh, who worked for the
video-sharing site Vimeo, orchestrated the incredibly ambitious fan film *Star
Wars Uncut* (2009) by inviting fans to "remake" short segments of *Star Wars:
A New Hope* (1977), which Pugh then stitched together to create a patchwork
scene-by-scene retelling of the original film.[22] In other cases, filmmakers may
solicit assistance with one aspect of production, seeking volunteers to contribute music or editing skills or even to assist in the promotion and marketing
of a movie. In his discussion of "media work," Mark Deuze traces the ways in
which "people seem to be increasingly willing to participate voluntarily in the
media-making process to achieve what can be called a 'networked reputation.' "[23]
In this sense, users might choose to participate in a project not out of a desire for
compensation but with a view toward building a reputation and being compensated for future work. Thus, participants in a project such as *Life in Day* or *Star
Wars Uncut* might choose to contribute for a variety of reasons, ranging from
the desire to be discovered to the pleasure of contributing to a larger collective
experiment in storytelling.

However, as Jonathan Gray argues, descriptions of crowdsourcing often
obscure the complexities of how movies and television shows are produced. As

Gray points out, workers in the media industry often imply that crowdsourced works are unlikely to achieve the status of art and therefore must be directed by a "benevolent dictator," who shepherds the project. This description of the production process ignores the fact that most Hollywood films are produced through the collective efforts of actors, writers, camera operators, lighting technicians, and other cast and crew who might be described as a "crowd." Gray goes on to argue that such an opposition merely reinforces the role of the individual artist and diminishes the contributions of an undifferentiated crowd. Gray's comments serve as an important reminder that our vocabulary for describing media production and reception will have a significant effect on how we conceptualize this process.[24]

KICKSTARTING DISTRIBUTION

Unlike crowdsourcing, crowdfunding focuses primarily on the practice of seeking donations from fans and other supporters in order to raise enough money to produce or distribute a film. Like crowdsourcing, crowdfunding relies upon social networking as a means of engaging an audience and getting individuals to contribute financially to a project. Crowdfunding sites like Kickstarter are built upon the assumption that people will support projects that excite or interest them. Donors pledge a specified amount and, depending on the amount, may receive gifts ranging from a copy of the DVD when the movie is completed to a souvenir from the set or even dinner with the cast and crew. As Kickstarter co-founder Yancey Strickler explained it, supporting an independent filmmaker offers an "emotional engagement" that is not available from simply buying a CD or DVD, one that is explicitly structured around ideologies of community and authorship.[25] This form of community often coalesces around shared tastes, values, or interests. For example, Gary Hustwit, who made *Helvetica* (2007), a documentary about the ubiquitous typeface, and *Objectified* (2009), which was about product design, uses an active social media profile, particularly on Twitter, to build an audience by reaching out to web designers and other creative workers who might be drawn to the issues addressed in his films.[26] Crowdfunding has, in fact, become an alternative source of support for a number of high-profile independent filmmakers, including Paul Schrader, David Lynch, Hal Hartley, Ira Sachs, and Mumblecore director Andrew Bujalski, who partially financed his 2011 feature *Computer Chess* using crowd donations. Even David Fincher, who directed *Fight Club* (1999) and *Girl with a Dragon Tattoo* (2011), sought donations for his adaptation of the comic book series *The Goon*, which was considered too controversial to be produced with studio funding. Given the grim financial realities, crowdfunding began to look like an increasingly viable alternative both for funding a movie and for generating interest that could be used once the film was completed.

The two major crowdfunding sites used by indie filmmakers are Kickstarter and IndieGoGo. The latter was launched at the 2008 Sundance Film Festival and was promoted as an opportunity for DIY filmmakers to gain funding in an increasingly competitive marketplace. The service collects a 4 percent fee on the amount raised, and filmmakers are allowed to keep the money raised, even if they fail to meet their stated goals. According to the *Wall Street Journal*, projects proposed on IndieGoGo have had limited success; only 10 percent met their financial goals, although 40 percent did manage to raise $500 or more.[27] By comparison, Kickstarter, founded in April 2009, requires project proposals to achieve their goals before funds will be released. Money is collected using Amazon Payments, and Kickstarter takes a 5 percent cut only if the project reaches its goal. Kickstarter projects have had a 43 percent success rate, and the service has become a useful tool not only for filmmakers but also for visual artists, musicians, designers, and other creative workers. Within two years of Kickstarter's launch, donors had pledged over $53 million to 20,371 projects.[28] More than $19 million of this total went to film-related projects, suggesting that it has been widely adopted by independent filmmakers seeking to secure funds and build an audience. Further, by April 2011 the website was supporting the launch of more than 2,000 new projects per month, indicating a broad level of participation.[29]

The appeals used to solicit donations range from relatively direct marketing techniques to earnest personal appeals and even naked self-promotion. Hal Hartley, the director of *Surviving Desire* (1993) and *Henry Fool* (1997), used Kickstarter after filming was completed to secure support for post-production work and for the release of a DVD version of his 2011 project *Meanwhile*. Hartley had originally planned the hour-long featurette as a pilot for a television miniseries. However, a lack of interest from cable channels spurred Hartley to use Kickstarter as a way of marketing the DVD. The video on his Kickstarter page serves primarily as a trailer for the movie, with *Meanwhile*'s lead actor, DJ Mendel, offering a short introduction to the film. Potential donors could choose from a variety of rewards: a *Meanwhile* lobby card for a $5 donation; a CD of music related to the film, $10; a copy of the completed DVD, $25; a signed copy of the DVD, $100. The largest donors would be given the opportunity to receive a "producer" credit and to attend the film's New York premiere and after-screening party.[30] Hartley was able to secure funding well before his scheduled deadline but continued to raise funds with the acknowledged hope of being able to claim a profit on the movie.

Even some relatively mainstream directors have used crowdfunding, intending not only to raise funds but also to position their projects as part of an alternative to Hollywood's production culture. Paul Schrader, best known for writing the screenplay for Martin Scorsese's *Taxi Driver* (1976), collaborated with novelist and screenwriter Bret Easton Ellis on *The Canyons* (2012), a feature about a group of power-hungry young adults living and working in contemporary Hollywood. In his pitch video, Schrader justified the use of Kickstarter by describing his project as participating in the process of "reinventing" film through the use of Indie 2.0 technologies, including online casting tools such as Let It Cast. Similarly, Ellis asserted that social media would allow the filmmakers to escape the "groupthink" that he associated with the studio system. The filmmakers set a goal of $100,000, an amount they reached well before their June 2012 deadline, thanks in part to their celebrity status. In fact, many of the thank-you gifts were related to Ellis and Schrader's status as stars: an autographed copy of the film's poster for a $50 donation, and an autographed copy of the shooting script of *The Canyons* for $150. A donation of $1,500 from a budding filmmaker would result in a promise from Schrader and Ellis to watch and "live-tweet" the donor's feature-length film, the kind of publicity that would otherwise be difficult to attract. The highest donor level was set at $10,000, and the individual who gave that amount was guaranteed dinner with the director and also the engraved belt buckle that was Robert DeNiro's set gift to Schrader from *Taxi Driver*.[31] In this way, Schrader and Ellis were able to promote *The Canyons* as a product that existed outside of the studio system and, to some extent, served as a critique of it, even while the movie was still in pre-production. But the use of Kickstarter by relatively mainstream directors like Schrader and Fincher often generates controversy, in part because they are seen as upsetting the site's perceived purpose to foster new and emerging artists. Even when Fincher defined his project as being in opposition to the normative values associated with Hollywood studios, his appeal left some indie film workers to speculate that the major studios themselves could begin to use crowdfunding techniques.

The most common Kickstarter pitch came from someone who was either an amateur filmmaker or someone who had little experience within the Hollywood or even Indiewood movie cultures. In many cases, filmmakers sought to appeal directly to the shared experiences or interests of potential donors. For example, Nathaniel Hansen, the director of *The Elders*, a planned documentary film and archive of interviews with senior citizens, emphasized his past experience with creating documentary portraits and explained the importance of "learning from" senior citizens and of creating oral histories that could be shared with future generations. Hansen was also explicit about how he would use the funds to pay for travel expenses and how the final project would be structured. The entire video consists of Hansen looking directly into the camera in a close-up and appealing to viewers' emotions about preserving the past. Although Hansen did include sample interviews on his Kickstarter page, the primary proposal highlighted the passion and commitment of the individual filmmaker and how his interests might reflect the needs and interests of a wider community.[32] Thus, in a number of cases, DIY filmmakers, especially those seeking to crowdsource or crowdfund films, have based their requests on ideas of community built around common interests or beliefs.

In other cases, directors have found success by mocking some of the conventions associated with this form of direct appeal or by coming up with innovative fundraising models. The Australian filmmakers behind *The Tunnel* financed their horror film by selling each digital frame for one dollar apiece before releasing the film on BitTorrent in conjunction with a more traditional release.[33] For her Kickstarter page for the movie *I Am I*, Jocelyn Towne presented an irreverent long-take introduction to the movie in which she explains the project as she leads the camera around her apartment and greets some of the other participants, including producers Cara Olsen and Jen Dubin, who pop up from behind Towne's couch, and actors Marianna Palka and Jason Ritter; the latter walks into her kitchen from off-screen as Towne pretends to call him on the phone to offer him a part in the movie. *I Am I* eventually became one of the highest-funded films in the history of Kickstarter, securing a reported $111,965 from more than 900 donors. Towne benefited not only from the presence of a couple of well-known actors in Jason Ritter and *Big Bang Theory*'s Simon Helberg but also from the publicity the movie received when it was featured in a story about Kickstarter that aired on CNN.[34] Similarly, animator Christopher Salmon was able to raise over $160,000 to adapt Neil Gaiman's story "The Price," largely because of the fan cultures around Gaiman, whose online presence complements his work in fantasy and graphic novels.

However, even though Kickstarter has generated a number of successes— seventeen films from the 2012 Sundance Film Festival and thirty-three from the 2012 South by Southwest received some support from crowdfunding—many other projects failed to achieve their funding objectives. A look at these unfunded projects can often tell us quite a bit about how indie and DIY cinema are being defined. As filmmaker Lucas McNelly points out, successful crowdfunding often depends on carefully managing the "perks" offered to potential donors. Further, successfully funded projects typically require directors to pay constant attention to social media, posting messages, photographs, and videos semi-daily on Facebook and Twitter and on microblogs such as Tumblr. This social media strategy also requires directors to identify the niche audiences that might be most interested in their work.[35] In other cases, fundraising has to be carefully timed to avoid conflicts with holidays and other distractions that will make a project less visible. Thus, while crowd productions seem to offer a more democratized approach to making movies—anyone can solicit funds on Kickstarter—there are some concerns about whether it is viable for most independent filmmakers. In addition, Indie 2.0 techniques can be adapted not only by amateur artists but also by mainstream commercial moviemakers. For them, the money raised through crowdfunding may matter less than the paratextual framing of their projects. By positioning their movies as products of the cultures of social media, these film-makers can present their work as existing outside of the mainstream.

Furthermore, as Graeme Turner argues, groups formed via digital media have come to redefine "community"; the term no longer refers to people living in a specific location but instead describes "a form of consciousness, a focus of belonging or identification."[36] Turner pointedly differentiates between national communities, which entail a range of entitlements and obligations, and fan-based communities, which are structured around affinities and taste cultures. He goes on to point out that when community is invoked in reference to fan practices, it has more to do with "enhancing the individual's experience of consumption," of navigating a pathway through all of the niche content choices available, rather than with the obligations and demands associated with traditional community.[37] However, Turner's alternative account, in which he describes these niche cul-tures as "zones of consumption," places too little emphasis on the voluntary, par-ticipatory contributions of the individuals who choose to support a DIY project. The practices of crowdfunding may enable new forms of hip consumption, allowing the crowdfunding model to serve as a substitute for more traditional forms of independent distribution through art-house theaters and alternative video stores. Nearly half of the people who supported Hal Hartley's *Mean-while* did so at the $25 level.[38] But the choice to contribute to Hartley directly entails an expression of support for his mode of independent production, one that appeared increasingly imperiled in 2011. In other cases, Kickstarter proj-ects offered contributors the opportunity to support projects that reinforced or advocated for social or political views they shared. In addition, crowdsourced projects may offer new ways of ensuring that marginalized voices and viewpoints are heard, particularly for groups living or working outside of the media indus-try. Thus, although these ad hoc groupings may not function as communities in the strictest sense of the term, they reflect a desire for sharing in the process of determining what kinds of messages and what forms of entertainment receive attention and support. And while the choice to support projects may be driven by individual interests, it is also rooted in a communitarian impulse that empha-sizes the value of expanding opportunities for independent voices.

PEDAGOGIES OF DIY PRODUCTION

The DIY approach to film distribution promoted the idea of community through the process of sharing resources and experiences, with the purpose of guiding others through the process of making and distributing movies. In an ear-lier discussion of Arin Crumley and Lance Weiler's website From Here to Awe-some, I noted that an online film "festival" would serve not merely as a means for filmmakers to promote their creations but also as a site where important "pedagogical" work was taking place.³⁹ In other words, these online resources become places where aspiring filmmakers can learn methods for promoting and exhibiting their work. Later, Weiler, who directed and self-distributed *The Last Broadcast* (1998) and *Head Trauma* (2006), helped to launch the Workbook Project, which billed itself as an open network for people who "want to be creative in the digital age." Like other DIY projects, the site encouraged participants to share resources and to view themselves as collaborators rather than competitors. Weiler's creative distribution practices—which include story worlds with vast transmedia extensions, such as the alternate-reality game (ARG) that accompanied the release of *Head Trauma*—positioned him as an expert capable of mentoring aspiring filmmakers. The Workbook Project hosted a series of conferences, "DIY Days," where independent filmmakers could meet to discuss distribution and promotional strategies. In addition, the site hosted a series of "Culture Hacker" blog posts and podcast interviews that explained how new media technologies inform storytelling. Beyond providing advice to potential filmmakers, these pedagogical approaches helped to define the parameters of DIY media production, establishing genres and modes of engaging with the audience, discussions that have helped to structure Kickstarter video appeals, for example.

Although it is easy to romanticize the DIY filmmaker and to view transmedia storytelling as a cutting-edge approach to promoting a film, a number of observers have questioned the implications that online self-distribution might have for the future of independent filmmaking. This marketing rhetoric permeates much of the pedagogical literature on DIY filmmaking. *Bomb It* director Jon Reiss, who characterizes himself as "an iconoclastic, ex punk rock anarchist neo Marxist," claims that filmmakers interested in pursuing a DIY approach must acknowledge that "the artificial divide between art and commerce must be eliminated."⁴⁰ Also lost in the hype about DIY filmmakers was the fact that practices of self-distribution existed long before the widespread use of digital media as a tool for promoting films. As Justin Wyatt observes, although the 1970s are typically associated with the growth of Hollywood blockbusters and the transition from platform to wide release patterns, a network of independent filmmakers used a variety of strategies to enter the theatrical marketplace. For example, a number of independently produced films, including Tom Laughlin's *Billy Jack* (1971), used four-walling distribution, whereby the filmmaker rents a theater, a technique that many DIY filmmakers have employed to ensure that their movies are viewed in a theater.⁴¹ In addition, Wyatt traces the production, distribution, and promotional history of Joe Camp's family-oriented feature *Benji* (1974), which used a variety of creative grassroots marketing techniques to build an audience gradually.⁴² Thus, although it is easy to view DIY filmmaking as a relatively recent phenomenon, many of the techniques used by independent filmmakers—renting movie screens, touring with a movie, using (social) networks to engage with audiences—actually have a much longer history. However, in the era of digital delivery, these practices have been reconceptualized. On the one hand, VOD distribution, whether through cable television, streaming video, or digital downloads, has opened up new ways for audiences to access independent content. On the other, these forms of independent filmmaking have placed new emphasis on collaboration and collective forms of production, distribution, and financing. Although many DIY movies continue to place emphasis on the creative visions of their directors, many of these projects also appeal to our desires for collaboration and participation.

WATCHING FOR *IRON SKY*

Pedagogical elements permeated many of the most successful Indie 2.0 projects, making them not merely movies but cinematic events that could be used to build community and even promote forms of political activism. One of the more influential crowd-produced projects was *Iron Sky*, by a film collective based in Finland, though supported by people around the globe. The collective, called Energia Productions and led by director Timo Vuorensela, first gained notoriety for making the *Star Wreck* film series, an ongoing cycle of *Star Trek* parodies. But the filmmakers also pioneered a crowdsourcing tool called Wreckamovie, which allowed people to streamline collaborative techniques by inviting contributors from around the world to submit ideas for a movie. One of the films in the series, *Star Wreck: In the Pirkinning*, was distributed through the Wreckamovie platform for free and was downloaded over three million times, suggesting that Energia Productions had built up a large international fan base that could be harnessed to help produce and distribute a film that was unrelated to an existing media franchise.

Iron Sky was based on a satirical alternate-reality premise in which a Nazi leader makes a major anti-gravity discovery in 1945 and launches several spaceships from a secret base in Antarctica that land on the moon. From there, the Nazis build an invasion fleet, and in the year 2018 they return to Earth. The film was tirelessly promoted throughout the pre-production and production processes through social media and web video sites such as Twitter, Facebook, and YouTube, where the crew released footage. A teaser trailer helped to establish the tone of the film and to illuminate the filmmaking process by employing an aesthetic that parodied the propaganda films of Leni Reifenstahl and the low-budget science fiction films of the 1950s. In other cases, short videos simulated news reports, complete with shaky video footage of the Nazi moon base. In all, Energia Productions posted more than 200 videos, some of them showing scenes from the movie or short videos that were part of the diegetic world of the film. In other cases, Energia posted interviews with the director and stars, clips from film festivals, and other news stories that allowed the filmmakers to remain visible to the people who were part of the cultures of anticipation surrounding the film. Like a number of other projects, they made an effort to use Google Maps and similar tools to visualize the locations where interest in the film might be the highest. They also encouraged fans to "buy war bonds," which involved small donations to the production of the film. Once the film was completed in 2012, investors would receive a copy of the DVD plus several other pieces of inexpensive memorabilia, including dog tags that tie into the war film premise.

SITA SINGS THE BLUES

One of the more innovative experiments in DIY distribution was Nina Paley's breathtaking and sharply inventive *Sita Sings the Blues*, an animated feature that faced unique challenges because of its complex relationship to copyright law due to its use of blues songs recorded by the 1930s musical artist Annette Hanshaw. Paley appealed to indie tropes, such as the idea of community and the desire for self-expression, which can be associated with her use of handmade animation techniques that give her film the appearance of authenticity. Like many other DIY filmmakers, Paley reinforced this sense of authenticity through a series of promotional paratexts and reviews that helped to characterize *Sita Sings the Blues* as a significant and unique independent film.

Sita Sings the Blues features a complex narrative that intercuts between two primary stories. First, we meet Nina and her boyfriend, Dave, happily in love, their cat Lexi contentedly sleeping on the foot of the bed, at least until it's time for that 5 a.m. feeding. Paley mixes intentionally crude animation here with photographic backgrounds that capture bits and pieces of San Francisco, establishing a visual motif that will be repeated throughout the film. These scenes use a technique that Paley calls "squigglevision." Soon after we are introduced to the couple, Dave gets a temporary job in India. When Nina flies out for a visit, Dave seems aloof, unwilling to show affection in public or, later, in private. Nina goes back to Brooklyn to take some freelance work and is greeted by an email from Dave telling her that he would like to end their relationship.

Alongside of Nina's story, we get the tale of Sita and Rama, based on the ancient Sanskrit epic *The Ramayana*. Sita endures a rejection similar to that experienced by Nina after Rama suspects that his wife has been unfaithful. Paley depicts this kidnapping and rescue plot with visual flair and wit. This narrative is mediated by a group of three modern-day Indian storytellers, who joke about Rama's decisions while gently debating when the story took place—"was it the eleventh century?" The modern-day narrators seem to undercut the self-seriousness of the epic and, in turn, Nina's break-up with Dave. But what

made *Sita Sings the Blues* feel so original to many viewers was Paley's decision to have Sita express her emotions by singing and dancing to recordings
of Hanshaw's songs of unrequited love and rejection, which match Sita's story
while also expressing the emotions experienced by Nina. To reinforce the connection with Hanshaw, Sita was drawn as a bluesy, sometimes brazen Betty
Boop–type figure.

And this is where the innovative distribution strategies came into play.
Because many of Hanshaw's recordings were still under copyright—even
though the songs themselves are in the public domain—Paley would have had
to pay thousands of dollars in fees to "decriminalize" the film.[43] She therefore
decided to distribute the film on the web under a Creative Commons license,
under the provision that "promotional" copies of movies and DVDs are not
subject to the same licensing fees as those sold in the marketplace. In addition
to these promotional copies, Paley chose to give away the film for free, both in
downloadable and streaming formats, accessible from her website.[44] Even when
Paley was given a "better" offer, she would have faced what was described as a
"step deal," in which she would have to pay gradually higher copyright fees if the
film became more profitable. So Paley ended up giving away the film, essentially
for free, on the web and sought to recover her costs through a limited-edition
DVD sale, through donations, and through the sale of ancillary materials, such as
T-shirts, charms, pins, and water bottles.

In addition, Paley courted publicity by reaching out to bloggers, offering to go
to lunch with any interviewer willing to buy her a meal and promising that she
would post a link when the interview was published. This ploy eventually caught
the attention of esteemed critic Roger Ebert, who succeeded in building interest in both Paley's film and the distribution dilemma she faced.[45] Although *Sita
Sings the Blues* no doubt benefited from Ebert's timely review and his decision to
highlight the film at his annual festival in Champaign, Illinois (which also happened to be Paley's hometown), Paley's carefully crafted grassroots distribution
and promotion plan had already established her film as an important case study
for both independent moviemakers and copyright activists.

THE AGE OF STUPID

Like *Sita Sings the Blues*, Franny Armstrong's *The Age of Stupid* (2009) made
use of a crowdsourced approach to distribution. The film is a hybrid documentary, with Pete Postlethwaite playing a librarian, identified as the Archivist,
who scolds the human race in the year 2055 for failing to take action to prevent global warming. The Archivist, who lives on the last remaining habitable
sliver of Earth on the Arctic Circle, curates a "Global Archive," a series of short
documentaries that convey symptoms of climate change. These short segments

depict the devastating effects of Hurricane Katrina, a Nigerian woman who fishes in oil-polluted waters, and an octogenarian mountaineer living in the Alps who has witnessed the receding of nearby glaciers. Armstrong skillfully weaves between these narrative threads to suggest that people were—to use the film's terminology—*stupid* to allow climate change to continue. The film is a bracing polemic, one that aggressively asserts the urgency of global warming. However, given its strident critique of corporations, it also presented a difficult challenge in terms of funding and distribution.

Having learned from her experiences with self-distributing her critique of the fast food industry, *McLibel* (2005), Armstrong chose to crowdfund *Age of Stupid*, in part because it would enable her to retain distribution rights. She speculates that millions of people saw the film because she kept control over when and where it would be seen.[46] Thus, even at the pre-production stage, Armstrong was able to engage audiences and get them involved in supporting the film and the cause associated with it.

This sense of participatory production also ensured that the film would receive an additional boost when it came time to promote and distribute it. Armstrong surmised that the crowds who had invested in her film would also likely offer it free publicity through blog posts, tweets, and other forms of word-of-mouth advertising. These collaborative activities were not completely disconnected from existing institutions. Armstrong worked with advocacy groups like MoveOn.org and Greenpeace in order to leverage their networks to build an audience for the film. Such techniques led Jon Reiss, a high-profile advocate of DIY filmmaking, to characterize *The Age of Stupid* as "the future of film, film culture and film distribution and marketing."[47] Reiss points out that the film premiered on 550 screens in forty-five countries, supported largely by a massive event screening in which the film's premiere party, featuring performances by Radiohead's Thom Yorke and others, was broadcast live, creating what Reiss called "a worldwide cinematic event." Although it would be difficult to measure the film's overall impact on climate change activism, the "event" status of the premiere helped to ensure more mainstream media coverage than a typical documentary would receive.

However, *The Age of Stupid* is perhaps more significant because of the ways in which Armstrong sought to offer a "transparent" model for crowdfunding and to share its environmentally friendly production techniques. The film's website contains extensive, if humorous, tips on how to crowdfund, such as publically releasing a film's budget, and offers templates for loan agreements and other financial and legal texts. In all cases, the filmmaker preaches the idea of involvement, suggesting that supporters want to be considered "part of the team." Thus, like other transmedia approaches, *The Age of Stupid* began with the recognition that audience participation could be mobilized, not merely to get people to attend the film but also to publicize it and to promote the political causes associated with it. Ultimately, *The Age of Stupid* not only presented an unfiltered message about climate change but also reinforced a narrative about the potential of social media technologies to enable independent filmmakers to reach a wider audience. This latter narrative was based on the idea of active movie audiences who were invested supporting movies and other forms of entertainment that mattered to them.

LOUIS C.K.

Entertainers have often relied on their popularity in order to market directly to consumers. This approach was popularized by the rock group Radiohead, which released its 2007 album, *In Rainbows*, directly through its website, allowing people to pay whatever amount they wished in order to download the entire album. The scheme fit neatly into an emerging culture of digital delivery, one that embraced the perception that entertainers could bypass traditional gatekeepers—record labels, movie theaters and studios, television channels—in order to address their audiences directly. Like many other DIY projects, this form of distribution expressed a longing for greater transparency. Bypassing gatekeepers, in this light, becomes more than simply allowing for more diverse content choices. It also served as a means of excluding various middlemen that would increase the costs of entertainment. At the same time, a "transparent" distribution approach could help turn consumers into producers by helping them to understand the economics of the entertainment industry.

Following this approach, the stand-up comedian and television star Louis C.K. announced that he would distribute a new comedy album, *Louis C.K. Live at the Beacon Theater*, through his website for $5 per download, a significantly cheaper cost than a new DVD sold in stores. Like many other DIY projects, C.K.'s distribution plan bypassed broadcast media and relied on word-of-mouth promotion, in part through sharing clips from the video on social media sites such as Facebook and Twitter. Further, as C.K. commented in an essay posted to his website, the video would be available worldwide, whereas a video distributed through more traditional channels might be restricted to the United States, with foreign distribution delayed, perhaps indefinitely.

C.K. placed tremendous emphasis on the desire for transparency, frankly discussing not only his distribution plan but also the actual financial numbers associated with *Beacon Theater*. This form of transparency often defies normal modes of doing business. As C.K. acknowledged, "there's power in exclusive ownership of information."[48] According to numbers on his website, the album was purchased 50,000 times in the first twelve hours after it was made available on December 10, 2011, which resulted in a gross income of $250,000. Within three days, the video had been downloaded 110,000 times, contributing to a gross of over half a million dollars. C.K. also noted that most of the production costs were covered by the ticket sales generated by the two live shows that provided the material for the video, suggesting again the potential benefits of linking DIY productions to one-time events. C.K. also pointed out that *Beacon Theater* was supported by "people in large numbers advocating this idea" of direct distribution. Thus, even a text not directly identified with a specific cause, such as climate change, could be caught up in the politics of distribution. In essence, creators recognized that centralized modes of distribution are undemocratic and that DIY methods could open up new forms of culture.

CONCLUSION

Although a number of DIY projects attracted attention from both the social media and the mainstream media, it is important to note that many similar projects went unnoticed. To some extent, successful films benefited from the involvement of figures who already had some celebrity, such as Kevin Smith, Louis C.K., or even Pete Postlethwaite. In other cases, DIY movies were able to achieve recognition thanks to the support of high-profile advocates, as when Roger Ebert wrote a glowing review of Nina Paley's *Sita Sings the Blues*. However, all these projects illustrate a powerful attempt to use digital delivery to redefine what it means to be an independent filmmaker.

In this sense, DIY culture not only placed emphasis on finding alternative distribution models but also served a larger pedagogical purpose, one that called for a more transparent relationship between producers and consumers of media content. This line was further blurred through references to the techniques of crowdsourcing and crowdfunding, by which filmmakers sought to tap the creative potential and financial support of movie audiences. Thus, although digital delivery practices have offered new avenues for media conglomerates to market directly to the consumer, these tools—and the discussions they have provoked—have also opened up new ways of thinking about the interactions between producers and consumers.

8 ▶ REINVENTING FESTIVALS
Curation, Distribution, and the Creation of Global Cinephilia

IN JULY 2010 STALWART directors Ridley Scott and Kevin Macdonald engaged in what was billed as "a historic cinematic experiment" when they invited YouTube users to submit video footage for a planned two-hour documentary entitled *Life in a Day*. The filmmakers stipulated only that the footage had to be recorded on July 24 (which, when delivered in shorthand, appeared as 24/7) and submitted to the *Life in a Day* YouTube page no later than July 31. Scott and Macdonald would then select footage to be compiled into a feature-length film, one that would draw on YouTube's worldwide reach to capture a snapshot of a global community linked by video sharing. The invitation included several enticements beyond the opportunity to be associated with a film produced by the directors of *Blade Runner* and *Last King of Scotland*, respectively. *Life in a Day* was guaranteed a slot at the 2011 Sundance Film Festival, and twenty contributors to the film would be invited to attend the film's premiere there and immerse themselves in the celebrity culture associated with Sundance. Participants whose footage was included in the final film would also receive a credit as co-directors, a recognition that seemingly confirmed the fantasy that cheap digital production tools would democratize cinema.

This model of democratized filmmaking has long been aligned with new technologies, and in the case of *Life in a Day* it proved especially alluring. Macdonald and Scott received well over 80,000 submissions, demonstrating how easy it had become to produce and share content. In fact, *Life in a Day* seemed to illustrate precisely the extent to which films fit neatly into an emerging on-demand culture, in which anyone could become a filmmaker and movies could be revised, downloaded, and shared at the click of a mouse. However, despite this new potential for movie fans to become involved in the production process, it was unclear how this energy could be used. In an interview about the submission process, Macdonald claimed that this foundational myth has been realized in practice only infrequently: "You can make a film now for nothing, effectively. If you've got a laptop and a camera you can make a film to a professional standard. And yet not a lot of people have done it. There are a lot of bad films being made, but the new Mozart hasn't come out."[1] Although Macdonald offered no direct solutions for the lack of visibility for DIY filmmaking, *Life in a Day* was positioned, in part, as an opportunity for budding filmmakers to be discovered. But underlying this narrative of discovery was the connection between YouTube, a video sharing site normally associated with fostering amateur content, and Sundance, a festival that balances uneasily between its role in facilitating the discovery of talented filmmakers and its status as an important component of the process by which independent films are able to obtain cultural capital. Although festivals such as Sundance historically have been linked to the production of exclusivity, the YouTube project *Life in a Day* was defined by the democratization not only of the tools of production but also of the modes of exhibition; anyone who wanted to see the film could do so while it was still playing at the festival.

Life in a Day, as its title implies, served as a video time capsule. The film was loosely structured around a small number of thematic, narrative, and ideological elements. On the narrative level, the clock time of everyday life allows the movie to depict the daily routines, rituals, and activities that ostensibly unite us—waking up, making coffee, reading the newspaper—treating us as part of a shared community. This sense of community is reinforced by the presence of a young Korean man who has traveled through 190 countries, many of them on a bicycle. The man imagines a future in which Korea will be reunified, and his story serves to bring together the myriad individual hopes and fears expressed by the movie's other participants. But the primary structuring force in *Life in a Day* is YouTube itself, particularly the early depictions of the site as space where an amateur user could "broadcast yourself." Reviews of the film often focused on the idea that the film's amateur contributions allowed for "some of the purest emotion" in recent film history; others described it as "intimate, startling, unsettling and often deeply moving."[2] As a result, *Life in a Day* not only fit into larger desires to be discovered but also linked to desires for a shared, global media event.

These questions about participatory filmmaking were given special emphasis due to the collaboration between the online video hub YouTube and the Sundance Film Festival. When *Life in a Day* premiered at Sundance on January 27, 2011, with many of the film's participants in attendance, it was simultaneously live-streamed on YouTube. Moreover, the streaming feed included access to the question-and-answer session held immediately after the film, allowing online audiences a brief glimpse of the celebrity cultures associated with a film festival.

Thus, the filmmakers sought to create a simultaneous global event, one in which YouTube—and the documentary itself—would be at the center. This type of simultaneity introduced a number of challenges, most notably the fact that the 5 p.m. Mountain Standard Time premiere meant that audiences in Eastern Europe and the Middle East would be tuning in at 3 a.m. local time. Although a second screening was scheduled for the following day so that more people could watch *Life in a Day* during the festival, some audience members outside the United States who were anticipating a shared media event expressed frustration about having to wake up in the middle of the night in order to attend the YouTube premiere.[3] Once these festival screenings ended, viewers would be unable to see the film until it was distributed in theaters, on cable, or on video. This distribution pattern allowed YouTube and Sundance to cultivate a wider culture of anticipation surrounding the film, building enthusiasm and word-of-mouth discussion that could then be used to promote future screenings.

Beyond the flurry of attention that culminated in a brief theatrical run and a series of screenings on the National Geographic Channel, the status of *Life in a Day* as a global media event was shaped by its relationship to Sundance. By allowing a global audience to "attend" the film's premiere, the festival opened up what is traditionally considered an exclusive event, a move that potentially redefines the role of the festival in mediating our relationship to a wider film culture. Sundance is just one of several major festivals that have used streaming video and social media to re-imagine the role of the film festival in the era of on-demand distribution. To begin, festivals have taken a more direct role in shaping the distribution patterns for independent films in particular, shifting from a model that emphasizes exclusive access to one that provides open—if temporary—access to movies playing at the festival. Festivals have also sought to cultivate active social media profiles that allow virtually anyone, regardless of geographic location, to interact with filmmakers and others attending the festival. This openness contributes to a new form of mobile cosmopolitanism, in which viewers can feel connected to the cutting edge of independent and art-house films, often from their homes.

Within this context, a number of film festivals have sought to fulfill the distribution and curatorial functions that have been upended in this moment of apparent crisis. In particular, festivals such as Sundance, Slamdance, Tribeca, and South by Southwest, which once served primarily as sites where new filmmaking talent could be discovered, have now become distributors, making selected films available online or on-demand through services such as YouTube or the Independent Film Channel (IFC) or platforms such as the XBox 360. As a result, these festivals have become involved in the process of redefining independent film and have begun to imagine new modes of distribution and exhibition. At the same time, they have changed the definition of festivals, transforming them from exclusive events grounded in a specific location into globalized social media phenomena. These new distribution models have changed the expectations of many independent directors, who now place less emphasis on live, collective moviegoing experiences and instead seek to use a range of distribution platforms to reach a wider audience. As Mumblecore filmmaker Joe Swanberg acknowledged, "I've come to realize that my festival run is my theatrical run."[4] Thus, rather than using festivals to gain theatrical screenings, Swanberg and many other low-budget filmmakers are now playing their films at festivals in order to support or promote online distribution through Netflix or iTunes or through on-demand options available through cable channels such as IFC. This focus on distribution works against the historic role festivals played in creating value for independent films through critical acclaim and through strategic exclusivity. As Marijke de Valck argues, festivals have traditionally relied upon a "media economy characterized by scarcity," in which a small number of festivals have exclusive access to new movies weeks or months before they are available through theaters, on DVD, or online.[5]

This chapter addresses the ways in which film festivals are being re-imagined in the era of digital delivery. Although festivals have a great deal of visibility in the entertainment press due to the presence of high-profile stars and famous directors, they often receive less attention compared with other aspects of film culture, likely because of their ephemeral nature. The "text" of a festival, unlike that of a movie or television show, may be more difficult to grasp, and textual materials, such as festival programs, reports, and reviews, only partially capture the experience of attending a film festival. Festivals are often held in improvised screening rooms, ranging from movie theaters to hotel ballrooms and even high school gymnasiums. In fact, as de Valck reminds us, "film festivals are transient events." They typically last only a few days, and the rituals and activities associated with festival participation often get lost in textual depictions of the festival experience.[6] These activities can include waiting in lines (many of which are determined by the hierarchies of different kinds of passes), dealing with vicissitudes of scheduling by viewing multiple movies in a single day, listening to volunteers introduce the movies that are about to screen, and cheering the many stars and directors who are attending the fest. In all cases, these activities help to shape the festival participants' expectations about film festivals and their social, political, and cultural roles. For example, the presence of filmmakers at post-screening interviews, the periods of waiting, and the organization of the schedule help to reinforce the perception of scarcity, the belief that viewers may have only a single chance to catch a film during the festival, potentially turning a movie screening into an event that cannot be re-created.

Some of the new distribution practices simply involve making certain films available to consumers during the festival, such as Slamdance's deal to show several films using the Microsoft Zune and XBox. Other approaches, such as the Sundance Next series, which began during the 2010 festival, played an important role in developing some of the key terms associated with independence. Next is a series of ultra-low-budget films curated by Sundance, where "independence" is defined as a voluntary choice that filmmakers embrace in order to express an artistic vision, rather than as a structural aspect of the film industry. Alongside the Next series, the festival helped YouTube to launch its movie rental service, through which it made five films available online for streaming rental, including several past successful Sundance films. Although many of these attempts at digital distribution have had little financial success—many of the Sundance films screened on YouTube generated only a few dozen views—they may indicate a new way of thinking not only about independent cinema but also about festivals themselves. This chapter will address the attempts to rebrand film festivals as distributors and the implications of this move for independent film distribution. Even though these models have met with only limited success thus far, they have a more significant role in rethinking film culture.

MEDIATING FESTIVALS

It is worth noting that the democratization of festival access has expanded to press coverage. With the decline in the number of critics employed by major newspapers, festivals have begun to open up press credentials to web journalists and film bloggers, who are now in a position to serve as tastemakers. As Jonathan Gray points out, interpretations of and expectations for all texts—whether movies, television shows, or books—are shaped by paratexts. Paratexts can be officially sanctioned by the distributors, the filmmakers, or the festival and are often created not only to expand awareness of a movie but also to promote preferred interpretations. In some cases, however, unofficial paratexts, such as reviews, gossip, or other texts not created by the distributors, can interfere with these sanctioned meanings, a challenge that has become especially difficult in the era of social media. In the case of movies, trailers, websites, and promotional tie-ins serve as a crucial framing device for alerting potential viewers about an upcoming movie, providing clues about its genre, subject matter, stars, director, and appearance.[7] We can then make choices about whether we are willing to spend $10 (or more) and two hours watching a particular movie. In the case of festivals, a dense layering of paratexts shapes both the festival experience and the wider sense of anticipation for a new movie. As Michael Z. Newman observes, "festival paratexts such as catalog descriptions and press materials articulate a discourse of legitimacy that contrasts them with the paratexts surrounding popular cinema."[8] On the one hand, festivals are often identified with the production of hype.[9] News articles identify a filmmaker or actress as a rising star or alert us to a new form of cinematic storytelling. People's experiences of *Life in a Day* were shaped well before the movie was completed, in part because of general familiarity with YouTube as a site for amateur self-expression, where anyone can post a video and potentially be heard by millions of others. All of the videos contained in the film release were also available on the *Life in a Day* YouTube channel. Finally, Kevin Macdonald's public comments about the film set up viewers to anticipate a film that would capture a fleeting glimpse of daily life across the globe. In essence, we were primed to expect a film that would depict what unites us—shared fears, pleasures, and activities—not what divides us. These official paratexts serve a vital role in the production of meaning; in the case of festivals, programs, posters, and other promotional materials help to reinforce the festival as a site of spectacle.

Alongside these officially sanctioned texts, critics play a vital role in conveying to a wider audience the hype surrounding a specific film or a film festival. Although there has been a distinct decline in the number of professional critics, the rise of the film blogosphere has allowed for the vast expansion of festival hype, especially given that many bloggers feel pressured to report on their festival favorites as quickly as possible in order to attract interested readers. As Gray points out, online critics have the potential to reach thousands of readers, allowing them to help define how a new movie will be received. They "hold the power to set the parameters for viewing," establishing why a film or filmmaker might be worthy of our time and attention.[10] As a result, festivals become sites for generating hype, for building anticipation around a film. As de Valck explains, "the more praise, prizes, and buzz a film attracts, the more attention it is likely to receive at other festivals."[11] And in the case of film festivals, these reviews tell us not only how to watch a specific movie (or whether to watch it in the first place) but also how to read the festival experience itself, providing us with textual clues about the nature of celebrity, about the concept of independent film, and in some cases about the film distribution process.

Just as online festival reports and other texts provide reviews of individual films and even shape our expectations of how film festivals function, we must also be attentive to the ways in which mobile phone apps can also transform the festival experience. Cell phones have provided attendees with a means of navigating festivals for some time. As early as 2007, South by Southwest participants were using Twitter to schedule impromptu parties or to find out what movies their friends were seeing. By 2009 a number of film festivals, including the Seattle International Film Festival and Sundance, had apps that not only helped users navigate the events but also reinforced their official interpretations. To some extent, the apps remediated the festival programs, taking aspects that had been common in the printed catalogs—plot summaries, cast lists, venue maps, and genre categorizations—and reworked them in a searchable format.[12] Attendees could even use the GPS device in their phones to find out what movies were playing closest to them. In addition, the apps alerted users to last-minute schedule changes and other bits of festival news, creating a real-time festival feed that could allow users to feel more connected. Like Twitter and other social media tools, the apps enabled a more interactive and participatory festival experience, appealing to a festivalgoer's desire to be part of the happenings by looking at and posting photographs, presumably of actors and directors attending films and walking the red carpet, thereby aligning the events with the cultures of celebrity and gossip.[13] In this sense, the apps appealed to discourses of personal mobility, providing festivalgoers with the ability to find out not only what's happening but also where.

SUNDANCE AS BRAND

To understand how digital delivery is reshaping film festivals, it is important to recognize how festivals serve to cultivate specific perceptions of independence. The role of the Sundance Film Festival in fostering a specific model of independent filmmaking in the 1980s and 1990s has been widely discussed. As Newman observes, indie cinema, as it came to be understood in the 1990s, is a historical concept, one that includes "not only movies but also institutions—distributors, exhibitors, festivals, and critical media—within which movies are circulated and experienced."[14] Festivals, awards ceremonies, public lectures, and trade publications often collaborate to establish definitions of what counts as an independent film, and these definitions are often in flux, especially as new distribution technologies and economic infrastructures shape how we access these movies. Formal definitions of independent film are often quite slippery and in most cases associated with the film's financing: a film was independent if not funded by a major studio. This financial independence, industry journalists implied, contributed to a filmmaker's freedom of expression. Without the constraints of a big budget, independent films could theoretically foster a more diverse and open film culture. Such definitions became especially blurry during what Newman calls the "Sundance-Miramax era," when most major studios owned a specialty division and when festivals often served as sites where studios could generate buzz for their films.

As Newman goes on to argue, these institutions help to cultivate expectations about the significance of independent films. In fact, as Alisa Perren points out, Miramax, the indie studio founded by Bob and Harvey Weinstein in 1979 and sold to Disney in 1993, used the buzz created at the 1989 Sundance Festival to launch Steven Soderbergh's debut film, *sex, lies, and videotape*, reinforcing the power of the festival and the distributor to bring critically acclaimed and edgy films to local theaters. Having purchased rights to the film soon after the 1989 festival, Miramax carefully built enthusiasm for it by positioning it as a "quality independent" through screenings at the Cannes Film Festival, a move that also helped to validate Sundance as a site that fostered these sorts of movies.[15] After the success of *sex, lies, and videotape*, Soderbergh publicly worried that the promotion of his film had changed the culture of Sundance, turning it into a site where filmmakers went to be discovered rather than a festival that fostered independent voices.[16]

More crucially, the success of the film festival helped to facilitate the extension of the Sundance brand via multiple cable channels, including the Sundance Channel and the Independent Film Channel, both of which are owned by AMC. The Sundance Channel shows a variety of independent films (loosely defined) alongside a number of documentaries and television series supporting a range of social and political causes, such as the series *Big Ideas for a Small Planet*, which showcases people and institutions working to be good stewards of the environment, and *Iconoclasts*, a series that pairs two prominent figures in different fields, such as Madeleine Albright and Ashley Judd or Charlize Theron and Jane Goodall, for a "conversation" designed to reveal unexpected similarities between them. Similar connections between film festivals and cable television influenced the programming of the Independent Film Channel. In his discussion of the relationship between IFC and Sundance, Robert Eberwein traces Robert Redford's attempts to extend the Sundance brand, noting that Redford felt the connection between the festival and IFC would provide "creative freedom" unavailable on other cable channels that specialized in broadcasting independent movies.[17]

These changing definitions—and fortunes—of independent film can be measured in shifting public assessments of the industry. By the mid-1990s, Sundance and festivals like it appeared to be part of the larger industry involved in the production of commercial mainstream fare. In his keynote address at the 1999 Independent Spirit Awards, acclaimed independent producer James Schamus—who had worked with filmmakers ranging from Ang Lee to Hal Hartley and Todd Haynes—proposed that the Spirit Awards be "immediately disbanded" because independent filmmakers were financed or distributed by major studios.[18] Schamus argued that movies nominated for the awards accounted for nearly $300 million in box office, a dramatic increase over the $20 million in 1986. In addition, high-profile festivals like Sundance and Cannes had helped to create a competitive marketplace in which all of the major studios competed for rights to distribute the independent films that played at them. Schamus concluded that independent films had "succeeded overwhelmingly in entering the mainstream system of commercial exploitation and finance."[19]

However, within less than a decade after Schamus's speech, the prospects for independent film appeared grim. Many major studios had closed their specialty divisions, and independent producers found it increasingly difficult to finance films. Thus, while digital delivery has often been promoted as making it easier for "long tail" filmmakers to get discovered, the combination of digital download-ing and an unstable economy combined to make financing of independent films far more challenging. As industry analyst Edward Jay Epstein notes, the collapse of the "foreign pre-sale" system was largely responsible for the crisis. Pre-sales, Epstein explains, are "essentially promissory notes from foreign distributors [that are used] as collateral to borrow the funds necessary to make a movie."[20] In this scenario, an independent producer secures a contract from a territorial buyer, most likely a foreign distributor based in Western Europe or Japan, who promises a specific sum once the film is completed. The filmmaker then takes this promise and a "completion bond," essentially a guarantee that the film will be completed using a specific script and stars, and borrows money from a bank. The bank, in most cases, is taking only a limited risk; if the film is not completed, the bank will be paid back by the completion bond. If the director finishes the film, the bank will be repaid by the foreign distributors, who would then have distribution rights to that movie in theaters, on television, and on DVD.[21] More recently, however, a series of factors combined to undercut the potential value of investing in independent film. First, the global financial crisis made banks more averse to risk, and in many cases institutions like Deutsche Bank simply stopped financing films. More crucially, the complications associated with digi-tal delivery realigned traditional distribution practices. As Epstein notes, DVD sales declined by more than 20 percent in 2008 in the countries where foreign pre-sales were most common, echoing a trend that was also in place in North America. The markets for independent films were also shaken by the decreased budgets of European television stations, owing to the financial crisis. Both of these factors were reinforced by spreading broadband access in Europe and Asia, which made it easier to download movies, both legally and illegally. As a result, theater owners and television stations were reluctant to pay for and screen films that were, in essence, already available for free online.[22] Such changes reflect the ongoing adjustment of the "window" system that determines when movies will be available and in what formats. As a result of these new digital delivery initia-tives, independent filmmakers are often under pressure to make films available quickly or risk losing sales when pirated versions of their movies become avail-able online. Thus, Mark Gill, the executive producer of *Next Stop Wonderland*, *Frida*, and *Law Abiding Citizen*, proclaimed at the 2008 Los Angeles Indepen-dent Film Festival that "the digital revolution is here. And boy does it suck."[23] Gill proposed that filmmakers preserve the existing model, encouraging his audience to focus on making films that cost around $15 million and to concentrate on pre-serving the platform release structure common to the Sundance-Miramax era, in which movies would gain advance publicity at festivals and then have a gradual theatrical release, starting in major metropolises before expanding to smaller cities and towns.

In response to this crisis of traditional distribution models, festivals helped to usher in new forms of digital delivery. By 2012 the Weinstein Company's Radius-TWC, Magnolia, and IFC, among other distributors, were buying festival films to be rented via video-on-demand (VOD) platforms; in many cases, VOD was used not just for low-budget films but also for movies with familiar Hollywood stars. Lars von Trier's *Melancholia* (2011), which featured Kirsten Dunst, generated $2 million in VOD rentals and another $3 million in theaters despite appearing on VOD a month *before* its theatrical release. *Margin Call* (2011), a timely narrative about Wall Street insider trading that starred Kevin Spacey and Zachary Quinto, earned approximately $5 million both in theaters and on VOD through a simultaneous day-and-date release.[24] Companies found that hybrid distribution, using festivals, VOD, and theaters, could serve as a viable alternative to more traditional models. Thus, while many in the industry were lamenting the role of digital delivery in altering the perceived value of independent films, festivals were quietly examining how digital tools could be used to cultivate on-demand markets for those same films.

SUNDANCE NEXT

Many problematic distribution issues were addressed in the Sundance Film Festival's attempts to redefine itself as engaged with social media and digital delivery. In addition, the festival was seeking to renew its image as a champion of independent filmmaking after many critics began to characterize the festival as a site that served to promote films produced by the major studios' specialty divisions. The Next series, launched during the 2010 festival, was designed to counter these claims by fostering extremely low-budget films. On the series website, the organizers touted the "independence" of the filmmakers, implying that the decision to make a movie on a minimal budget was a choice motivated by the desire for personal expression: "If a filmmaker wants to create his or her own idiosyncratic vision, it's often not worth looking around for a big budget, waiting for others to say it's ok to make it. You have to stand up and make the film yourself. Small scale filmmaking imparts a freedom that any artist would pay for; the audience experience is priceless."[25] Implied in the description of the series is that a low-budget film is the product of an individual artist, a form of personal expression that might be tarnished by a larger budget, and that story elements were "amped up by their smaller means." In his keynote address, Sundance Festival founder Robert Redford extolled the Next program as a way for the festival to go "back to its roots."[26] In fact, Redford borrowed heavily from the utopian language associated with digital media in describing how the festival was in the process of renewing itself; at the same time, he positioned the festival—and the future of festivals in general—in terms of new forms of distribution.

The films selected for the 2010 Sundance Next series shared several key characteristics. Most notably, all were made for less than $500,000. A number reflected a range of interests and styles consistent with the programming at previous festivals; others sought to connect with the social media networks associated with the Mumblecore filmmakers. One of the more prominent films was Katie Aselton's *The Freebie*, a film that followed a couple's decision to allow each partner to sleep with one other person without any consequences. Aselton, who had previously appeared in Mark and Jay Duplass's *The Puffy Chair* (2005), provided the series with a specific connection to the Mumblecore movement that emerged from the 2007 South by Southwest festival. Other films included Linas Phillips's *Bass Ackwards*, also focused on the experiences of young adults dealing with a relationship crisis.

Although the Sundance Next series seemed to offer an alternative to more commercial forms of independent film, a number of journalists and critics responded cynically to the festival's efforts to recover its origins. Karina Longworth remarked, "If NEXT is partly a marketing gimmick—an institutional intervention to make it easier for a press corps easily distracted by shiny objects to care about starless films—perhaps it's fitting that its first incarnation feels less like a revolution than a rebranding."[27] Roger Ebert generally praised the festival for its attempts to embrace "new distribution channels such as the net and regional art cinemas," but noted that the one Next film he attended was shared mainly with friends of the filmmaker.[28] Although Ebert was a little more generous toward the attempts to rebrand Sundance, both he and Longworth seemed to recognize that the festival was struggling to define itself in relation to the emerging DIY and on-demand cinemas typically associated with festivals like South by Southwest and Slamdance, as well as a changing independent film marketplace.

Sundance later expanded its focus on social media and low-budget filmmaking by distributing a small number of current and past festival films on a range of digital platforms, including iTunes, Amazon, Hulu, and Netflix, as well as the festival's own distribution hub, Sundance Now. This approach allowed the filmmakers to retain rights to their movies but to take advantage of the Sundance brand. Sundance also created a streaming catalog of films made by its 6,000 alumni and worked with the online crowdfunding service Kickstarter to help filmmakers raise money to make and market their movies. Each of these initiatives furthered the festival's shift toward supporting digital delivery.[29] Streaming versions of movies could be rented for $3.99 to $6.99 and were typically available for purchase as digital downloads for $18 to $20. Notably, the website appeals to audience desires to be "in the know," caught up with a wider culture of independent film fans, and in some cases offers the opportunity to watch a movie before it is available on DVD. As Anne Thompson observed, this online distribution model seemed to provide an alternative for an overcrowded independent film marketplace: "So many films these days wind up lost in a heap of films, no matter how well they played or were reviewed—that are deemed unreleasable in the current unforgiving marketplace."[30] However, given the competition with other digital platforms, it is not clear how the Sundance offerings will fare with consumers. To some extent, Sundance sought to align itself with the emerging "Indie 2.0" culture described by Kevin Smith, even if Smith's comments were intended to distance himself from the Miramax-Sundance system that had dominated independent distribution. Although many of the Sundance Next films were sparsely attended, the rebranding of the festival helped to position it as a site for promoting—and distributing—indie film. At the same time, the online screenings offered a way for "outsiders" to feel more connected to the festival.

SOUTH BY SOUTHWEST

Like Sundance, South by Southwest (SXSW) has served as a "discovery" festival, one that has become increasingly defined by its relationship to the discourses of interactivity and participation. But SXSW explicitly promotes itself as the place to find less commercial and more independent alternatives to the mostly mainstream films on the screens at Sundance. As Dennis Lim noted, many of the films that play at SXSW were rejected by Sundance, allowing the festival to cast itself as a home for "underdog outsiders."[31]

This orientation was expressed in part by the festival's 2010 slogan, "Tomorrow Happens Here," a phrase that reviewer Karina Longworth sarcastically described as "slick marketing shorthand for the event's reputation as a test tube for new cinematic trends and a breeding ground for incestuous indie collaborations."[32] That year SXSW, like Sundance, sought to introduce limited forms of digital delivery, a practice that seemed to undermine the traditional role of film festivals, prompting Longworth to decry the contradictions that seemed inherent in SXSW's emphasis on producing an online festival alongside its live screenings. However, SXSW, already famous as the festival where Twitter was launched in 2007, reworked the desire for community through its emphasis on social media. Like Sundance, SXSW sought to redefine the nature of the film festival and transform it from an exclusive event into one associated with online distribution. Non-attendees could view themselves as virtual participants, capable of using online media to keep up with the latest buzz regarding new movies and new forms of communication. This focus on creating alternative distribution models was reinforced by Janet Pierson, producer of the South by Southwest Film Conference and Festival, who remarked that festivals can function "as a marketplace of invention, where filmmakers can shop for varying distribution strategies, deciding which approach—theater, DVD, Internet, on-demand—makes the most sense for their project."[33]

In addition to serving as an important site for promoting social media, SXSW also became known as a destination festival for low-budget independent films. The festival is perhaps best known for helping to launch the careers of the filmmakers associated with the Mumblecore movement, including Joe Swanberg, Mark and Jay Duplass, Andrew Bujalski, and Susan Buice and Arin Crumley, whose *Four Eyed Monsters* (2005) pioneered the use of video podcasts, YouTube, and other forms of social media in the promotion of DIY films.[34] Although critics remain ambivalent about the movement's aesthetics, the distribution strategies of Mumblecore veterans reflect the changing relationship between independent filmmaking and festivals.[35] Swanberg's career was launched after a successful screening of his debut film, *Kissing on the Mouth*, at the 2005 festival, where the term "Mumblecore" was coined by Andrew Bujalski's sound editor, Eric Masunaga, to describe its talky, improvisational style. More crucially, Mumblecore films were grounded in the challenges of depicting intimacy in the age of digital media, in which human communication often is mediated by social networking and video sharing tools. As Aymar Jean Christian observes, Mumblecore "reflects a generation's constant computer use, engagement with social networking, and consumption of bodies through digitally mediated spaces."[36] The intimacy and immediacy of these films, Christian argues, reflect the changing modes of distribution and representation associated with digital media. Similarly, Robert Sickels views the Mumblecore filmmakers as being "at the forefront of a technological movement" that will challenge traditional distribution practices for independent—and even studio—films.[37] Thus, although some of the filmmakers associated with Mumblecore have since moved on to work with studios, the promotion of the label helped to establish the idea of distributing movies through digital formats.

Mumblecore's use of digital delivery became even more explicit during the 2009 South by Southwest Film Festival, when Joe Swanberg's *Alexander the Last* played at the festival one day after it premiered on the Independent Film Channel's video-on-demand service, IFC in Theaters. As Sickels pointed out, the on-demand service was available at that time in more than 55 million American homes, allowing users to watch films currently playing in festivals or, in some cases, in limited release in theaters.[38] For Swanberg, festival distribution provided new forms of access to a wider audience than would be available through theatrical distribution: "I feel like I can say this is a watershed moment. The promise of the digital revolution, this democratization of movies, is now really happening."[39] This revolution often involved skipping theatrical screenings and opting instead to use festivals to generate just enough attention—in the form of film reviews from major newspapers, alternative weeklies, and high-profile film blogs—to attract attention to the movie. Instead of a brief theatrical run in major cities and college towns, followed months later by a DVD release, the festival window helped to redefine not only the distribution process but also the definition of an independent "hit."

By 2010 SXSW had expanded its experiments with online distribution by making five films available online during the festival. Two of the movies, *Breaking Upwards* and *The Overbrook Brothers,* had played at past festivals, but the other three, Bryan Poyser's *Lovers of Hate,* Shane Meadows's *Le Donk and Scor-Zay-Zee,* and Emmett Malloy's documentary *The White Stripes under the Great Northern Lights*—premiered at the 2010 festival, allowing audiences at home "a chance to catch a piece of the festival experience."[40] This effort to bring connected viewers into the festival experience expanded in 2011 with the use of live streaming software such as Ustream to bring audiences an even more immersive experience of some of the more ephemeral aspects of the festival: keynote addresses, concerts, filmmaker interviews, and even question-and-answer sessions. Many of these events were featured on the South by Southwest website; others appeared on the website for the Independent Film Channel and on Facebook Live.[41] The role of liveness remains a crucial element of the virtual festival experience. Although viewers who watched online may not have had full participation in the festival, they were able to follow these sessions in real time, allowing them the experience of being in the know about the newest movies and technologies.

This form of festival distribution is not without controversy, especially given that streaming video and VOD open up new points of access before viewers can see movies on more traditional platforms or even in other festivals. Tom Hall, the director of programming for the Sarasota Film Festival, addressed this issue directly in response to the announcement that *Alexander the Last* would premiere simultaneously at SXSW and on IFC's Festival Direct VOD series. Calling the decision a "seismic shift," Hall argued that offering the film via VOD "calls into question the value of subsequent festival screenings."[42] In other words, if a movie is readily available at home, at a cost that is competitive with the price of a movie ticket, festival programmers may see little incentive to show that movie. Hall speculated that some value could be added to a festival screening if audiences were made aware that the film's director and stars would be in attendance; for lesser-known films, however, this type of experience might not compete with watching at home. In addition, given IFC's extensive acquisitions, Hall worried that the extended menu of movies available to users at home would make it difficult for festivals to find movies not already released in other formats, undermining the exclusivity model under which most festivals operate. Ultimately, these new practices change the cultural role of festivals, rewriting their importance in shaping film taste and even the value of regional festivals for the communities where films play after their national or international premieres. As Hall wrote, "the relative value of the film festival may be dimming, and we all should begin looking to find ways to reinvent ourselves in this new world."[43] Thus, although the festival window was promoted as offering new opportunities for filmmakers to be discovered, festivals also faced the possibility that new forms of access could diminish the their own value.

TRIBECA

In what is considered to be the first time a festival released films during the event, Tribeca's involvement with digital delivery dates back to 2007, when it collaborated with the video platform Jaman, a service that offers movies in both download rental and ad-supported streaming formats. Six films were made available for free, worldwide, for seven days during the festival. Later, Jaman also developed a partnership with the San Francisco International Film Festival, which also made several films available during an exclusive worldwide window, practices that aligned Tribeca and Jaman with a global, mobile, movie-loving public. This distribution model allowed Jaman to advertise itself as being "like a Sundance on the Web," a means of discovering, watching, and discussing popular films.[44]

More recently, these practices have expanded to make Tribeca one of the most visible participants in the reinvention of festivals as online events shaped by digital delivery and social media tools. Like Sundance and SXSW, the Tribeca Film Festival sought to extend its cultural and geographic reach in 2011 through the use of online distribution.[45] Through a wide range of promotional discourse, Tribeca was able to create a link between the idea of innovative technologies and the cutting-edge nature of film festivals, which tend to be positioned as sites of discovery where new professional careers can be launched and where audiences can discover and discuss films months in advance of their appearance in theaters. To promote itself as immersed in the future of film distribution, Tribeca launched several online initiatives that would open up the festival to a wider online public, many of which were promoted in a video featuring festival director Geoff Gilmore that was posted to the festival's main webpage.

Perhaps most notably, the website hosted what it called a "Festival Streaming Room," where six feature-length films and eighteen short films were available for viewers to stream. Half of them debuted at the 2011 festival; the others were older films that had played at past festivals. However, the Streaming Room was not available on-demand. Instead, viewers were required to reserve a "virtual seat" in advance, and the films would stream during three to five windows posted on the Streaming Room web page.[46] This ability to watch the festival from home, of course, encourages a form of virtual attendance at the festival. Film fans who live outside of New York or who might otherwise be unable to attend the festival could see a limited slate of films online. Gilmore also emphasized that the Streaming Room featured an adaptive screening player that would adjust to the needs and specifications of individual devices, whether laptops, tablets, or mobile phones, ensuring that viewers would not be constrained or limited to a specific location or device and that the festival itself fit into discourses of mobility. Tribeca also worked with YouTube to make several films available through that website's Screening Room rental program for a three-week period in May 2011. The potential to stream festival movies offered everyone a chance to participate in the sense of anticipation associated with being at a film festival. This distribution practice was continued in 2012; Tribeca offered four movies on a variety of VOD platforms, including cable and satellite providers, as well as iTunes, Amazon Watch Instantly, Vudu, and Samsung Media Hub.

Tribeca also created a sense of remote presence at the 2011 festival by offering a live feed of the red carpet area, question-and-answer sessions, award shows, panels, and other special events ("see what's happening in real time"). Viewers were given the additional ability to switch among cameras. However, even as Tribeca sought to create these models of virtual festival participation, the practice of appointment viewing, typically associated with festivals, ran counter to the convenience models offered by sites such as YouTube. As the Independent Film Channel's Matt Singer remarked, "Generally the appeal of streaming is as the impulse buy of the movie world: it's an instant gratification, available on demand sort of thing."[47] Users who were accustomed to watching movies on their own time were forced to adjust their schedules to the films', potentially limiting access, especially for audiences outside the Eastern Time Zone.

In addition to serving as a distributor of several of the films playing at the festival, Tribeca made use of a wide range of social media tools to create the experience of being a participant in the festival. For example, a "Filmmaker Feed" for each director with a movie at the festival "connects you with filmmakers in a way that wouldn't be possible if you were attending the festival in person." Thus, in some sense, Tribeca was implying that social media actually expanded the festival experience beyond merely being there. A typical "Filmmaker Feed" page includes a picture of the director next to a link for the Tribeca page for the film, along with a short biography and list of prior credits. Below that are a series of social media widgets that show the filmmaker's Twitter and Facebook postings, a feature that allowed the festival to persist beyond the screening dates, given that the widgets would continue to update after the festival was done. Each director could also post an embedded YouTube video on his or her page. One director who took advantage of this opportunity was Scott Rettberg, whose documentary *New York Says Thank You* concerns a volunteer organization dedicated to transforming the anniversary of the September 11 attacks into a day of national service. Soon after the festival ended, Rettberg posted footage of jubilant New

Yorkers at Ground Zero, just a few blocks from the location of the Tribeca Film Festival, celebrating the killing of Osama bin Laden on May 2, 2011. It was an especially apt use of embedded video, linking the subject of Rettberg's documentary, the location of the festival, and the immediacy of the events in a powerful way.

Users were also invited to post questions to participating filmmakers. Many came from aspiring filmmakers, who asked more established directors, such as David Gordon Green (*All the Real Girls, Pineapple Express*) for advice on how to break into the movie industry or whether festivals were a valuable experience for independent filmmakers. To some extent, these questions emulate the question-and-answer sessions typically found at film festivals; however, the use of social media reinforces the idea that the festival is no longer tied to a geographic space but is, instead, a global phenomenon, one that invites everyone with internet access to participate.

CONCLUSION

The enhanced role of Tribeca's on-demand offerings was depicted in a 2012 Time Warner Cable advertisement featuring festival co-founder Robert De Niro, an actor often associated with his gangster persona from films like *The Godfather* and *Goodfellas*. The advertisement shows De Niro settling in on a couch with a middle-class but apparently hip African-American couple to watch a Tribeca film. True to his persona, De Niro waits impatiently while the husband and wife pop some popcorn before asking them, "Do you want to check the dog again? Do you want a little sippy drink, you know with a little bendy straw? It's all hunk-dory?" After receiving assurances from the couple, De Niro assumes the role of festival host, picking up the remote and saying, "OK, then, Tribeca Film On-Demand Proudly Presents," before being interrupted by the couples' cell phones going off simultaneously. From there, a voice-over tells us that Time Warner can "bring Tribeca to your home whenever you want." The advertisement seems to imply that a subscription to the cable television service would allow users to bring a small slice of celebrity into their homes. The situation is notably different from the advertisements depicting families with children. Instead of platform mobility as a means to promote family harmony, we see that on-demand technologies can allow us to attend film festivals, even if the interruptions of daily life have the potential to disrupt that special screening experience.

Festivals remain an important part of the film industry, even if the majority of films that play there fail to achieve any kind of theatrical distribution. Furthermore, they continue to promote celebrity spectacle through red carpet events and reinforce auteur filmmaking through their emphasis on the director as the primary author of a film. Even the valorization of the low-budget Mumblecore filmmakers at South by Southwest serves as an attempt to locate new "indepen-dent" voices that are operating outside the studio system. For major festivals, such as Sundance, South by Southwest, and Tribeca, the festival process become a means of configuring attention, shaping not only how a film is experienced by festival goers but also how that film is received in a wider movie culture. At the same time, these paratextual elements help to define the role of festivals in a wider cinematic culture.

Given the changing place of independent film in the era of digital delivery, film festivals have become crucial sites for theorizing the production, distribu-tion, exhibition, and reception of movies. In all cases, festivals continue to serve as places where hype or buzz emerges. But at the same time, we are introduced to a wide range of production and distribution narratives that help to define the practice of independent moviemaking. Thus, the hype surrounding the Mumblecore filmmakers at South by Southwest not only promoted their mov-ies but also introduced a set of practices to go along with them. These practices might include the naturalistic film techniques and talky scripts favored by many Mumblecore filmmakers, but they are also linked to the cultural status of the festival itself. Rather than using a successful festival screening to launch a the-atrical run, independent film distribution has been redefined to entail a wide variety of digital delivery platforms, including streaming services such as Net-flix and video-on-demand services such as IFC Festival Direct. Furthermore, distributing films during a festival—creating what might be called a "festival window"—profoundly alters the traditional window system that has guided distribution since the popularization of VHS during the 1980s. Finally, festi-vals have deepened their use of social media tools in order to expand the festi-val experience, allowing people not attending the festival to gain admission to events that were once considered exclusive and providing those who attend the festival with a more interactive experience. These practices reinforce the percep-tion of a globalized, engaged movie culture while also expanding the circulation of cinematic hype.

CONCLUSION: DIGITAL FUTURES

Digital delivery not only affects the economic models of the movie industry but also promotes an on-demand culture, in which the practices of moviegoing and the perceptions of media culture are transformed. Movie viewers are now re-imagined as individualized and mobile, able to watch practically anywhere or anytime they wish, while having access to aspects of film culture—such as film festivals and art-house movies—that have in the past been available only in specific locations. In this sense, platform mobility seems to be an extension of models of active spectatorship that have informed both media scholarship and industry discourse. Many of these questions about mobility, personalization, and fragmentation were addressed in a comedy sketch about the TV Hat, a baseball cap that could be converted into a mobile personal theater, on Comedy Central's *The Colbert Report*. The TV Hat, a product marketed on late-night television, allowed users to tuck an iPod or iPhone into a pocket inside a baseball cap with a giant brim. Users could then lower side blinders and a magnifying lens, allowing them to become "immersed in a private multimedia entertainment zone." The comedy segment showed Colbert trying on the cap and marveling, in an echo of the TV Hat advertisement, that the hat provided "a motion picture experience absolutely anywhere"; viewers watching the segment saw a stock image of the interior of a movie palace, suggesting that mobile video now offers the full sensory pleasures of seeing movies on the big screen. Cutting back to the advertisement, we see a range of possible uses for the hat: a woman tanning on the beach, a man exercising in the gym, a traveler sitting in the airport, and a commuter stuck in traffic (presumably in the back of a taxi), all locations associated with boredom and forced waiting.

Colbert's satirical commentary on the TV Hat served not merely as an opportunity to send up a genuinely silly product—the TV Hat was widely mocked in tech blogs such as *Wired* and *Gizmodo*—but also as a sharp critique of other forms of personalized entertainment.[1] Seizing on the image of the woman tanning on the beach, Colbert joked that he enjoyed hearing the sounds of the ocean "while watching *Hawaii 5-0*." And pointing out that the hat came in a range of colors, including "camouflage," he added that a user could "watch TV while you're hunting." In both cases, portable television seems to take us away from the natural world of genuine experience, isolating us in a media bubble where we are oblivious to our surroundings. While these comments reinforce a simplistic opposition between real and artificial experience, they also help to establish the ways in which portable media devices are often seen as supporting a culture defined by platform mobility, one in which normally private activities—such as watching television—encroach upon the public world and where users are constantly distracted by entertainment to the point that they neglect the people around them.

Colbert's slyest commentary was reserved for the ways in which the TV Hat, like other forms of platform mobility, would fit into family life, and he echoed the promotional discourse used to sell mobile devices. Initially noting that the side blinders would allow users to "focus on what matters most by blocking out unnecessary distractions, like your spouse or your children," Colbert cut back to images from the advertisement depicting a father wearing a TV Hat while his daughter watches a living-room set and a husband wearing the hat in bed while his wife reads a book beside him. The TV Hat advertisement also seemed to imply that the hat could help to restore family harmony, allowing the father to "watch the game while kids watch cartoons," phrasing that directly echoed imagery from UltraViolet and other digital delivery services. While it would be easy to dismiss the TV Hat as a quirky or misguided product marketed to insomniacs on late-night television, Colbert's observations about the advertisement helped to highlight how the hat fit into wider desires and fears about personal media technologies and their relationship to a culture marked by fragmented and individualized media consumption practices.

But the privatized mobility of the TV Hat isn't the full story when it comes to our emerging on-demand culture. Instead, despite the proliferation of smaller screens, digital delivery also reinforces a number of traditional practices associated with media consumption. The depiction of the TV Hat fits neatly into concerns that platform mobility contributes to a degraded screen culture, in which viewers reportedly are willing to accept the idea of watching movies on smaller screens and an experience that is less than fully immersive. Such fears were reinforced in a wide range of movie industry discourse that sought to emphasize the importance of moviegoing, often by depicting mobile technologies as offering an incomplete experience. In this context, Randall Stross, while tracing the evolution of cinema from stand-alone Kinetoscopes through the era of widescreen cinema to today's iPod culture, worried that the social and aesthetic aspects of moviegoing were being replaced by a situation in which "movie watching is, again, a solitary experience, involving small images on a laptop, a tablet and, tinier still, a cellphone. The convenience is wonderful, of course, but it comes at a price: the loss of the immersive cinematic experience." Stross reported ominously that Americans would pay to watch an estimated 3.4 billion movies online in 2012 alone, adding that it would be impossible to calculate how many of those would be watched on one of the many smaller screens movie fans carry with them.[2] However, despite these concerns, platform mobility has often been used to promote watching movies on relatively big screens. Stross's article obscures the fact that subscription video-on-demand (VOD) services are often consumed on big-screen television sets through gaming systems such as an Xbox or Wii, rather than laptops. In addition, social media and movie apps place emphasis on the idea of going out, of using mobile devices to supplement the big-screen cinematic experience. The Sundance Film Festival app is designed to assist moviegoers as they seek to navigate the festival; others, including Flixster and Fandango, promote the sale of movie tickets and even help users to arrange gatherings with friends. Similarly, users can log into sites like Gathr and Tugg in order to request screenings of movies that might not normally play in theaters in their community. As Cinedigm CEO Chris McGurk reported, these services identified an untapped resource—fewer than 5 percent of seats in most theaters are used on Monday through Thursday—and built a social media tool that can be used to facilitate the practice of watching movies on the big screen.[3]

Users of mobile devices such as the iPhone and Kindle Fire may be capable of isolating themselves in a media bubble, but platform mobility can also enable new forms of interactivity and participation in a wider media culture as audiences connect with each other and sometimes with the producers of the entertainment they watch. In some cases, this activity may be related to the promotion of a Hollywood franchise, as we saw with the use of Twitter to help foster a culture of anticipation around the forthcoming *Hunger Games*. At the same time, these tools can contribute to wider practices of using popular culture as a means of identifying and engaging with the political meanings of texts; for example, a number of bloggers and critics discussed whether Christopher Nolan's *The Dark Knight* served as an endorsement or critique of the Bush administration's actions in response to the terrorist attacks of September 11.[4] Although social media technologies can be used to exploit the free labor of fans to promote Hollywood films, these tools also contribute to what Henry Jenkins has described as a "participatory culture," in which fan communities develop new techniques for collaboration, whether combining skills to assemble a picture puzzle or producing a shot-by-shot remake of *Star Wars*, as Casey Pugh and thousands of others did with *Star Wars Uncut*.[5] At the same time, this participatory culture has contributed to a virtual reinvention of indie culture, in which filmmakers and others can use the skills and resources of the multitude in processes known as crowdsourcing and crowdfunding, practices that often help to reveal interests and tastes that have not been served adequately and have the potential to open up what actor and director Matthew Lillard hopes will be a "golden age of filmmaking." Lillard himself tapped into these social networks in a powerful way, raising funds on Kickstarter and using methods such as a marathon "Ask Me Anything" chat on

Reddit to support the production of *Fat Kid Rules the World*.[6] In this sense, indie film fans are positioned to "demand" films of their choice and even to use their personal resources to see that they get made. Often these practices of crowd-sourcing and crowdfunding are driven by deep emotional and political commitments. Even though mainstream directors have taken up crowdfunding as a form of early promotion, these techniques have also been used to support vitally important political issues, most notably Franny Armstrong's *Age of Stupid*, which brought much needed attention not only to climate change but also to the tools that might empower other aspiring filmmakers. In short, even if an on-demand distribution system allows studios greater control over how their films circulate, it also allows audiences to "demand" titles that might be of interest to them.

Many of these shifts are taking place within what I have called an "on-demand culture," in which much of our entertainment is available at the click of a mouse, often via mobile devices that allow us to watch movies or participate in discussions about entertainment while on the go. In this sense, on-demand culture is not simply about the circulation of movies and television shows. It is also about the circulation of ideas and expectations about media culture and the role of entertainment in our daily lives, what Lisa Gitelman has called the social protocols that shape our habits, behaviors, and expectations about media technologies. Thus, platform mobility becomes linked to a set of changing social behaviors and economic practices that work to redefine media culture. These protocols have contributed to the increased informality of watching movies, allowing a viewer to start a movie on one device, perhaps an iPhone, and pick it up later using another device, such as a laptop or television set. The persistent availability of a wide, if incomplete, menu of movie choices also guarantees that something is always "on," allowing users to make more spontaneous choices about what they watch or, in some cases, to schedule catch-up viewings of television shows they might have missed. As a result, the viewing protocols associated with film and television have become conflated, even if viewers continue to maintain clear distinctions between the two media. At the same time, this on-demand culture is not linked to a specific technology, medium, or location. Instead, the ability to access content on demand affects both film and television, not only our expectations about where we can watch but also the time frames that inform when we can watch, often in ways that involve constant renegotiation.

This shift to on-demand delivery contributes to a culture in which media consumers become active participants in the process of navigating their entertainment choices. In tracking the changing practices of movie and television distribution in the era of digital delivery, this book has sought to make sense of the contradictions between the promises of fast, inexpensive, and ubiquitous access to a wide variety of entertainment and the actual experience of these delivery models. Contrary to promises made by media and technology companies concerning platform mobility, audiences often encounter constrained choices and limited mobility, due to practices such as geo-blocking and rights management. Thus, the promises of liberation and freedom are constrained by market fragmentation, limited choice, and, quite often, consumer confusion. Alongside these questions about distribution models, digital delivery also helped to perpetuate concerns about the fragmentation of movie and television audiences. Such concerns reflect a longstanding trend in television associated with what Amanda Lotz calls the "multichannel transition."[7] But as users increasingly became segmented into "tribes" of viewers, both movies and television became more capable of delivering niche media, raising deeply complicated questions about the fragmentation of media audiences and the implications for national and global media cultures.[8]

These questions about delivery systems often ignore the continued importance of residual media forms. As Raymond Williams reminds us, the residual addresses "areas of human experience, aspiration, and achievement which the dominant culture neglects, undervalues, opposes, represses, or even cannot recognize."[9] Williams's concept of the residual helps to challenges the hype surrounding different forms of digital delivery and even points to aspects of culture that may be neglected in the celebrations of convenience and freedom that have become central to the discourses of platform mobility. Although digital delivery has been promoted as the future of media consumption, the persistence of physical media—through phenomena such as Redbox kiosks and the Qwikster-inspired revolt against Netflix—seems to suggest that user practices may, in fact, be more complicated. In his discussion of digital delivery, Lucas Hilderbrand worries that "unless users figure out a way to hack, download, and store the material, we are moving toward a model where there is no longer fixity and the assurance of long-term access that a videotape or a DVD allows." Such a scenario, Hilderbrand adds, takes us "away from a collector model," in which users purchase and own physical media.[10] However, even though a number of services support a streaming model, in which users pay for temporary access to a film or television show, studios are also attempting to reshape consumption habits by enticing people into buying discs with digital copies that allow them to transition into the era of cloud storage. This enticement of immateriality seems to challenge traditional fears about planned obsolescence: if the movie is stored in the cloud, then it will be possible for users to avoid the risks associated with disc wear and other forms of physical degradation while preserving a "collector's model" whereby enthusiasts could still display, watch, and share their DVDs with others. Yet, the DVD and other material formats continue to retain value for many film fans. These questions of archivability and collectability are not merely about changing norms for hobbyists or changing distribution practices. As Roger Ebert and others have noted, the shift to digital delivery raises significant questions about what aspects of our digital cinema history will be preserved, given that digital platforms face frequent upgrades that have the potential to render older formats obsolete.[11]

Another challenging question about the future of digital delivery involves the alteration of the perceived value of the film text. Although DVDs came to serve as one of the primary revenue streams for film distributors, the persistent online availability of movies has changed what audiences are willing to pay for on-demand rentals and purchases. Recognition of this trend has resulted in the rise of inexpensive distribution models such as Redbox kiosks and Netflix streaming subscriptions, which allow users to make more deliberate choices about what they buy. In turn, on-demand culture contributes to a changing level of engagement with movie culture, allowing users to navigate menus of films and television shows by genre, turning streaming video into an updated form of flipping channels to seek out content that can fill an empty moment; if a show or movie fails to hook the viewer immediately, she can move on to something else with minimal investment. Users can sample, explore, taste, and in some cases skip movies or make plans to watch them later, compiling queues of films that often extend well into the hundreds. Such a shift may demand that filmmakers ensure that they have opening sequences designed to capture the audience's attention or that their films fit neatly into a familiar category that may not challenge the audience's expectations too radically.[12]

On-demand culture also complicates ideas of when and where movies can be consumed. As Barbara Klinger documents, the 1990s saw the popularization of home theater systems that allowed movie buffs to emulate the big-screen experience in the family home, a practice that she aligned with a wider distaste for going out.[13] Klinger points out that the home became a primary site for what she called "nontheatrical exhibition," and she traces the emergence of what she calls "home film cultures."[14] These home film cultures became characterized not just by an embrace of new technologies but also by the practices of movie collecting, which in turn contributed to the cultivation of a popular film canon. Also, the desire for DVD extras helped to broaden the perception that movies can be recognized as "high art."[15] But with the emergence of platform mobility, we are shifting to a culture characterized by increasingly informal practices of movie watching, practices that often have significant implications for film culture, changing our expectations about the processes of cinematic engagement. Rental DVDs, especially those used by Netflix and Redbox, are often stripped of the special features that had contributed to the construction of cinematic knowledge. Similarly, VOD sites such as Hulu offer few if any of these so-called extras. These practices are intended to encourage consumers to purchase DVDs or Blu-Ray discs; however, as Edward Jay Epstein has documented, DVD sales continue to decline as users adjust to VOD models.[16] As a result, digital delivery may contribute to a changed relationship with film culture, one in which movies are framed not by supplemental features on DVD but by the materials on VOD menus, and even by the very organization of those menus into genres and other easily identifiable categories. This trend should not be taken to imply that movie fans are becoming less informed about entertainment culture. Instead, we are witnessing an ongoing evolution of the sites where informal cinematic education takes place.

Thus, despite guarantees of digital delivery, mobility, access, and plenitude, it is impossible to view these utopian promises without some degree of skepticism and uncertainty, a situation that led Brian David Johnson to acknowledge that the entire future of entertainment is "up in the air."[17] Ultimately, then, one of the key questions addressed in this book, the future of movies, proves to be difficult to answer. What we are witnessing instead is the ongoing volatility of entertainment culture. On the one hand, it is tempting to imagine, in an era of collapsing distribution windows, that the practice of going to theaters is endangered, especially given the increasing average cost of a movie ticket, a problem that has been exacerbated by the "3D surcharge." As Edward Jay Epstein argues, movie theaters have often served as little more than "launching platforms" for videos, DVDs, and other products related to the films shown, although, given the decrease in DVD sales, theatrical box office remains an important component of a film's profitability.[18] On the other hand, digital delivery has been used to transform movie theaters, turning them into sites of multimedia activity that extends well beyond filmed entertainment to special events such as live concert and sports broadcasts. A number of filmmakers, including Kevin Smith (*Red State*) and Franny Armstrong (*The Age of Stupid*), have used digital delivery to create a simultaneous global premiere that allowed thousands, if not millions, of viewers to share in the excitement of attending such an event. Certainly, digital projection in theaters has been used to show 3D films, many of them sequels, remakes, or reboots of existing Hollywood blockbuster franchises, and movie events such as the release of James Cameron's *Avatar* held a tremendous power over the cultural imagination as audiences were left to speculate whether the director had revolutionized cinematic storytelling. And although 3D quickly ceased to be a novelty, the perception remained that the format served as an "upgrade" over 2D, one that depended on viewing movies on the big screen but also one that contributed to the redefinition of projectors as computers. This idea of the "upgrade" haunts our definitions of digital cinema, reminding us that files and formats are always vulnerable to updates as technologies improve. As David Bordwell argues, now that cinema has become digital, it follows the logic of the "platform," one that is subject, like all information technologies, to "innovation, development, and obsolescence."[19] Furthermore, movies, like the technologies themselves, are produced under the idea of the upgrade, with blockbuster franchises available to be rebooted when the technology improves.

All of these changes point to a transformation in movie and television culture as users attempt to navigate the new delivery formats. At the same time, the social role of movies maintains some continuity with the past, as moviegoers worldwide continue to attend theatrical premieres in vast, if not record-breaking, numbers. These events remind us that for millions of people movies still hold a significant place in our cultural imagination, even if their social role has been altered by the accelerated velocity with which they pass through theaters and into other formats. Audiences still hold out hope that a movie will excite, challenge, engage, or entertain them. Thus, even though digital delivery contributes to the rise of the more casual viewing arrangements associated with platform mobility, movies still have a tremendous amount of power to provoke excitement, discussion, anticipation, and reflection. At the same time, thanks to the techniques of crowdsourcing and crowdfunding, digital cinema opens up new questions about what it means to be a producer or participant in film culture. While remaining cautious about the ways in which multinational corporations have used digital delivery to gain greater control over movie distribution, we might also begin to recognize the ways in which on-demand culture opens up new ways of thinking about how we find, watch, share, and discuss movies. On-demand culture is still emerging, but many of the practices, habits, and distribution models associated with it are taking form now, and consumers are adjusting to these new formats and even reworking them to satisfy their own specific, localized needs. Although media conglomerates are playing a major role in shaping these changes, consumers will also play a vital role, not just in the distribution, promotion, and circulation of movies but also in the ongoing struggles over the role of media and technologies in everyday life. Therefore, we must remain attentive not only to the various distribution channels where movies and television shows circulate but also to the practices of consumers as they attempt to navigate them.

NOTES

INTRODUCTION: ON-DEMAND CULTURE

1. Janko Roettgers, "The Day Netflix Met Its Heaviest User," *New Tee Vee*, June 12, 2012, http://gigaom.com/video/the-day-netflix-met-its-heaviest-user/.

2. Adrian Johns, *Piracy: The Intellectual Property Wars from Gutenberg to Gates* (Chicago: University of Chicago Press, 2009), 457.

3. Roettgers, "The Day Netflix Met Its Heaviest User."

4. Philip Drake, "Distribution and Marketing in Contemporary Hollywood," in *The Contemporary Hollywood Film Industry*, ed. Paul McDonald and Janet Wasko (Malden, MA: Blackwell, 2008), 63.

5. David Bordwell, *Pandora's Digital Box: Films, Files, and the Future of Movies* (Madison, WI: Irvington Way Institute Press, 2012), 8.

6. Lucas Hilderbrand, *Inherent Vice: Bootleg Histories of Videotape and Copyright* (Durham: Duke University Press, 2009), 20–25.

7. Chris McGurk, "Production and Distribution Revolution," *Thompson on Hollywood*, June 16, 2012, http://blogs.indiewire.com/thompsononhollywood/laff-keynote-chris-mcgurk.

8. Vincent Mosco, *The Digital Sublime: Myth, Power, and Cyberspace* (Cambridge, MA: MIT Press, 2004). See also Randall Livingstone, "The Myth of Classlessness in Apple's 'Get a Mac' Campaign," *Flow TV* 13, no. 11 (April 8, 2011), http://flowtv.org/2011/04/myth-of-classlessness/. Livingstone, in particular, is attentive to the ways in which the "Get a Mac" ads reinforce myths of classlessness by depicting the laid-back, leisured, and hip Justin Long as a Mac, while John Hodgman, dressed in drab, stodgy work clothes, embodies the personal computer.

9. Sarah Banet-Weiser, Cynthia Chris, and Anthony Freitas, eds., *Cable Visions: Television Beyond Broadcasting* (New York: New York University Press, 2007), 1.

10. For a discussion of the portability of videotapes and DVDs, see Daniel Herbert, *Videoland: Movie Culture at the American Video Store* (Berkeley: University of California Press, forthcoming).

11. For a thoughtful discussion of how users negotiate these four different kinds of screens, see Henry Blodget, "Don't Mean to be Alarmist, But the TV Business May Be Starting to Collapse," *Business Insider*, June 2, 2012, http://www.businessinsider.com/tv-business-collapse-2012-6.

12. Henry Jenkins, *Convergence Culture: Where Old and New Media Collide* (New York: New York University Press, 2006), 14–15.

13. Sheila C. Murphy, *How Television Invented New Media* (New Brunswick: Rutgers University Press, 2012), 88.

14. Charles Acland, "Theatrical Exhibition: Accelerated Cinema," in McDonald and Wasko, eds., *Contemporary Hollywood Film Industry*, 84.

15. Tom Schatz, "The Studio System and Conglomerate Hollywood," in McDonald and Wasko, eds., *Contemporary Hollywood Film Industry*, 27.

16. Schatz, "Studio System," 36–37.

17. Jennifer Holt, *Empires of Entertainment: Media Industries and the Politics of Deregulation, 1980–1996* (New Brunswick: Rutgers University Press, 2011), 2.

18. Holt, *Empires of Entertainment,* 177.

19. Yinka Adegoke and Dan Levine, "Comcast Completes NBC Universal Merger," Reuters, January 9, 2011, http://www.reuters.com/article/2011/01/29/us-comcast-nbc-idUSTRE70S2 WZ20110129.

20. Jennifer Holt, "Platforms, Pipelines, and Politics: The iPhone and Regulatory Hangover," in *Moving Data: The iPhone and the Future of Media,* ed. Pelle Snickars and Patrick Vonderau (New York: Columbia University Press, 2012), 143.

21. Schatz, "Studio System," 53; Jenkins, *Convergence Culture,* 114.

22. Matt Hills, *Fan Cultures* (London: Routledge, 2002), 178. See also, Chuck Tryon, "TV Time Lords: Fan Cultures, Narrative Complexity, and the Future of Science Fiction Television," in *The Essential Science Fiction Television Reader,* ed. J. P. Telotte (Lexington: University Press of Kentucky, 2008), 308.

23. Acland, "Theatrical Exhibition," 94.

24. Frederick Wasser, *Veni, Vidi, Video: The Hollywood Empire and the VCR* (Austin: University of Texas Press, 2001), 102.

25. Wasser, *Veni, Vidi, Video,* 80.

26. David Harvey, *The Condition of Postmodernity: An Enquiry into the Origins of Cultural Change* (London: Blackwell, 1989).

27. Manuel Castells, *The Rise of the Networked Society,* 2nd ed. (Malden, MA: Blackwell, 2000), 467–468.

28. Max Dawson and Lynn Spigel, "Television and Digital Media," in *American Thought and Culture in the Twenty-First Century,* ed. Catherine Morley and Martin Halliwell (New York: Columbia University Press, 2008), 281.

29. Mubi founder Efe Cakarel famously asserted that he came up with the idea for the service when he was unable to watch Wong Kar Wei's *In the Mood for Love* in a café in Tokyo. See http://mubi.com/about.

30. Acland, "Theatrical Exhibition," 83.

31. Anne Balsamo, "I Phone, I Learn," in Snickars and Vonderau, eds., *Moving Data,* 252–253.

32. Steven Shaviro, *Post-Cinematic Affect* (Washington, D.C.: Zero Books, 2010), 2.

33. Michel Foucault, *Discipline and Punish: The Birth of the Prison,* trans. Alan Sheridan (New York: Vintage, 1979). Gilles Deleuze, "Postscript on the Societies of Control," *October* 59 (Winter 1992): 3–7.

34. George F. Will, "iPod's Missed Manners," *Washington Post,* November 20, 2005, http://www.washingtonpost.com/wp-dyn/content/article/2005/11/18/AR2005111802400.html.

35. Anna McCarthy, *Ambient Television: Visual Culture and Public Space* (Durham: Duke University Press, 2001), 5.

36. Hilderbrand, *Inherent Vice,* xiii.

37. Charles R. Acland, *Screen Traffic: Movies, Multiplexes, and Global Cultures* (Durham: Duke University Press, 2003), 238.

38. Acland, *Screen Traffic,* 20.

CHAPTER 1. COMING SOON TO A COMPUTER NEAR YOU

1. Quoted in Erik Gruenwedel, "Blockbuster Canada Shutting Down," *Home Media Magazine,* September 2, 2011, http://www.homemediamagazine.com/.

2. Chris Tribbey, "Exclusive: Study Stresses Staying Power of Disc," *Home Media Magazine*, April 6, 2011, http://www.homemediamagazine.com/redbox/exclusive-study-stresses-staying-power-disc-23570.

3. Erick Schonfield, "Netflix Now the Largest Single Source of Internet Traffic in North America," *Tech Crunch*, May 17, 2011, http://techcrunch.com/2011/05/17/netflix-largest-internet-traffic/.

4. Mike Hale, "On-Demand Options for Hard-to-Find Films," *New York Times*, August 3, 2010, http://www.nytimes.com/2010/08/04/movies/04vengeance.html.

5. See for example, "Beta Male: The Auteurs' Efe Cakarel Interviewed by Paul Fileri," *Film Comment* (January/February 2009), http://www.filmlinc.com/fcm/jf09/uncutauth.htm.

6. Instawatcher.com, accessed June 18, 2012.

7. David Poland, "New Toys—July 2010," August 2, 2010, http://www.mcnblogs.com/thehotblog/archives/2010/08/new_toys_july_2.html.

8. David Poland, "DUH!"—Starz Says It Will Not Be Renewed," *Movie City News*, September 1, 2011, http://moviecitynews.com/2011/09/duh%E2%84%A2-starz-says-it-will-not-be-renewed/.

9. Janet Wasko, *How Hollywood Works* (New York: Sage, 2003).

10. Paul McDonald, *Video and DVD Industries* (London: BFI, 2007), 145. See also Dan Fost, "Divx's Death Pleases Opponents," *San Francisco Chronicle*, June 18, 1999, http://www.sfgate.com/cgi-bin/article.cgi?file=/chronicle/archive/1999/06/18/BU89741.DTL.

11. McDonald, *Video and DVD Industries*, 149.

12. McDonald, *Video and DVD Industries*, 146.

13. Wasko, *How Hollywood Works*, 144.

14. Wasko, *How Hollywood Works*, 145.

15. Wasko, *How Hollywood Works*, 145.

16. John McMurria, "A Taste of Class: Pay-TV and the Commodification of Television in Postwar America," in *Cable Visions: Television Beyond Broadcasting*, ed. Sarah Banet-Weiser, Cynthia Chris, and Anthony Freitas (New York: New York University Press, 2007), 44.

17. McMurria, "A Taste of Class," 45.

18. Jennifer Holt, *Empires of Entertainment: Media Industries and the Politics of Deregulation, 1980–1996* (New Brunswick: Rutgers University Press, 2011), 42–43.

19. David Bordwell, "Creating a Classic, with a Little Help from Your Pirate Friends," *Observations on Film Art*, February 21, 2008, http://www.davidbordwell.net/blog/2008/02/21/creating-a-classic-with-a-little-help-from-your-pirate-friends/.

20. Holt, *Empires of Entertainment*, 161.

21. Holt, *Empires of Entertainment*, 163.

22. "Netflix and Lionsgate Unite for Exclusive Syndication Arrangement to Stream Up to Seven Seasons of Acclaimed Series 'Mad Men' to Netflix Members," *Futon Critic*, April 5, 2011, http://www.thefutoncritic.com/.

23. Paul Bond, "Netflix's Reed Hastings Calls HBO His Primary Competition," *Hollywood Reporter*, December 6, 2011, http://www.hollywoodreporter.com/news/netflix-reed-hastings-hbo-go-270172.

24. Derek Kompare, *Rerun Nation: How Repeats Invented American Television* (New York: Routledge, 2005).

25. Amanda D. Lotz, *The Television Will Be Revolutionized* (New York: New York University Press, 2007), 78–80.

26. Shawn Shimpach, *Television in Transition: The Life and Afterlife of the Narrative Action Hero* (Malden, MA: Blackwell, 2010), 15.

27. Daniel Frankel, "Thor Hits Netflix as Content Drought Eases," *Paid Content,* June 11, 2012, http://paidcontent.org/2012/06/11/thor-hits-netflix-as-content-drought-eases/.

28. Chris Albrecht, "YouTube Screening Room: AtomFilms Redux," *New Tee Vee,* June 19, 2008, http://gigaom.com/video/youtube-screening-room-atomfilms-redux/.

29. Andrew Wallenstein, "YouTube, Lionsgate in Ad Pact," *Ad Week,* July 17, 2008, http://www.adweek.com/news/technology/youtube-lionsgate-ad-pact-96397.

30. David Carr, "The Evolving Mission of Google," *New York Times,* March 20, 2011, http://www.nytimes.com/2011/03/21/business/media/21carr.html.

31. Dawn C. Chmielewski, "YouTube Strikes Movie Rental Deal with Paramount," *Los Angeles Times,* April 4, 2012, http://latimesblogs.latimes.com/.

32. By August 2012, Netflix reported that it had about 5,200 movies and more than 20,000 television episodes available for Prime members. See David Pogue, "Potluck for the Eyeballs: Amazon's Streaming Service," *New York Times,* August 29, 2012, http://www.nytimes.com/2012/08/30/technology/personaltech/amazons-streaming-movie-service-offers-its-own-potluck-state-of-the-art.html.

33. Tim Stevens, "Amazon Prime Instant Video Hands-On," *Endgadget,* February 22, 2011, http://www.engadget.com/2011/02/22/amazon-prime-instant-videos-hands-on/.

34. Dan Sabbagh, "Amazon's Lovefilm Deal Could Turn Every Home into a Multiplex," *The Guardian,* January 24, 2011, http://www.guardian.co.uk/media/2011/jan/24/amazon-lovefilm-deal-films?INTCMP=ILCNETTXT3487.

35. Michael Learmonth, "Store Wars!" *Variety,* November 14–20, 2005, pp. 1, 62. Quoted in Acland, "Theatrical Exhibition," 85.

36. Miguel Bustillo and Karen Talley, "For Wal-Mart, a Rare Online Success," *Wall Street Journal,* August 29, 2011, http://online.wsj.com/.

37. For a discussion of web video's role in reviving sketch comedy, see Tim Anderson, " 'TV Time' Is Now the New 'Playtime,' " *Flow* 4, no. 1 (2006), http://flowtv.org/2006/03/tv-time-is-now-the-new-playtime/.

38. David Ehrlich, "The Criterion Collection Is Coming to Hulu Plus," *Cinematical,* February 15, 2011, http://blog.moviefone.com/2011/02/15/the-criterion-collection-hulu-plus/.

39. Ryan Lawler, "As Netflix Goes after TV Fans, Hulu Chases Movie Buffs," *New Tee Vee,* February 15, 2011, http://gigaom.com/video/hulu-criterion-collection/.

40. Peter Becker, "A Long Time Coming," *Criterion Blog,* February 15, 2011, http://www.criterion.com/current/posts/1753-a-long-time-coming. For a discussion of Criterion's efforts to "package" film history, see Nathan Carroll, "Unwrapping Archives: DVD Restoration Demonstrations and the Marketing of Authenticity," *Velvet Light Trap* 56.1 (2005): 18–31.

41. Matt Singer, "Criterion Comes to Hulu Plus," *Independent Film Channel News,* February 15, 2011, http://www.ifc.com/news/2011/02/criterion-comes-to-hulu-plus.php.

42. David Poland, "Hulu Pays for High Loyalty Content that Mainstream-Chasing Netflix Can't Afford," *Movie City News,* February 15, 2011, http://moviecitynews.com/2011/02/hulu-pays-for-high-loyalty-content-that-mainstream-chasing-netflix-cant-afford/.

43. Ben Parr, "Is Netflix the Next HBO?" *Mashable,* March 16, 2011, http://mashable.com/2011/03/16/is-netflix-the-next-hbo/.

44. Tim Arango, "Time Warner Views Netflix as a Fading Star," *New York Times,* December 12, 2010, http://www.nytimes.com/2010/12/13/business/media/13bewkes.html.

45. Sheila C. Murphy, *How Television Invented New Media* (New Brunswick: Rutgers University Press, 2012), 76.

46. Michael Learmonth, "Hulu Enters Original Programming with Morgan Spurlock Series," *Ad Age,* August 3, 2011, http://adage.com/article/digital/hulu-acquires-morgan-spurlock-series/229066/.

47. Quoted in Paul Fileri and Ruby Cheng, "Spotlight on MUBI: Two Interviews with Efe Cakarel, Founder and CEO of MUBI," in *Digital Disruption: Cinema Moves On-Line*, ed. Dina Iordinova and Stuart Cunningham (St. Andrews, Scotland: St. Andrews Film Studies, 2012), 174.

48. Fileri and Cheng, "Spotlight on MUBI," 176.

49. For a discussion of documentaries and digital distribution, see Chuck Tryon, "Digital Distribution, Participatory Culture, and the Transmedia Documentary," *Jump Cut* 53 (2011), http://www.ejumpcut.org/currentissue/TryonWebDoc/index.html.

50. Quoted in Ryan Kearney, "Ted Leonsis' SnagFilms Aims to Make 'Filmanthropy' Profitable," *TBD Arts*, March 18, 2011, http://www.tbd.com/.

51. Edward Jay Epstein, *The Big Picture: Money and Power in Hollywood* (New York: Random House, 2006), 20.

52. Edward Jay Epstein, *The Hollywood Economist: The Hidden Financial Reality Behind the Movies* (Brooklyn: Melville House, 2010), 173–175.

53. Jeff Ulin, *The Business of Media Distribution: Monetizing Film, TV, and Video Content* (New York: Focal Press, 2010), 173.

54. Ulin, *Business of Media Distribution*, 182.

55. Barbara Klinger, *Beyond the Multiplex: Cinema, New Technologies, and the Home* (Berkeley: University of California Press, 2006), 154.

56. Ryan Lawler, "Amazon Getting Serious about Competing with Netflix," *New Tee Vee*, July 28, 2011, http://gigaom.com/video/amazon-prime-netflix-competition/.

57. Sean Ludwig, "Netflix Now Testing Awesomely Easy Interface Targeted at Kids," *Media Beat*, August 11, 2011, http://venturebeat.com/2011/08/12/netflix-now-testing-awesomely-easy-interface-targeted-at-kids/.

58. David M. Ewalt, "Microsoft Xbox is Winning the Living Room War. Here's Why," *Forbes*, June 4, 2012, http://www.forbes.com/sites/davidewalt/2012/06/04/microsoft-xbox-is-winning-the-living-room-war-heres-why/.

59. Michael Cieply, "Scuffle over On-Demand Portends Battles to Come," *New York Times*, April 24, 2011, http://www.nytimes.com/2011/04/25/business/media/25vod.html.

60. Michael Cieply, "'Avatar' Director Cautions Against Early Video-on-Demand Release," *New York Times*, April 8, 2011, http://www.nytimes.com.

61. For a discussion of day-and-date distribution, see Chuck Tryon, *Reinventing Cinema: Movies in the Age of Media Convergence* (New Brunswick: Rutgers University Press, 2009), 104–106.

62. Anthony Breznican, Josh Rottenberg, and Benjamin Svetkey, "10 Ways to Save Movies," *Entertainment Weekly*, May 28, 2011, http://www.ew.com/ew/gallery/0,,20484512,00.html.

63. Eric Kohn, "Cable Gets Behind Indie Pics VOD," *Variety*, November 1, 2010, http://www.variety.com/article/VR1118026276.

64. Steve Pond, "The New Indie Film Arthouse: Is It Moving Online?" *The Wrap*, March 31, 2011, http://www.thewrap.com/movies/column-post/new-indie-film-arthouse-it-moving-online-26048.

65. Anthony Kaufman, "Industry Beat: Why VOD is Turning into a Profitable Avenue for Indie Filmmakers," *Filmmaker Magazine* (Fall 2009): 20.

66. According to Box Office Mojo, the budget for *Just Go With It* was $80 million, while *Unknown* cost $30 million. Of course, these estimates likely do not count prints and advertising costs.

67. For one of the most thorough accounts of the launch of premium VOD, see Marc Graser, "WB, Sony, U and Fox Cue Premium VOD," *Variety*, March 31, 2011, http://www.variety.com/article/VR1118034714.

68. Patrick Goldstein, "Universal's 'Tower Heist' VOD Fiasco: What Went Wrong?" *Los Angeles Times*, October 12, 2011, http://latimesblogs.latimes.com/.

69. One of the entertainment pundits most critical of premium VOD is David Poland, who frequently complains that studios are failing in their efforts to market digital delivery. See, for example, David Poland, "The Massive DirecTV Campaign for Home Premiere," *Hot Blog*, April 21, 2011, http://moviecitynews.com/2011/04/the-massive-directv-campaign -for-home-premiere/.

70. Roger Ebert, "Summer Movie Special: Sequel Madness," *Newsweek* May 15, 2011, http://www .newsweek.com/2011/05/15/summer-movie-special-sequel-madnes.html. See also Robert Putnam, *Bowling Alone: The Collapse and Revival of American Community* (New York: Simon and Schuster, 2001).

71. David Burke, "'Cedar Rapids' Movie Made (Mostly) in Michigan," *Quad City Times*, February 21, 2011, http://qctimes.com/news/local/article_b7491eb8–3d68–11e0-b394–001cc4c03286 .html.

72. Patrick Goldstein, "Is DirecTV's $30 Movie Rental Test a Flop of 'Ishtar'-Like Proportions?" *Los Angeles Times*, July 11, 2011, http://latimesblogs.latimes.com/the_big_picture/.

73. Ben Fritz, "Not Much Demand Yet for Premium Video-on-Demand," *Los Angeles Times*, July 8, 2011, http://latimesblogs.latimes.com/.

74. Anthony Kaufman, "Here's the 6 Reasons Why You Don't Know More about VOD Numbers," IndieWire, April 4, 2012, http://www.indiewire.com/.

CHAPTER 2. RESTRICTING AND RESISTANT MOBILITIES

1. Will Richmond, "Fox's New 8-Day Window Obsoletes Hulu's Simple User Experience," *VideoNuze*, August 16, 2011, http://www.videonuze.com/.

2. Greg Sandoval, "Will Hollywood's 'UltraViolet' Plan Replace the DVD?" *CNet News*, January 5, 2011, http://news.cnet.com/8301-31001_3-20027507-261.html.

3. Brent Lang, "Hollywood Unveils 'UltraViolet'—The All-Platform Video Player," *The Wrap*, January 5, 2011, http://www.thewrap.com/. Mike Snider, "Blu-Ray Grows, but DVD Slide Nips Home Video Sales," *USA Today*, January 9, 2012, http://www.usatoday.com/tech/ news/story/2012-01-10/blu-ray-sales-2011/52473310/1.

4. Ben Fritz, "DVD Revenue Plummets 44% in 2010, SNL Kagan Study Says," *Los Angeles Times*, May 12, 2011, http://latimesblogs.latimes.com/.

5. David Poland, "Hulu Pays for High Loyalty Content That Mainstream-Chasing Netflix Can't Afford," *Movie City News*, February 15, 2011, http://moviecitynews.com/.

6. Alisa Perren and Karen Petruska, "Big Hollywood, Small Screens," in *Moving Data: The iPhone and the Future of Media*, ed. Pelle Snickars and Patrick Vonderau (New York: Columbia University Press, 2012), 117. See also Marc Hachman, "UltraViolet Cloud Movies Nearly Here: Here's Why You Should Care," *PC Magazine*, September 2, 2011, http://www.pcmag.com/ article2/0,2817,2392250,00.asp.

7. Greg Sandoval, "Replacing DVD, a Hollywood Cliffhanger," *CNet News*, March 14, 2011, http://news.cnet.com/8301-31001_3-20042731-261.html?tag=mncol;txt.

8. Sandoval, "Will Hollywood's 'UltraViolet' Plan Replace the DVD?"

9. Hachman, "UltraViolet Cloud Movies."

10. Phil Keys, "Vudu/UltraViolet: Make or Break Moment for UltraViolet and Walmart," *Forbes*, March 16, 2012, http://www.forbes.com/.

11. Wheeler Winston Dixon, "How Long Will It Last, and Do You Really Own It?" *Flow TV* 14, no. 7 (September 3, 2011), http://flowtv.org/2011/09/how-long-will-it-last/.

12. Dixon, "How Long Will It Last?"

13. Quoted in Jon Silver, Stuart Cunningham, and Mark David Ryan, "Mission Unreachable: How Jaman is Shaping the Future of On-line Distribution," in *Digital Disruption: Cinema Moves On-line*, ed. Dina Iordinova and Stuart Cunningham (St. Andrews, Scotland: St. Andrews Film Studies, 2012), 133.

14. Patrick Frater, "Jaman Firms Up Indie Pacts," *Variety*, September 28, 2007, http://www.variety.com/article/VR1117972978?refCatId=19.

15. Silver, Cunningham, and Ryan, "Mission Unreachable," 136–137.

16. Silver, Cunningham, and Ryan, "Mission Unreachable," 137.

17. Stuart Cunningham and Jon Silver, "On-line Film Distribution: Its History and Global Complexion," in Iordinova and Cunningham, eds., *Digital Disruption*, 34.

18. Ben Fritz, "Netflix Expanding into Latin America," *Los Angeles Times*, July 6, 2011, http://articles.latimes.com/2011/jul/06/business/la-fi-ct-netflix-expands-20110706.

19. Ryan Lawler, "Netflix Could Beat Cable TV in Latin America," *New Tee Vee*, July 11, 2011, http://gigaom.com/video/netflix-cable-latin-america/.

20. Janko Roettgers, "Can Netflix Beat Latin America's Pirates?" *New Tee Vee*, September 6, 2011, http://gigaom.com/video/netflix-brazil-mexico-piracy/.

21. Roettgers, "Can Netflix Beat Latin America's Pirates?"

22. Matthew Garrahan, "Netflix Sets Latin American Expansion," *Financial Times*, July 5, 2011 http://www.ft.com/cms/s/0/5e4f39ca-a733-11e0-b6d4-00144feabdco.html#axzz1S8IsRF8V.

23. Rochelle King, "Netflix Launches in Latin America," *Netflix Blog*, September 5, 2011, http://blog.netflix.com/2011/09/netflix-launches-in-latin-america.html.

24. Lawler, "Netflix Could Beat Cable."

25. Janko Roettgers, "Jason Kilar: Hulu Plus Is Becoming Major Money Maker," *New Tee Vee*, October 5, 2011, http://gigaom.com/.

26. Janko Roetggers, "Why Hulu Is Doubling Down on Its Latino Audience," *New Tee Vee*, December 13, 2011, http://gigaom.com/.

27. Andrew Wallenstein and Diana Lodderhose, "Netflix Preps Euro Launch in 2012," *Variety*, July 15, 2011, http://www.variety.com/article/VR1118039987.

28. Wallenstein and Lodderhose, "Netflix Preps Euro Launch."

29. Associated Press, "US Online Streaming Site Hulu Expands to Japan," *MSNBC.com*, September 1, 2011, http://www.msnbc.msn.com/.

30. Joe Karaganis, "Introduction," in *Media Piracy in Emerging Economies*, ed. Joe Karaganis (New York: Social Science Research Council, 2011), 1.

31. Christopher Dodd, "MPAA's Chris Dodd: Piracy Is 'Single Biggest Threat We Face as an Industry,'" *Hollywood Reporter*, March 29, 2011, http://www.hollywoodreporter.com/news/mpaas-chris-dodd-piracy-is-172346.

32. David Rosen, "The New Hollywood," *Filmmaker Magazine*, May 10, 2012, http://www.filmmakermagazine.com/. See also Steven Zeitchik and Jonathan Landreth, "Hollywood Gripped by Pressure System from China," *Los Angeles Times*, June 12, 2012, http://www.latimes.com/entertainment/news/movies/la-et-china-censorship-20120612,0,6399621,full.story.

33. Dodd, "MPAA's Chris Dodd."

34. Quoted in Adrian Johns, *Piracy: The Intellectual Property Wars from Gutenberg to Gates* (Chicago: University of Chicago Press, 2009), 454.

35. John Thornton Caldwell, *Production Culture: Industrial Reflexivity and Critical Practice in Film and Television* (Durham: Duke University Press, 2008), 79.

36. J. D. Lasica, *Darknet: Hollywood's War against the Digital Generation* (Hoboken, NJ: John Wiley & Sons, 2005), 41

37. Frederick Wasser, *Veni, Vidi, Video: The Hollywood Empire and the VCR* (Austin: University of Texas Press, 2001), 102.

38. Daniel Frankel, "Federal Judge Slaps Injunction on VOD Service Zediva," *The Wrap*, August 1, 2011, http://www.thewrap.com/.

39. Tom Kulik, "Zediva: Streaming Through a Copyright Loophole in the Digital Domain," *Legal Intangibles*, April 12, 2011, http://legalintangibles.com/2011/04/zediva-streaming-through-a-copyright-loophole-in-the-digital-domain/.

40. Timothy B. Lee, "Judge Orders Shutdown of DVD-Streaming Service Zediva," *Ars Technica*, August 2, 2011, http://arstechnica.com/.

41. Ryan Singel, "Is Zediva's New-Release Movie Streaming Service Legal?" *Wired.com*, March 23, 2011, http://www.wired.com/threatlevel/2011/03/zediva-copyright.

42. Ryan Singel, "Federal Judge Orders Shutdown of Innovative DVD-Streaming Service Zediva," *Wired.com*, August 2, 2011, http://www.wired.com/epicenter/2011/08/zediva-preliminary-injunction.

43. Larkin, *Signal and Noise*, 220.

44. Larkin, *Signal and Noise*, 225.

45. Mike Masnick, "Dark Knight . . . Both Most Pirated and Highest Earning Movie," *Tech Dirt*, November 21, 2008, http://www.techdirt.com/articles/20081118/0400182867.shtml.

46. Daniel Frankel, "Nielsen: 1.5M U.S. Households Cut the Cord in 2011," *Paid Content*, May 2, 2012, http://paidcontent.org/.

47. Ryan Lawler, "Cord Cutters not Replacing Cable TV with Online Video," *New Tee Vee*, July 23, 2011, http://gigaom.com/broadband/cord-cutters-not-replacing-cable/.

48. Henry Blodget, "Don't Mean to Be Alarmist, But the TV Business May Be Starting to Collapse," *Business Insider*, June 2, 2012, http://www.businessinsider.com/tv-business-collapse-2012-6.

49. It's worth noting that sports channels were able to demand ten of the highest twenty-five affiliate fees. See David Goetzi, "ESPN Trumps All Cable Fees, CPMs," *Media Daily News*, January 27, 2012, http://www.mediapost.com/publications/article/166754/espn-trumps-all-cable-fees-cpms.html.

50. "Fox's 8-Day Delay on Hulu Triggers Piracy Surge," *Torrent Freak*, August 22, 2011, https://torrentfreak.com/foxs-8-day-delay-on-hulu-triggers-piracy-surge-110822/.

51. Claire Atkinson, "Gaming the System," *New York Post*, April 28, 2012, http://www.nypost.com/p/news/business/gaming_the_system_L20Rd15dXullvEoAbLPeAJ.

52. Claire Atkinson, "TV in Real Dime: Hulu, Networks to Change Model of Free Streaming," *New York Post*, April 30, 2012, http://www.nypost.com/p/news/business/tv_in_real_dime_phoGiKk7rC9agDUEkHae2I.

53. Ryan Lawler, "How Much Would the Average Person Pay for a Standalone HBO GO Subscription? About $12 a Month," *Tech Crunch*, June 5, 2012, http://techcrunch.com/2012/06/05/hbo-go-without-hbo/.

CHAPTER 3. "MAKE ANY ROOM YOUR TV ROOM"

1. For a discussion of how DVDs affected television viewing, see Derek Kompare, "Publishing Flow: DVD Box Sets and the Reconception of Television," *Television and New Media* 7.4 (November 2006): 335–360.

2. For a recent discussion of this comparison, see Sheila C. Murphy, *How Television Invented New Media* (New Brunswick: Rutgers University Press, 2012), 93–94.

3. Charles R. Acland, "Curtains, Carts, and the Mobile Screen," *Screen* 50.1 (2009): 149. For a discussion of the "black box fallacy," see Henry Jenkins, *Convergence Culture: Where Old and New Media Collide* (New York: New York University Press, 2006), 14–16.

4. This point is underscored by the fact that most studios are scheduled to stop using film as a delivery system by the end of 2013.

5. Jonathan Sterne, "Formatted to Fit Your Screen," *FlowTV* 15.5 (January 2012), http://flowtv.org/2012/01/formatted-to-fit-your-screen/.

6. Lynn Spigel, *Make Room for TV: Television and the Family Ideal in Postwar America* (Chicago: University of Chicago Press, 1992), 36.

7. Spigel, *Make Room for TV*, 37. In fact, Spigel notes that the term "togetherness" was coined by *McCall's* magazine in 1954, reflecting the emphasis on the nuclear family.

8. Spigel, *Make Room for TV*, 38.

9. Spigel, *Welcome to the Dreamhouse: Popular Media and Postwar Suburbs* (Durham: Duke University Press, 2001), 52.

10. Spigel, *Welcome to the Dreamhouse*, 62, 73–75.

11. Spigel, *Welcome to the Dreamhouse*, 61. See also Jeffrey Sconce, *Haunted Media: Electronic Presence from Telegraphy to Television* (Durham: Duke University Press, 2000).

12. Spigel, *Welcome to the Dreamhouse*, 67.

13. Barbara Klinger, *Beyond the Multiplex: Cinema, New Technologies, and the Home* (Berkeley: University of California Press, 2006), 9, 24–25.

14. Klinger, *Beyond the Multiplex*, 23.

15. Klinger, *Beyond the Multiplex*, 35.

16. Klinger, *Beyond the Multiplex*, 45. See also Ann Gray, *Video Playtime: The Gendering of a Leisure Technology* (London: Routledge, 1992).

17. Chuck Tryon, "Pushing the (Red) Envelope: Portable Video, Platform Mobility, and Pay-Per-View Culture," in *Moving Data: The iPhone and the Future of Media*, ed. Pelle Snickars and Patrick Vonderau (New York: Columbia University Press, 2012), 124–139.

18. Kristen Daly, "Cinema 3.0: The Interactive Image," *Cinema Journal* 50.1 (Fall 2010): 82.

19. Francesco Cassetti, "Back to the Motherland: The Film Theatre in the Postmedia Age," *Screen* 52.1 (Spring 2011): 6.

20. Cassetti, "Back to the Motherland," 9.

21. Dan Schiller, *How to Think about Information* (Urbana: University of Illinois Press, 2007), 141.

22. Vincent Mosco, *The Political Economy of Communication*, 2nd ed. (Los Angeles: Sage, 2009), 136. See also Mark Andrejevic, *iSpy: Surveillance and Power in the Interactive Era* (Lawrence: University of Kansas Press, 2007), 11.

23. John Seabrook, "Streaming Dreams: YouTube Turns Pro," *The New Yorker*, January 16, 2012, http://www.newyorker.com/reporting/2012/01/16/120116fa_fact_seabrook.

24. As Shawn Shimpach notes, similar problems are challenging the TV industry, as well. See Shimpach, *Television in Transition: The Life and Afterlife of the Narrative Action Hero* (Malden, MA: Wiley-Blackwell, 2010), 23.

25. For a discussion of the role of the VCR and other new media technologies in enabling time-shifting, see Anne Friedberg, *Window Shopping: Cinema and the Postmodern* (Berkeley: University of California Press, 1994).

26. Acland, "Curtains," 149.

27. Cassetti, "Back to the Motherland," 3.

28. See for example, Catherine Grant, "Auteur machines? Auteurism and the DVD," in *Film and Television after DVD*, ed. James Bennett and Tom Brown (London and New York: Routledge, 2008), 101–115.

29. Jeff Ulin, *The Business of Media Distribution: Monetizing Film, TV, and Video Content* (New York: Focal Press, 2010), 196. Edward Jay Epstein, "Hollywood's Death Spiral: The Secret Numbers Tell the Story," *Slate*, July 25, 2005, http://www.slate.com/id/2123286/.

30. Ulin, *Business of Media Distribution*, 189.

31. "State of the Media: Trends in TV Viewing—2011 TV Upfronts," Nielsen Wire Blog, April 2011, http://blog.nielsen.com/nielsenwire/wp-content/uploads/2011/04/State-of-the-Media-2011 -TV-Upfronts.pdf.

32. Gerard Goggin, *Global Mobile Media* (London: Routledge, 2011), 80–98.

33. Harry McCracken, "TV Everywhere? Cable on the Net Isn't There Yet," *Time*, May 5, 2011, http://www.time.com/time/business/article/0,8599,2069693,00.html.

34. Niki Strange, "Multiplatforming Public Service: The BBC's 'Bundled Project,'" in *Television as Digital Media*, ed. James Bennett and Niki Strange (Durham: Duke University Press, 2011), 132.

35. Mark Saltzman, "The Dark Knight: App Edition Fuses Movies with Social Media," *USA Today*, February 24, 2011, http://content.usatoday.com/communities/technologylive/post/ 2011/02/dark-knight-warner-bros-app-ipad/1.

36. William Fenton, "Warner Debuts First Movie Apps for iOS, *Inception* and *The Dark Knight*," *PCMag.com*, February 16, 2011, http://www.pcmag.com/article2/0,2817,2380445,00 .asp.

37. The concept of digital myths is borrowed here from Vincent Mosco and is meant to describe the ways in which digital discourses often take on mythological overtones. As Mosco is quick to point out, myth, as it is used here, does not imply falsehood. Instead, myth reflects deep-seated cultural desires for mobility, agency, and community. See Vincent Mosco, *The Digital Sublime: Myth, Power, and Cyberspace* (Cambridge, MA: MIT Press, 2004).

38. Mike Masnick, "Hollywood's Kinder, Gentler DRM: UltraViolet, Getting Slammed in Reviews," *Tech Dirt*, October 26, 2011, http://www.techdirt.com/.

39. Molly Wood, "UltraViolet: DRM by any other Name Still Stinks," *C-Net*, March 16, 2012, http://news.cnet.com/.

40. Spigel, *Welcome to the Dreamhouse*, 67.

41. Anne Balsamo, "I Phone, I Learn," in Snickars and Vonderau, eds., *Moving Data*, 253.

42. Anne Balsamo, "I Phone, I, Learn," 253.

43. William Boddy, "'Is It TV Yet?' The Dislocated Screens of Television in a Mobile Digital Culture," in Bennett and Strange, eds., *Television as Digital Media*, 96.

44. Shaun Moores, "Media Uses & Everyday Environmental Experiences: A Positive Critique of Phenomenological Geography," *Participations* 3, no. 2 (November 2006), http:// www.participations.org/volume%203/issue%202%20-%20special/3_02_moores.htm.

CHAPTER 4. BREAKING THROUGH THE SCREEN

1. James Cameron, "TI DLP Cinema™, George Lucas and James Cameron to Highlight Digital Cinema and 3D Movies at ShoWest 2005," *DCinema Today*, March 15, 2005, http://www .dcinematoday.com/dc/pr.aspx?newsID=228.

2. David Bordwell, *Pandora's Digital Box: Films, Files, and the Future of Movies* (Madison, WI: Irvington Way Institute Press, 2012).

3. Rebecca Keegan, *The Futurist: The Life and Times of James Cameron* (New York: Crown, 2009), xi.

4. Bordwell, *Pandora's Digital Box*, 210.

5. All box office numbers are taken from Box Office Mojo. See http://boxofficemojo.com/. For a discussion of the *Beowulf* adaptation, see Chuck Tryon, *Reinventing Cinema: Movies in the Age of Media Convergence* (New Brunswick: Rutgers University Press, 2009), 71–72.

6. Lisa Kernan, *Coming Attractions: Reading American Movie Trailers* (Austin: University of Texas Press, 2004), 5–6.

7. Jonathan Gray, *Show Sold Separately: Promos, Spoilers, and Other Media Paratexts* (New York: New York University Press, 2010), 47.

8. Gray, *Show Sold Separately*, 48. See also John Ellis, *Visible Fictions: Cinema, Television, Video* (New York: Routledge, 1993), 54.

9. Charles R. Acland, "*Avatar* as Technological Tentpole," *Flow TV* 11, no. 6 (January 22, 2010), http://flowtv.org/2010/01/avatar-as-technological-tentpole-charles-r-acland-concordia-university/.

10. Neil Miller, "Review: 'Avatar' Delivers on Its Promise," *Film School Rejects*, December 11, 2009, http://www.filmschoolrejects.com/reviews/review-avatar-neilm.php.

11. Jeffrey Sconce, "Avatard," *Ludic Despair*, January 4, 2010, http://ludicdespair.blogspot.com/2010/01/avatard.html.

12. Geoff Boucher, "USC Professor Creates an Entire Alien Language for 'Avatar,'" *Los Angeles Times*, November 20, 2009, http://latimesblogs.latimes.com/herocomplex/2009/11/usc-professor-creates-alien-language-for-avatar.html.

13. Joshua Davis, "James Cameron's New 3D Epic Could Change Film Forever," *Wired*, November 17, 2009, http://www.wired.com/magazine/2009/11/ff_avatar_cameron/all/1.

14. It's worth noting that the cover of the book gives the title as *James Cameron's Avatar: An Activist Survival Guide*, suggesting that Cameron even maintained a certain amount of authorship over virtually every text associated with the film.

15. Maria Wilhelm and Dirk Mathison, *Avatar: A Confidential Report on the Biological and Social History of Pandora* (New York: HarperCollins, 2009).

16. Gray, *Show Sold Separately*, 113.

17. Keegan, *The Futurist*, x.

18. Quoted in Anne Thompson, "Geeking Out with Cameron at the 3D Summit: *Titanic, Avatar*, Theme Parks," *IndieWire*, September 23, 2011, http://blogs.indiewire.com/.

19. Bordwell, *Pandora's Digital Box*, 74–75. *Avatar*'s success was especially important overseas in that it helped to encourage China to build more theaters capable of digital projection.

20. For a detailed discussion of *Avatar*'s relationship to the processes of DVD versioning, see Charles R. Acland, "You Haven't Seen *Avatar* Yet," *Flow TV* 13, no. 8 (February 11, 2011), http://flowtv.org/2011/02/you-havent-seen-avatar/.

21. Richard Corliss, "Avatar on DVD Review: Pandora's Skimpy Box," *Time*, April 24, 2010, http://www.time.com/time/arts/article/0,8599,1984304,00.html. Emphasis in the original.

22. Acland, "You Haven't Seen *Avatar* Yet."

23. Acland, "You Haven't Seen *Avatar* Yet."

24. Acland, "*Avatar* as Technological Tentpole."

25. Barbara Klinger, *Beyond the Multiplex: Cinema, New Technologies, and the Home* (Berkeley: University of California Press, 2006), 45.

26. Jill Serjeant, "'Avatar' Director Cameron in Bid to Bring 3D to TV," Reuters, April 11, 2011, http://www.reuters.com/article/2011/04/12/us-3d-idUSTRE73A5NR20110412.

27. Mike Snider, "At Home Review: Watching the World Cup in 3D," *USA Today*, June 17, 2010, http://content.usatoday.com/.

28. Brian Stelter and Brad Stone, "Television Begins a Push into the 3rd Dimension," *New York Times*, January 5, 2010, http://www.nytimes.com/2010/01/06/business/media/06tele.html.

29. Edward C. Baig, "3D TV Showing of World Cup Is Nifty, If Not Without Issues," *USA Today*, June 17, 2010, http://www.usatoday.com/.

30. "The Future of the DVD," *Home Media Magazine*, March 2011, 6, http://www.homemediamagazine.com/research/physical-media-study.

31. Kristin Thompson, "Has 3D Already Failed? The Sequel, Part 2: Real Dsgusted," *Observations on Film Art*, January 25, 2011, http://www.davidbordwell.net/blog/2011/01/25/has-3d-already-failed-the-sequel-part-2-realdsgusted/.

32. See also David Itzkoff, "Eye-Popping for Art's Sake: An Advocate for 3-D Films," *New York Times*, October 19, 2010, http://movies.nytimes.com/2010/10/20/movies/20cameron.html.

33. Edward Jay Epstein, *The Hollywood Economist: The Hidden Financial Reality Behind the Movies* (Brooklyn: Melville House, 2010).

34. See Mike Fleming, "OSCAR: Chris Nolan Q&A about 'Inception,'" *Deadline Hollywood Daily*, January 7, 2011, http://www.deadline.com/.

35. Steven Zeitchik, "With 'Glee' 3-D Concert Movie, Lea Michele Will Sing on the Big Screen," *Los Angeles Times*, May 3, 2011, http://latimesblogs.latimes.com/. See also Steven Zeitchik, "As It Seeks a Big-Event Feel, 'Glee' 3-D Movie Adds Advance Screenings," *Los Angeles Times*, July 11, 2011, http://latimesblogs.latimes.com/.

36. Rick Porter, "More 'Lost' Finale Events: Theater Simulcast, Comedy Shows," *Zap 2 It*, April 20, 2010, http://blog.zap2it.com/.

37. Steve Pond, "Alternative Content Rides Digital Delivery into Theaters," *The Wrap*, April 5, 2011, http://www.thewrap.com/movies/column-post/alternative-content-rides-digital-delivery-theaters-26174.

38. Charles R. Acland, *Screen Traffic: Movies, Multiplexes, and Global Cultures* (Durham: Duke University Press, 2003), 222.

39. Andrew Barker, "The Lion of Judah," *Variety*, June 2, 2011, http://www.variety.com/review/VE1117945372/. See also Kirk Honeycutt, "The Lion of Judah: Film Review," *Hollywood Reporter*, June 3, 2011, http://www.hollywoodreporter.com/review/lion-judah-film-review-193901.

40. Quoted in Anne Thompson, "James Cameron and Michael Bay Talk State of 3D, Avatar, Dark of the Moon: 'Not an Afterthought,'" *Thompson on Hollywood*, May 19, 2011, http://blogs.indiewire.com/thompsononhollywood/.

41. Anne Friedberg, *Window Shopping: Cinema and the Postmodern* (Berkeley: University of California Press, 1994), 175–176.

42. Tom Russo, "Seven Hit Hollywood Reboots," *Boston Globe*, July 1, 2012, http://articles.boston.com/2012-07-01/ae/32496554_1_andrew-garfield-emma-stone-gwen-stacy.

43. William Proctor "Beginning Again: The Reboot Phenomenon in Comic Books and Film," *Scan* 8, no. 2 (2012), http://scan.net.au/scan/journal/display.php?journal_id=163.

44. Anne Thompson, "What Will *Tron: Legacy*'s 3D VFX Look Like in 30 Years?" *Popular Mechanics*, December 9, 2010, http://www.popularmechanics.com/.

45. Jason Sperb, "A Few Thoughts on *Tron*'s Blu-Ray Release," *Jamais Vu: Thoughts on Cinema and Media*, April 8, 2011, http://lightpalimpsest.blogspot.com/2011/04/few-thoughts-on-trons-blu-ray-release.html.

46. Dan North, *Performing Illusions: Cinema Special Effects and the Virtual Actor* (London: Wallflower Press, 2001), 145.

47. North, *Performing Illusions*, 145–146.

48. Steven Zeitchik, "'Star Wars' and 'Titanic' 3D: How Much Is Too Much?" *Los Angeles Times*, October 1, 2010, http://latimesblogs.latimes.com/movies/2010/10/star-wars-3d-george-lucas-titanic-james-cameron.html.

49. Anne Thompson, "Paramount, Fox, Cameron Relaunch Titanic Again in Retro-3D," *Thompson on Hollywood*, May 19, 2011, http://blogs.indiewire.com/thompsononhollywood/.

50. Thompson, "Retro 3D."

51. Will Brooker, *Using the Force: Creativity, Community, and Star Wars Fans* (New York: Continuum, 2002), 90. See also, Chuck Tryon, "Fan Films, Adaptations, and Media Literacy," in *Science Fiction Film, Television, and Adaptation: Across the Screens*, ed. J. P. Telotte and Gerald Duchovnay (New York: Routledge, 2012), 181.

52. Jay A. Fernandez and Kim Masters, "'Star Wars' Saga Set for 3D Release Starting 2012," *Hollywood Reporter*, October 14, 2010, http://www.hollywoodreporter.com/news/star-wars-saga-set-3d-28485.

53. Stephen Kelly, "3D Is Not the Answer to Cinema's Problems. How about Better Films?" *The Guardian*, May 24, 2012, http://www.guardian.co.uk/commentisfree/2012/may/24/3d-cinema-problems.

54. Ty Burr, "A Movie Lover's Plea: Let There Be Light," *Boston Globe*, May 22, 2011, http://www.boston.com/.

55. Roger Ebert, "The Dying of the Light," *Chicago Sun-Times*, May 24, 2011, http://blogs.suntimes.com/ebert/2011/05/the_dying_of_the_light.html.

56. Kristin Thompson, "Do Not Forget to Return Your 3D Glasses," *Observations on Film Art*, July 27, 2011, http://www.davidbordwell.net/blog/2011/07/27/do-not-forget-to-return-your-3d-glasses/. See also David S. Cohen, "'Transformers' to Pump Up 3D Brightness," *Variety*, June 22, 2011, http://www.variety.com/article/VR1118038975?refCatId=13.

57. Thompson, "Return Your 3D Glasses."

58. David Poland, "Friday Estimates by Yo Ho Yo Ho Klady," *Movie City News*, May 21, 2011, http://moviecitynews.com/2011/05/friday-estimates-by-yo-ho-yo-ho-klady/.

59. In fact, China's box office increased by 35 percent to $2 billion from 2010 to 2011. See Joshua L. Weinstein, "Global Box Office Up, Domestic Box Office Down in 2011 (Updated)," *The Wrap*, March 22, 2012, http://www.thewrap.com/movies/article/global-box-office-domestic-box-office-down-2011-36467.

60. Quoted in Pamela McClintock, "CinemaCon 2012: Fox Will Stop U.S. 35mm Film Distribution Within Two Years," *Hollywood Reporter*, April 24, 2012, http://www.hollywoodreporter.com/.

61. Brent Lang, "CinemaCon: James Cameron Ramps Up His Calls for Higher Frame Rates," *The Wrap*, March 31, 2012, http://www.thewrap.com/.

62. Carolyn Giardina, "Peter Jackson Responds to 'Hobbit' Footage Critics, Explains 48-Frames Strategy," *Hollywood Reporter*, April 28, 2012, http://www.hollywoodreporter.com/.

63. Bordwell, *Pandora's Digital Box*, 208.

64. Bordwell, *Pandora's Digital Box*, 209. As Bordwell notes, Cameron stands to profit tremendously from the adoption of 3D equipment, given that his company works with both ESPN and CBS Sports.

CHAPTER 5. REDBOX VS. RED ENVELOPE, OR CLOSING THE WINDOW ON THE BRICKS-AND-MORTAR VIDEO STORE

1. Janko Roetttgers, "Netflix Just Became Cable's Biggest TV Network," *New Tee Vee*, July 3, 2012, http://gigaom.com/video/netflix-june-one-billion-hours/.

2. See, for example, Anne Friedberg, *Window Shopping: Cinema and the Postmodern* (Berkeley: University of California Press, 1994), and Derek Kompare, "Publishing Flow: DVD Box Sets and the Reconception of Television," *Television & New Media* 7.4 (2006): 335–360.

3. Jeff Ulin, *The Business of Media Distribution: Monetizing Film, TV, and Video Content* (New York: Focal Press, 2010), 3.

4. "The Future of the DVD," *Home Media Magazine*, March 2011, http://www.home mediamagazine.com/research/physical-media-study.

5. Ted Striphas, *The Late Age of Print: Everyday Book Culture from Consumerism to Control* (New York: Columbia University Press, 2009), 5. Striphas's concept is informed by Henri Lefebvre. See *Everyday Life in the Modern World*, trans. Sacha Rabinovitch (New Brunswick, NJ: Transaction Publishers, 1984), 68–109.

6. Ulin, *Business of Media Distribution*, 4.

7. Ulin, *Business of Media Distribution*, 4–36.

8. Ulin, *Business of Media Distribution*, 31.

9. Frederick Wasser, *Veni, Vidi, Video: The Hollywood Empire and the VCR* (Austin: University of Texas Press, 2001), 117.

10. Edward Jay Epstein, "Hollywood's Death Spiral: The Secret Numbers Tell the Story," *Slate*, July 25, 2005, http://www.slate.com/id/2123286.

11. Edward Jay Epstein, *The Big Picture: Money and Power in Hollywood* (New York: Random House, 2006), 216.

12. Edward Jay Epstein, *The Hollywood Economist: The Hidden Financial Reality Behind the Movies* (Brooklyn: Melville House, 2010), 185.

13. Chris Anderson, *The Long Tail: Why the Future of Business Is Selling Less of More* (New York: Hyperion, 2006).

14. Ryan Lawler, "Netflix: The Future Is Streaming," *NewTeeVee*, May 27, 2010, http://newteevee .com/2010/05/27/netflix-the-future-is-streaming/. See also "Netflix Business Opportunity," http://www.netflix.com/Jobs.

15. Ben Fritz, "Netflix to Lose Starz, Its Most Valuable Source of New Movies," *Los Angeles Times*, September 1, 2011, http://latimesblogs.latimes.com/.

16. David Poland, "Delivelution 71311: Welcome to Netflix 3.0," *The Hot Blog*, July 13, 2011, http://moviecitynews.com/2011/07/delivelution-71311-welcome-to-netflix-3-0/.

17. Will Richmond, "Netflix's DVD Split Is Yet Another Self-Inflicted Wound," *Video Nuze*, September 19, 2011, http://www.videonuze.com/article/netflix-s-dvd-split-is-yet-another-self -inflicted-wound.

18. Jefferson Graham, "Netflix Looks to Future but Still Going Strong with DVD Rentals," *USA Today*, July 1, 2009, http://www.usatoday.com/tech/products/2009-06-30-netflix-future_N .htm.

19. Janko Roettgers, "Good News for Netflix: Shaw Raises Bandwidth Caps," *New Tee Vee*, May 26, 2011, http://gigaom.com/broadband/netflix-shaw-bandwidth-caps/.

20. David Poland, "More Anything Anywhere," *The Hot Blog*, August 15, 2010, http://www .mcnblogs.com/thehotblog/archives/2010/08/more_anything_a.html.

21. Chuck Tryon, *Reinventing Cinema: Movies in the Age of Media Convergence* (New Brunswick: Rutgers University Press, 2009), 16–37. See also Barbara Klinger, "The DVD Cinephile: Viewing Heritages and Home Film Cultures," in *Film and Television after DVD*, ed. James Bennett and Tom Brown (London: Routledge, 2008), 19–44.

22. Barbara Klinger, *Beyond the Multiplex: Cinema, New Technologies, and the Home* (Berkeley: University of California Press, 2006), 73.

23. Klinger, *Beyond the Multiplex*, 87.

24. Catherine Grant, "Auteur Machines? Auteurism and the DVD," in Bennett and Brown, eds., *Film and Television after DVD*, 101–115.

25. For a discussion of the role of television as a "babysitting machine," see Ellen Seiter, *Sold Separately: Children and Parents in Consumer Culture* (New Brunswick: Rutgers University Press, 1993), 26.

26. Ulin, *Business of Media Distribution*, 171–174. See also Epstein, *Hollywood Economist*, 174–175. The concept of home video as an "electronic babysitter" dates back to at least the 1980s. See Joshua M. Greenberg, *From Betamax to Blockbuster: Video Stores and the Invention of Movies on Video* (Cambridge, MA: MIT Press, 2008), 94.

27. Ryan Lawler, "New Netflix Streams Are Child's Play," *NewTeeVee*, July 27, 2010, http://gigaom.com/video/new-netflix-streams-are-childs-play/.

28. Janko Roettgers, "Netflix Adds *Yo Gabba Gabba* & *iCarly*," *NewTeeVee*, May 23, 2011, http://gigaom.com/video/netflix-yo-gabba-gabba-icarly/.

29. David Milstead, "Forget the Futurists—Coinstar is a Cash Machine," *Globe and Mail*, 9 April 2011, B10. By May 2012, there were still around 37,000 Redbox kiosks.

30. Ben Fritz, "Blockbuster Tells Hollywood Studios It's Preparing for Mid-September Bankruptcy," *Los Angeles Times*, August 26, 2010, http://latimesblogs.latimes.com/entertainmentnewsbuzz/.

31. Janet Wasko, *How Hollywood Works* (London: Sage, 2003), 131.

32. "Movie Gallery to Close All U.S. Stores: Report," Reuters, May 2, 2010, http://www.reuters.com/article/idUSTRE6412SR20100502.

33. Erik Gruenwedel, "Blockbuster Canada Shutting Down," *Home Media Magazine*, September 2, 2011, http://www.homemediamagazine.com/.

34. Brooks Barnes, "Movie Studios See a Threat in the Growth of Redbox," *New York Times*, September 6, 2009, http://www.nytimes.com/2009/09/07/business/media/07redbox.html.

35. Carla DiOrio, "$1 DVD Rentals Costing Biz $1 Bil: Study," *Hollywood Reporter*, December 7, 2009, http://www.hollywoodreporter.com/.

36. Chris Tribbey, "Six Questions: Redbox's Mitch Lowe," *Home Media Magazine*, July 31, 2009, http://www.homemediamagazine.com/.

37. Ben Fritz, "'Just Go with It' Tops 2011 Redbox Rentals," *Los Angeles Times*, December 29, 2011, http://latimesblogs.latimes.com/entertainmentnewsbuzz/2011/12/just-go-with-it-tops-2011-redbox-rentals.html.

38. Redbox Press Room, http://redboxpressroom.com/#, accessed February 20, 2011.

39. Brian Winston, *Media, Technology, and Society, A History: From the Telegraph to the Internet* (London: Routledge, 1998).

40. Winston, *Media Technology, and Society*, 11.

41. For a discussion of Lowe's early career as a video retailer, see Greenberg, *From Betamax to Blockbuster*, 76.

42. David Lieberman, "DVD Kiosks Like Redbox Have Rivals Seeing Red," *USA Today*, 11 August 2009, http://usatoday30.usatoday.com/money/media/2009-08-11-rental-dvd-redbox_N.htm?loc=interstitialskip.

43. Diane Garrett, "Redbox Analysis: Kiosks vs. Studios," *Thompson on Hollywood*, August 24, 2009, http://blogs.indiewire.com/thompsononhollywood/.

44. Andrew Miller, "Rental Advisory: A Redbox Etiquette Primer," *The Andrew Miller*, January 31, 2010, http://theandrewmiller.com/rental-advisory-a-redbox-etiquette-primer/.

45. Brooks Barnes mentions that Redbox president Mitch Lowe experimented with a VHS vending machine in the 1980s, which, as a *Star Wars* buff, he called Video Droid. He sold sixty of the machines in the United States and Japan in 1984. The concept failed in part due to a more credit-conscious customer base and because of the fragility of VHS tapes. Barnes, "Movie Studios See a Threat." See also Redbox.com.

46. Wheeler Winston Dixon, "Red Boxes and Cloud Movies," *Flow* 14, no.4 (July 2011).

47. Saul Hansell, "Buying Movies on Flash Drives: A Nice Idea That Doesn't Work," *New York Times*, February 22, 2008, http://bits.blogs.nytimes.com/2008/02/22/buying-movies-on-flash-cards-nice-idea-that-doesnt-work/.

48. "Movies from an ATM," *Irish Times*, September 7, 2007, Finance, 6.

49. Jon Healey, "CES: PortoMedia's Video Kiosks," *Los Angeles Times*, April 5, 2008, http://opinion.latimes.com/bitplayer/2008/01/ces-portomedias.html.

50. John Cook, "Digiboo Takes Flight: Movie Kiosks at Seattle Airport Offer New Releases for $3.99 (Video)," *Tech Crunch*, March 23, 2012.

51. Jill Kipnis, "DVDs Now Showing at Your Local Kiosk," *Billboard*, August 7, 2004.

52. Personal interview, Enrico Donà.

53. Sherwin Loh, "DVD Rentals at Your Fingertips," *Straits Times* (Singapore), September 10, 2004.

54. Jessica Lim, "DVD Kiosk Concept Stalls," *Straits Times* (Singapore), June 7, 2011.

55. Blake Williams, "Movie Magic Brings Redbox-Like DVD Rentals to Toronto," *BlogTO*, May 1, 2011, http://www.blogto.com/.

56. "Best Buy Bringing Online Video Service to Canada," *CBC News*, June 16, 2011, http://www.cbc.ca/fp/story/2011/06/16/4956666.html.

57. Adam Dawtrey, "Odeon Ends Alice in Wonderland Boycott," *The Guardian*, February 25, 2010, http://www.guardian.co.uk/film/2010/feb/25/odeon-alice-in-wonderland-boycott.

58. Eugene Novikov, "What's This Hullaballoo over AMC Theatres and 'Alice in Wonderland?'" *Cinematical*, February 21, 2010, http://www.cinematical.com/.

59. Ryan Paul, "Studio Makes Redbox an Offer It Can't Refuse, Redbox Sues," *Ars Technica*, October 28, 2008, http://arstechnica.com/tech-policy/news/2008/10/universal-studios-attacks-dvd-rental-kiosks.ars.

60. Erik Gruenwedel, "Analyst: Dismissal of Redbox Claims Could Undermine Kiosk Viability," *Home Media Magazine*, October 5, 2009, http://www.homemediamagazine.com/.

61. Olga Kharif, "Wal-Mart, Target Put Squeeze on Redbox," *Business Week*, February 2, 2010, http://www.businessweek.com/.

62. Ryan Lawler, "Paramount: Redbox Had 'Minimal Impact' on DVD Sales," *NewTeeVee*, June 15, 2010, http://newteevee.com/2010/06/15/paramount-redbox-had-minimal-impact-on-dvd-sales/.

63. Ben Fritz, "Universal Keeps Pace with Redbox, Spurning Warner Bros.," *Los Angeles Times*, March 1, 2012, http://latimes.com/.

64. Cited in Dawn Taylor, "Could 1$ Redbox Rentals Cripple iTunes?" *Cinematical*, September 4, 2009, http://www.cinematical.com.

65. Erik Gruenwedel, "Analyst: Consumers Prefer Movie Rentals to Purchase, Theatrical," *Home Media Magazine*, May 25, 2011, http://www.homemediamagazine.com/market-share/analyst-consumers-prefer-movie-rentals-purchase-theatrical-24044.

66. Brooks Barnes, "Movie Studios See a Threat."

67. Thomas K. Arnold, "Is Warner Trying to Remake the Video Rental Business?" *Home Media Magazine*, January 18, 2010, http://www.homemediamagazine.com/warner/warner-trying-remake-video-rental-business-18123.

68. Trefis Team, "Dish Aiming for New Subscribers with Blockbuster Promotion," *Forbes*, May 25, 2011, http://blogs.forbes.com/greatspeculations/2011/05/25/dish-aiming-for-new-subscribers-with-blockbuster-promotion/.

69. Chris Anderson, *Free: The Future of a Radical Price* (New York: Hyperion, 2009).

70. Ben Fritz, "Blockbuster Switches to Redbox-Style Single Day Rental Pricing," *Los Angeles Times*, May 27, 2011, http://latimesblogs.latimes.com/.

CHAPTER 6. THE TWITTER EFFECT

1. Charles R. Acland, *Screen Traffic: Movies, Multiplexes, and Global Cultures* (Durham: Duke University Press, 2003), 242.

2. Metrics for counting the number of tweets containing a given keyword are often unreliable, and numbers vary widely. One commonly cited tracking service, Tweebeat, counted 400,000 Oscar-related tweets, while another service, TweetReach, estimated the number of Oscar postings at nearly 1.3 million. See Christina Warren, "The Oscars & Social Media by the Numbers," *Mashable*, February 28, 2011, http://mashable.com/2011/02/28/oscars-by-the-numbers/.

3. Warren, "Oscars & Social Media."

4. Andrew Hampp, "Forget Ebert: How Twitter Makes or Breaks Movie Marketing Today," *Ad Age*, October 5, 2009, http://adage.com/article/madisonvine-news/social-media-twitter-makes-breaks-movie-marketing/139444/.

5. Brooks Barnes, "A Plea for Tolerance in Tight Shorts. Or Not," *New York Times*, June 11, 2009, http://www.nytimes.com/2009/06/14/movies/14barn.htm.

6. Nick Douglas, "Twitter Blows Up at SXSW Conference," *Gawker*, March 12, 2007, http://gawker.com/.

7. Ross Mayfield, "Twitter Tips the Tuna," *Ross Mayfield's Weblog*, March 12, 2007, http://ross.typepad.com/blog/2007/03/twitter_tips_th.html.

8. THR Staff, "THR Poll: 9 out of 10 Call Social Media New Form of Entertainment; Young People Want Texting in Movies," *Hollywood Reporter*, March 21, 2012, http://www.hollywoodreporter.com/.

9. Alexander Zaitchik, "Twitter Nation Has Arrived: How Scared Should We Be?" *AlterNet*, February 21, 2009, http://www.alternet.org/media/127623. For a response to Zaitchik's complaints, see Chuck Tryon, "Why You Should Be on Twitter," *AlterNet*, March 4, 2009, http://www.alternet.org/media/129319.

10. Dalia Colon, "Weave a Web of Success," *St. Petersburg Times*, July 20, 2008, 1F.

11. Sharon Waxman, "Social Networking Making Friday the Only Day That Counts," *The Wrap*, July 9, 2009, http://www.thewrap.com/movies/article/summer-box-office-twitter-effect_4229.

12. Hampp, "Forget Ebert."

13. Richard Corliss, "Box-Office Weekend: Brüno a One-Day Wonder?" *Time*, July 13, 2009, http://www.time.com/time/arts/article/0,8599,1910059,00.html.

14. Cara Pring, "100 Social Media Statistics for 2012," *The Social Skinny*, January 11, 2012, http://thesocialskinny.com/100-social-media-statistics-for-2012/.

15. Brian David Johnson, *Screen Future: The Future of Entertainment, Computing, and the Devices We Love* (Santa Clara, CA: Intel Press, 2010), 104.

16. Axel Bruns and Jean Burgess, "New Methodologies for Researching News Discussion on Twitter," *Mapping Online Publics*, 2011 http://snurb.info/files/2011/New%20Methodologies%20for%20Researching%20News%20Discussion%20on%20Twitter%20(final).pdf.

17. THR Staff, "THR Poll."

18. Acland, *Screen Traffic*, 239.

19. Acland, *Screen Traffic*, 242.

20. "Watching Together: Twitter and TV," *The Twitter Blog*, May 4, 2011, http://blog.twitter.com/2011/05/watching-together-twitter-and-tv.html.

21. Graeme Turner, "'Liveness' and 'Sharedness' Outside the Box," *Flow TV* 13.11 (April 8, 2011), http://flowtv.org/2011/04/liveness-and-sharedness-outside-the-box/.

22. Ryan Lawler, "Want to Make a Show More Social? Start with the Script," *New Tee Vee*, July 21, 2011, http://gigaom.com/video/social-tv-broadcasters/.

23. The video is available online at http://www.youtube.com/watch?v=1L3eeC2lJZs.

24. David Lieberman, "Is It Time to Let Moviegoers Send Texts during a Film?: CinemaCon," *Deadline Hollywood Daily*, April 25, 2012, http://www.deadline.com/.

25. THR Staff, "THR Poll."

26. Pierre Lévy, *Collective Intelligence: Mankind's Emerging World in Cyberspace*, trans. Robert Bononno (Cambridge, MA: Perseus, 1997).

27. Henry Jenkins, *Convergence Culture: Where Old and New Media Collide* (New York: New York University Press, 2006), 25–58.

28. Jason Mittell, "Narrative Complexity in Contemporary American Television," *Velvet Light Trap* 58 (2006): 29–40. See also Jason Mittell, "Sites of Participation: Wiki Fandom and the Case of Lostpedia," *Transformative Work and Cultures* 3 (2009), http://journal.transformativeworks.org/index.php/twc/article/view/118/117.

29. Jenkins, *Convergence Culture*, 30.

30. Brooks Barnes, "How 'Hunger Games' Built Up Must-See Fever," *New York Times*, March 18, 2012, http://www.nytimes.com/2012/03/19/business/media/how-hunger-games-built-up-must-see-fever.html.

31. Barnes, "Hunger Games."

32. Kimberly Ann Owczarski, "*Batman*, Time Warner, and Franchise Filmmaking in the Conglomerate Era" (Ph.d. diss., University of Texas, 2008), http://www.lib.utexas.edu/etd/d/2008/owczarskik22644/owczarskik22644.pdf.

33. Brenna Ehrlich, "Fans Crack Twitter Code for Sneak Peek at New Batman Film," *Mashable*, May 20, 2011, http://mashable.com/2011/05/20/batman-twitter/.

34. Johnson, *Screen Future*, 149.

35. Erik Gruenwedel, "Vudu Bows 99-Cent 'Movie of the Day,'" *Home Media Magazine*, July 26, 2011, http://www.homemediamagazine.com/.

36. Mike Shields, "Simultaneous Viewing and Surfing Commonplace," *Adweek*, July 8, 2010, http://www.adweek.com/.

37. Lynn Spigel, *Welcome to the Dreamhouse: Popular Media and Postwar Suburbs* (Durham: Duke University Press, 2001). Raymond Williams, *Television: Technology and Cultural Form* (New York: Schocken, 1974).

38. Lisa Parks, "Flexible Microcasting: Gender, Generation, and Television-Internet Convergence," in *Television after TV: Essays on a Medium in Transition*, ed. Lynn Spigel and Jan Olsson (Durham: Duke University Press, 2004), 137.

39. Ryan Lawler, "How Big Data Could Change What You Watch on TV," *New Tee Vee*, July 20, 2011, http://gigaom.com/video/whats-watched/.

40. Christina Warren, "GetGlue Gets Slick New Dashboard for TV Marketers," *Mashable*, September 8, 2011, http://mashable.com/2011/09/08/getglue-business/.

41. Mike Shields, "GetGlue Checking in with Sports Fans," *Adweek*, March 30, 2011, http://www.adweek.com/news/technology/getglue-checking-sports-fans-126103.

42. Doug Gross, "New Apps Let Couch Potatoes and Bookworms Check In, Too," CNN.com, August 23, 2010, http://cnn.com/.

43. Jon Healey, "Miso Offers Another Version of TV's Second Screen," *Los Angeles Times*, September 6, 2011, http://latimesblogs.latimes.com/.

44. Chuck Tryon, *Reinventing Cinema: Movies in the Age of Media Convergence* (New Brunswick: Rutgers University Press, 2009), 81.

45. David Bordwell, *Pandora's Digital Box: Films, Files, and the Future of Movies* (Madison, WI: Irvington Way Institute Press, 2012), 213.

46. Matt Goldberg, "Tugg.com Letting Customers Control What Comes to Their Local Theaters," *Collider*, February 22, 2012, http://collider.com/tugg-movie-theaters-online-service/147338/.

47. Jordan Poast, "Interview: Matthew Lillard Transmogrified," *Cultural Transmogrifier Magazine*, June 7, 2012, http://www.ctzine.com/interview-matthew-lillard-transmogrified/.

48. Richard Whittaker, "The Way We Watch Now: Case Studies," *Austin Chronicle*, June 22, 2012, http://www.austinchronicle.com/screens/2012-06-22/the-way-we-watch-now-case-studies/print/.

49. Scott Macauley, "Scott Glosserman Explains Gathr and Theatrical-on-Demand," *Filmmaker Magzine*, March 9, 2012, http://www.filmmakermagazine.com/.

50. Quoted in Ted Hope, "Sheri Candler on 'New Online Distribution Service: Prescreen,'" *IndieWire*, August 19, 2011, http://blogs.indiewire.com/.

51. Peter Martin, "Will Prescreen Change the Way Indie Films are Distributed?" *Movies.com*, August 26, 2011, http://www.movies.com/movie-news/prescreen-indie-films/4227.

52. Rip Empson, "Timing Is Everything: Indie Movie Discovery Platform Prescreen to Close Its Doors," *Tech Crunch*, May 31, 2012, http://techcrunch.com/2012/05/31/prescreen-suspends-beta/.

53. Scott Macauley, "Talking New Distribution Thinking at Cannes," *Filmmaker Magazine*, May 24, 2011, http://www.filmmakermagazine.com/news/2011/05/talking-new-distribution-thinking-at-cannes-2/.

54. Jon Fougner, "Guest Post by Jon Fougner: Cinema Profitability Part 3," *IndieWire*, May 13, 2011, http://blogs.indiewire.com/.

55. David Lieberman, "Will Social Media Re-Invigorate Moviegoing?: CinemaCon," *Deadline Hollywood Daily*, April 26, 2012, http://www.deadline.com/2012/04/will-social-media-re-invigorate-movie-going-cinemacon/.

56. Georg Szalai, "Warner Bros. to Acquire Rotten Tomatoes Owner Flixster," *Hollywood Reporter*, May 4, 2011, http://www.hollywoodreporter.com/news/warner-bros-acquire-rotten-tomatoes-185237.

57. Sharon Waxman, "Is Hollywood Finally Joining the Information Age? With Flixster, Warner Bros. Has a Plan," *The Wrap*, May 22, 2011, http://www.thewrap.com/.

58. Nick DeMartino, "Can Data Save the Studios in the Age of Social Media?" *Tribeca Future of Film Blog*, May 23, 2011, http://www.tribecafilm.com/tribecaonline/future-of-film/Can-Data-Save-the-Studios.html.

59. Adam Clark Estes, "Why Robert Bork (Indirectly) Kept Netflix Off Facebook," *Atlantic Wire*, July 26, 2011, http://www.theatlanticwire.com/.

60. For a discussion of the Netflix contest, see Tryon, *Reinventing Cinema*, 114–115. See also Jordan Ellenberg, "The Netflix Challenge," *Wired* 16.3 (March 2008): 114–122.

61. Ryan Singel, "Netflix Spilled Your Brokeback Mountain Secret, Lawsuit Claims," *Wired*, December 17, 2009, http://www.wired.com/.

62. Peter Kafka, "Please Don't Tell Me What You're Watching on Netflix," *All Things D*, March 13, 2012, http://allthingsd.com/20120313/please-dont-tell-me-what-youre-watching-on-netflix/.

63. Lance Whitney, "Netflix to Offer Facebook Integration (Outside U.S.)," *CNet*, July 26, 2011, http://news.cnet.com/.

64. Estes, "Robert Bork."

65. Kashmir Hill, "Good on You, Hulu: More 'Frictionless-Sharing' Companies Should Follow This Lead," *Forbes*, May 3, 2012, http://www.forbes.com/.

CHAPTER 7. INDIE 2.0

1. Patrick Goldstein, "Sundance 2011: Kevin Smith Says Goodbye to His Indie Movie Career," *Los Angeles Times*, January 24, 2011, http://latimesblogs.latimes.com/.

2. Karina Longworth, "Kevin Smith: 'I Am So, Like, Sick of Movies and Shit,'" *LA Weekly*, April 7, 2011, http://www.laweekly.com/.

3. The Sundance Film Festival reportedly receives 12,000 film submissions annually, while South by Southwest received 2,000 in 2012 alone. Although many films were likely submitted to both festivals, these numbers suggest that thousands of films go undistributed.

4. Lucas Hilderbrand, "Reports on Digital Innovations in Arthouse Distribution," *Film Quarterly* 64, no. 2 (2010): 31.

5. Michael Z. Newman, *Indie: An American Film Culture* (New York: Columbia University Press, 2011), 51.

6. Geoff King, *Indiewood, USA: Where Hollywood Meets Independent Cinema* (New York: I. B. Taurus, 2009), 20.

7. Newman, *Indie*, 51. For a more detailed discussion of the role of paratexts in constructing meanings around specific television shows and movies, see Jonathan Gray, *Show Sold Separately: Promos, Spoilers, and Other Media Paratexts* (New York: New York University Press, 2010).

8. Michael Z. Newman, "Indie Culture: In Pursuit of the Authentic Autonomous Alternative," *Cinema Journal* 48.3 (Spring 2009): 16–34. The idea that indie culture offers a more authentic form of expression than commercial media is suggested by analyses of independent productions such as Kaya Oakes, *Slanted and Enchanted: The Evolution of Indie Culture* (New York: Holt, 2009).

9. Yannis Tzioumakis, "From the Business of Film to the Business of Entertainment: Hollywood in the Age of Digital Technology," in *American Film in the Digital Age*, ed. Robert C. Sickels (Santa Barbara: Praeger, 2011), 29.

10. Henry Jenkins, *Convergence Culture: Where Old and New Media Collide* (New York: New York University Press, 2006), 95–134.

11. Longworth, "Kevin Smith."

12. Daren Brabham, "The Myth of Amateur Crowds," *Flow TV* 13, no. 6 (January 2011), http://flowtv.org/2011/01/the-myth-of-amateur-crowds/.

13. Chris Holmlund, "Introduction: From the Margins to the Mainstream," in *Contemporary American Independent Film: From the Margins to the Mainstream*, ed. Chris Holmlund and Justin Wyatt (New York: Routledge, 2005), 1.

14. Edward Jay Epstein, *The Hollywood Economist: The Hidden Financial Reality Behind the Movies* (Brooklyn: Melville House, 2010), 206–211.

15. Holmlund, "Introduction," 9.

16. Chris Anderson, *Free: The Future of a Radical Price* (New York: Hyperion, 2009), 3.

17. Smith's term calls attention to an underlying and often ignored feature of the 1990s independent boom: its continued emphasis on a film culture rooted in youthful masculinity.

18. Eric Kohn, "Cable Gets Behind Indie Pics VOD," *Variety*, November 1, 2010, http://www.variety.com/article/VR1118026276?refcatid=2199.

19. Jon Reiss, *Think Outside the Box Office: The Ultimate Guide to Film Distribution in the Digital Era* (Los Angeles: Hybrid Cinema Publishing, 2010), 38.

20. Jordan Ellenberg, "The Netflix Challenge," *Wired* 16.3 (March 2008): 114–122.

21. Jeff Howe, "The Rise of Crowdsourcing," *Wired* 14.6 (June 2006), http://www.wired.com/wired/archive/14.06/crowds.html.

22. For a discussion of *Star Wars Uncut* as an adaptation, see Chuck Tryon, "Fan Films, Adaptations, and Media Literacy," in *Science Fiction Film, Television, and Adaptation: Across the Screens*, ed. J. P. Telotte and Gerald Duchovnay (New York: Routledge, 2012), 176–190.

23. Mark Deuze, "Convergence Culture and Media Work," in *Media Industries: History, Theory, and Method*, ed. Jennifer Holt and Alissa Perren (London: Wiley-Blackwell, 2009), 152.

24. Jonathan Gray, "Crowds, Words, and the Futures of Entertainment Conference," *Antenna Blog*, November 15, 2011, http://blog.commarts.wisc.edu/.

25. Mike Musgrove, "At Play: Kickstarter Is a Web Site for the Starving Artist," *Washington Post*, March 7, 2010, http://www.washingtonpost.com/.

26. Jamie Dobie, "DOCNYC Report: Is Crowd Sourcing the Future?" *POV Blog*, November 5, 2010, http://www.pbs.org/.

27. Emily Maltby, "Tapping the Crowds for Funds," *Wall Street Journal*, December 8, 2010, http://online.wsj.com/.

28. Eric Schonfield, "Kickstarter, Two Years and 20,000 Projects Later: $53 Million Pledged, $40 Million Collected," *Tech Crunch*, April 28, 2011, http://techcrunch.com/2011/04/28/kickstarter-53-million/.

29. Yancey Strickler, "Happy Birthday Kickstarter!" *Kickstarter Blog*, April 28, 2011, http://www.kickstarter.com/blog/happy-birthday-kickstarter.

30. See the *Meanwhile* Kickstarter page, http://www.kickstarter.com/projects/260302407/meanwhile.

31. Elisabeth Holm, "Kickstarter's Elisabeth Holm Breaks Down 'The Canyons,'" *Sundance Blog*, May 23, 2012, http://www.sundance.org/.

32. For a discussion of a typical Kickstarter appeal, see Chuck Tryon, "Learning from *The Elders*: Crowdfunding, Transmedia, and Documentary," *In Media Res*, http://mediacommons.futureofthebook.org/.

33. Pip Bulbeck, "Australian Crowd-Fund Feature 'The Tunnel' Gets BitTorrent Release," *Hollywood Reporter*, May 18, 2011, http://www.hollywoodreporter.com/.

34. Anthony Kaufman, "Has Kickstarter Reached Its Goal of Changing the Way Movies Are Made?" *IndieWire*, June 2, 2011, http://www.indiewire.com/.

35. Lucas McNelly, "Crowdfunding 201: Anatomy of a Failure," *Turnstyle*, June 8, 2012, http://turnstylenews.com/2012/06/08/crowdfunding-201-anatomy-of-a-failure/.

36. Graeme Turner, "Media, Community, and Zones of Consumption," *Flow TV* 15, no. 3 (November 2011), http://flowtv.org/2011/11/zones-of-consumption/.

37. Turner, "Media, Community, and Zones of Consumption."

38. As of November 16, 2011, 451 people had pledged to support *Meanwhile*, with 193 of those promising $25. Another 139 people had offered $35, which meant they would receive a gift package including both the DVD and a CD with songs featured in the film.

39. Chuck Tryon, *Reinventing Cinema: Movies in the Age of Media Convergence* (New Brunswick: Rutgers University Press, 2009), 178–179.

40. Jon Reiss, "We Are in the Midst of a New World Order or Crisis," *IndieWire*, November 17, 2009, http://www.indiewire.com/article/jon_reiss_we_are_in_the_midst_of_a_new_world_order_or_crisis/.

41. Justin Wyatt, "Revisiting 1970s Independent Distribution and Marketing Strategies," in Holmlund and Wyatt, eds., *Contemporary American Independent Film*, 229.

42. Wyatt, "Revisiting," 236–241.

43. Nina Paley, "Sita's Distribution Plan," *NinaPaley.com*, December 28, 2008, http://blog.ninapaley.com/2008/12/28/sitas-distribution-plan/.

44. Eric Kohn, "'Sita' Singing the Distribution Blues," *The Wrap*, August 4, 2009, http://www.thewrap.com/.

45. Roger Ebert, "Having a Wonderful Time, Wish You Could Hear," *Chicago Sun-Times*, December 23, 2008, http://blogs.suntimes.com/.

46. See "Crowdfunding FAQ," *Spanner Films*, accessed May 18, 2011, http://www .spannerfilms.net/money_faq.

47. Jon Reiss, "*The Age of Stupid* Is the Future of Film," *Huffington Post*, September 21, 2009, http://www.huffingtonpost.com/.

48. Louis C.K., "A Statement from Louis C.K.," *Louis C.K.*, December 13, 2011, https://buy .louisck.net/statement.

CHAPTER 8. REINVENTING FESTIVALS

1. Joe Utichi, "Interview: Kevin Macdonald of 'Life in a Day,'" *Cinematical*, July 23, 2010, http://www.cinematical.com/2010/07/23/interview-kevin-macdonald/.

2. Megan O'Neill, "Reminder: 'Life in a Day' Premiere Streaming Live Tonight 8PM ET [Update: Review]," *Social Times*, January 27, 2011, http://socialtimes.com/life-in-a-day -premiere_b36249. Marc Lee, "Life in a Day, DVD Review," *The Telegraph*, October 28, 2011, http://www.telegraph.co.uk/.

3. O'Neill, "Reminder: 'Life in a Day' Premiere."

4. Michael Cieply, "Movies Sell Slowly at Sundance," *New York Times*, January 25, 2009, http://www.nytimes.com/2009/01/26/business/media/26sundance.html.

5. Marijke de Valck, "Conversion, Digitization, and the Future of Film Festivals," in *Digital Disruption: Cinema Moves On-Line*, ed. Dina Iordinova and Stuart Cunningham (St. Andrews, Scotland: St. Andrews Film Studies, 2012), 120.

6. Marijke de Valck, *Film Festivals: From European Geopolitics to Global Cinephilia* (Amsterdam: Amsterdam University Press, 2007), 21–22.

7. Jonathan Gray, *Show Sold Separately: Promos, Spoilers, and Other Media Paratexts* (New York: New York University Press, 2010), 47–52.

8. Michael Z. Newman, *Indie: An American Film Culture* (New York: Columbia University Press, 2011), 61.

9. Gray, *Show Sold Separately*, 5–6.

10. Gray, *Show Sold Separately*, 167.

11. Valck, *Film Festivals*, 35.

12. I use the term "remediation" here in the full sense discussed by Jay David Bolter and Richard Grusin to describe how new media often adapt and rework older media. See Bolter and Grusin, *Remediation: Understanding New Media* (Cambridge, MA: MIT Press, 2000).

13. David H. Lawrence XVII, "The Sundance App Puts the Festival at Your Fingertips," *Backstage*, January 18, 2012, http://www.backstage.com/.

14. Michael Z. Newman, *Indie*, 1.

15. Alisa Perren, "Sex, Lies, and Marketing: Miramax and the Development of the Quality Indie Blockbuster," *Film Quarterly* 55, no. 2 (2001–2002): 34.

16. Perren, "Sex, Lies, and Marketing," 35.

17. Robert Eberwein, "The IFC and Sundance: Channeling Independence," in *Contemporary American Independent Film: From the Margins to the Mainstream*, ed. Chris Holmlund and Justin Wyatt (London: Routledge, 2005), 267.

18. James Schamus, "A Rant," in *The End of Cinema as We Know It*, ed. Jon Lewis (New York: New York University Press, 2001), 253.

19. Schamus, "A Rant," 254.

20. Edward Jay Epstein, *The Hollywood Economist: The Hidden Financial Reality Behind the Movies* (Brooklyn: Melville House, 2010), 207.

21. Epstein, *Hollywood Economist*, 207–208.

22. Epstein, *Hollywood Economist*, 207–209.

23. Mark Gill, "Mark Gill on Indie Film Crisis," *Variety*, June 21, 2008, http://weblogs.variety.com/thompsononhollywood/2008/06/laff-mark-gill.html.

24. Gregg Goldstein, "Distribs Go Multiplatform Diving," *Variety*, May 19, 2012, http://www.variety.com/article/VR1118054273. See also Daniel Miller, "Sundance 2012: The Day-and-Date Success Story of 'Margin Call,'" *Hollywood Reporter*, January 18, 2012, http://www.hollywoodreporter.com/. David Poland questions the enthusiasm for VOD, suggesting that after advertising and production costs, *Margin Call* likely barely broke even. See David Poland, "Margin Call Math," *Movie City News*, January 18, 2012, http://moviecitynews.com/2012/01/margin-call-math/.

25. Mike Plante, "Meet the Next," Sundance Film Festival, January 12, 2010, http://festival.sundance.org/2010/news/article/meet_the_next/.

26. Quoted in Jay Fernandez, "Redford: Sundance Going Back to Its Roots," *Hollywood Reporter*, January 21, 2010, http://www.hollywoodreporter.com/.

27. Karina Longworth, "Sundance: What's Happening NEXT?" *LA Weekly*, January 21, 2010, http://www.laweekly.com/2010–01–21/film-tv/sundance-what-s-happening-next/.

28. Roger Ebert, "Sundance and Five Sundance-Style Movies," *Roger Ebert's Journal*, January 22, 2010.

29. Anne Thompson, "Sundance Institute Pushes Deeper into Digital Distribution Alternatives—Analysis," *IndieWire*, July 29, 2011, http://blogs.indiewire.com/.

30. Anne Thompson, "Sundance Institute Pushes Deeper."

31. Dennis Lim, "A Generation Finds Its Mumble," *New York Times*, August 19, 2007, http://www.nytimes.com/2007/08/19/movies/19lim.html.

32. Karina Longworth, "2010: The Year SXSW Film Broke," *Village Voice*, March 24, 2010, http://www.villagevoice.com/.

33. S. James Snyder, "The Film Festival Comes to Your Living Room," *Time*, March 18, 2009, http://www.time.com/time/arts/article/0,8599,1885670,00.html.

34. Chuck Tryon, *Reinventing Cinema: Movies in the Age of Media Convergence* (New Brunswick: Rutgers University Press, 2009), 117–119.

35. In one of the most productive readings of Mumblecore, Aymar Jean Christian argues that Mumblecore should be read as a style or movement rather than a genre. Aymar Jean Christian, "Joe Swanberg, Intimacy, and the Digital Aesthetic," *Cinema Journal* 50, no. 4 (Summer 2011): 119.

36. Christian, "Joe Swanberg," 121.

37. Robert C. Sickels, *American Film in the Digital Age* (Santa Barbara: Praeger, 2011), 170.

38. Sickels, *American Film*, 173.

39. Joe Swanberg, quoted in Snyder, "Film Festival Comes to Your Living Room."

40. Marc Eastman, "IFC Films & SXSW Present 2nd Annual On-Demand Film Festival," *Are You Screening*, March 5, 2010, http://www.areyouscreening.com/.

41. Ryan Lawler and Janko Roettgers, "Where to Watch SXSW Live Online," *New Tee Vee*, March 11, 2011, http://gigaom.com/video/where-to-watch-sxsw-live-online/.

42. Tom Hall, "Sundance 2009: You, Me, and VOD," *IndieWire*, January 21, 2009, http://blogs.indiewire.com/twhalliii/sundance_2009_you_me_and_vod.

43. Hall, "You, Me, and VOD."

44. Jon Silver, Stuart Cunningham, and Mark David Ryan, "Mission Unreachable: How Jaman is Shaping the Future of On-line Distribution," in Iordinova and Cunningham, eds., *Digital Disruption*, 133–134.

45. Brian Brooks, "Update: Tribeca Moves into Distribution, Launches Virtual Film Fest," *IndieWire*, March 2, 2010, http://www.indiewire.com/.

46. For a good discussion of how the Streaming Room worked, see Stephen Holden, "Visiting the Festival from Home," *New York Times*, April 11, 2011, http://www.nytimes.com/2011/04/15/movies/tribeca-festival-online-and-on-demand.html.

47. Matt Singer, "Tribeca Launches Online Film Festival," *IFC Blog*, March 22, 2011, http://www.ifc.com/news/2011/03/tribeca-launches-online-film-f.php.

CONCLUSION: DIGITAL FUTURES

1. Charlie Sorrel, "TV-Hat, the Dork-Tastic Head-Mounted Theater," *Wired*, April 16, 2010, http://www.wired.com/. Dan Nosowitz, "Review: The As-Seen-on-TV Hat, an iPhone-Viewing Visor," *Gizmodo*, January 8, 2010, http://gizmodo.com/.

2. Randall Stross, "Yes, Norma Desmond, The Pictures Are Getting Small Again," *New York Times*, July 7, 2012, http://www.nytimes.com/2012/07/08/technology/movie-screens-small-to-big-to-small-again-digital-domain.html.

3. Chris McGurk, "LAFF Keynote Speaker Cinedigm CEO Chris McGurk: Production and Distribution Revolution," *Thompson on Hollywood*, June 12, 2012, http://blogs.indiewire.com/.

4. For a more nuanced response to the politics of Batman, see Scott Mendelson, "Debunking the 'Dark Knight Endorses Bush/Cheney' Myth," *Salon*, August 31, 2008, http://open.salon.com/.

5. Henry Jenkins, *Convergence Culture: Where Old and New Media Collide* (New York: New York University Press, 2006).

6. Lucas McNelly, "Crowdfunding 201: Matthew Lillard Talks Campaign Secrets of 'Fat Kid,'" *Turnstyle*, June 1, 2012, http://turnstylenews.com/.

7. Amanda D. Lotz, *The Television Will be Revolutionized* (New York: New York University Press, 2007), 37.

8. Lotz's arguments about niche media build from Joseph Turow's powerful analyses of the rise of niche magazines and the resulting fragmentation that Turow sees as endangering community and democracy. See Joseph Turow, *Breaking Up America: Advertisers and the New Media World* (Chicago: University of Chicago Press, 2007).

9. Raymond Williams, *Marxism and Literature* (Oxford: Oxford University Press, 1978), xxi.

10. Lucas Hilderbrand, "From the VCR to YouTube: An Interview with Lucas Hilderbrand (Part One)," *Confessions of an Aca-Fan*, April 14, 2011, http://henryjenkins.org/2011/04/from_the_vcr_to_youtube_an_int.html.

11. Roger Ebert, "The Sudden Death of Film," *Chicago Sun-Times*, http://blogs.suntimes.com/ebert/2011/11/the_sudden_death_of_film.html.

12. Edward Jay Epstein speculates that new movies will have to contain "universally appealing elements," in part due to the vast global audience for Hollywood films. See Epstein, *The Hollywood Economist: The Hidden Financial Reality Behind the Movies* (Brooklyn: Melville House, 2010), 218.

13. Barbara Klinger, *Beyond the Multiplex: Cinema, New Technologies, and the Home* (Berkeley: University of California Press, 2006), 17–53.

14. Klinger, *Beyond the Multiplex*, 243.

15. Klinger, *Beyond the Multiplex*, 72.

16. Epstein, *Hollywood Economist*, 208.

17. Brian David Johnson, *Screen Future: The Future of Entertainment, Computing, and the Devices We Love* (Santa Clara, CA: Intel Press, 2010), 6.

18. Epstein, *Hollywood Economist*, 213.

19. David Bordwell, *Pandora's Digital Box: Films, Files, and the Future of Movies* (Madison, WI: Irvington Way Institute Press, 2012), 209.

SELECT BIBLIOGRAPHY

Acland, Charles. "*Avatar* as Technological Tentpole." *Flow TV* 11.6 (January 22, 2010).

———. "Curtains, Carts, and the Mobile Screen." *Screen* 50.1 (2009): 148–66.

———. *Screen Traffic: Movies, Multiplexes, and Global Cultures.* Durham: Duke University Press, 2003.

———. "Theatrical Exhibition: Accelerated Cinema." In McDonald and Wasko, eds., *Contemporary Hollywood Film Industry*, 83–105.

———. "You Haven't Seen *Avatar* Yet." *Flow TV* 13.8 (February 11, 2011).

Anderson, Chris. *Free: The Future of a Radical Price.* New York: Hyperion, 2009.

———. *The Long Tail: Why the Future of Business Is Selling Less of More.* New York: Hyperion, 2006.

Andrejevic, Mark. *iSpy: Surveillance and Power in the Interactive Era.* Lawrence: University of Kansas Press, 2007.

Balsamo, Anne. "I Phone, I Learn." In Snickars and Vonderau, eds., *Moving Data*, 251–64.

Banet-Weiser, Sarah, Cynthia Chris, and Anthony Freitas, eds. *Cable Visions: Television Beyond Broadcasting.* New York: New York University Press, 2007.

Bennett, James, and Tom Brown, eds. *Film and Television after DVD.* London: Routledge, 2008.

Bennett, James, and Niki Strange, eds. *Television as Digital Media.* Durham: Duke University Press, 2011.

Boddy, William. "'Is It TV Yet?' The Dislocated Screens of Television in a Mobile Digital Culture." In Bennett and Strange, eds., *Television as Digital Media*, 76–101.

Bolter, Jay David, and Richard Grusin. *Remediation: Understanding New Media.* Cambridge, MA: MIT Press, 2000.

Bordwell, David. "Creating a Classic, with a Little Help from Your Pirate Friends." *Observations on Film Art*, February 21, 2008.

———. *Pandora's Digital Box: Films, Files, and the Future of Movies.* Madison, WI: Irvington Way Institute Press, 2012.

Brabham, Daren. "The Myth of Amateur Crowds." *Flow* 13.06 (January 2011).

Brooker, Will. *Using the Force: Creativity, Community, and "Star Wars" Fans.* New York: Continuum, 2002.

Bruns, Axel. *Blogs, Wikipedia, Second Life and Beyond: From Production to Produsage.* New York: Peter Lang, 2009.

Bruns, Axel, and Jean Burgess. "New Methodologies for Researching News Discussion on Twitter." *Mapping Online Publics*, 2011.

Caldwell, John Thornton. *Production Culture: Industrial Reflexivity and Critical Practice in Film and Television.* Durham: Duke University Press, 2008.

Carroll, Nathan. "Unwrapping Archives: DVD Restoration Demonstrations and the Marketing of Authenticity." *Velvet Light Trap* 56.1 (2005): 18–31.

Cassetti, Francesco. "Back to the Motherland: The Film Theatre in the Postmedia Age." *Screen* 52.1 (Spring 2011): 1–12.

Castells, Manuel. *The Rise of the Networked Society.* 2nd ed. Malden, MA: Blackwell, 2000.

Chamberlin, Daniel. "Scripted Spaces: Television Interfaces and the Non-Places of Asynchronous Entertainment." In Bennett and Strange, eds., *Television as Digital Media*, 230–54.

Christian, Aymar Jean. "Joe Swanberg, Intimacy, and the Digital Aesthetic." *Cinema Journal* 50.4 (Summer 2011): 117–35.

Cubitt, Sean. *Videography: Video Media as Art and Culture.* Houndmills, UK: MacMillan, 1993.

Cunningham, Stuart, and Jon Silver. "On-line Film Distribution: Its History and Global Complexion." In Iordinova and Cunningham, eds., *Digital Disruption*, 33–66.

Daly, Kristen. "Cinema 3.0: The Interactive Image." *Cinema Journal* 50.1 (Fall 2010): 81–98.

Dawson, Max, and Lynn Spigel. "Television and Digital Media." In *American Thought and Culture in the Twenty-First Century*, ed. Catherine Morley and Martin Halliwell, 275–89. New York: Columbia University Press, 2008.

Dayan, Daniel. "Looking for Sundance: The Social Construction of a Film Festival." In *Moving Images, Culture, and the Mind*, ed. Ib Bondebjerg, 43–52. London: University of Luton Press, 2000.

Deleuze, Gilles. "Postscript on the Societies of Control." *October* 59 (Winter 1992): 3–7.

Deuze, Mark. "Convergence Culture and Media Work." In *Media Industries: History, Theory, and Method*, ed. Jennifer Holt and Alissa Perren, 144–56. London: Wiley-Blackwell, 2009.

Dixon, Wheeler Winston. "How Long Will It Last, and Do You Really Own It?" *Flow* 14.7 (September 3, 2011).

———. "Red Boxes and Cloud Movies." *Flow* 14.4 (July 21, 2011).

Douglas, Susan J. *Listening In: Radio and the American Imagination.* Minneapolis: University of Minnesota Press, 2004.

Drake, Philip. "Distribution and Marketing in Contemporary Hollywood." In McDonald and Wasko, eds., *Contemporary Hollywood Film Industry*, 63–82.

Ebert, Roger. "The Dying of the Light." *Chicago Sun-Times*, May 24, 2011.

———. "Having a Wonderful Time, Wish You Could Hear." *Chicago Sun-Times*, December 23, 2008.

Eberwein, Robert. "The IFC and Sundance: Channeling Independence." In Holmlund and Wyatt, eds., *Contemporary American Independent Film*, 231–47.

Epstein, Edward Jay. *The Big Picture: Money and Power in Hollywood.* New York: Random House, 2006.

———. *The Hollywood Economist: The Hidden Financial Reality Behind the Movies.* Brooklyn: Melville House, 2010.

Fileri, Paul, and Ruby Cheng. "Spotlight on MUBI: Two Interviews with Efe Cakarel, Founder and CEO of MUBI." In Iordinova and Cunningham, eds., *Digital Disruption*, 167–80.

Foucault, Michel. *Discipline and Punish: The Birth of the Prison.* Translated by Alan Sheridan. New York: Vintage, 1979.

Friedberg, Anne. *Window Shopping: Cinema and the Postmodern.* Berkeley: University of California Press, 1994.

Gill, Mark. "Mark Gill on Indie Film Crisis." *Variety*, June 21, 2008.

Goggin, Gerard. *Global Mobile Media.* London: Routledge, 2011.

Grant, Catherine. "Auteur Machines? Auteurism and the DVD." In Bennett and Brown, eds., *Film and Television after DVD*, 101–15.

Gray, Ann. *Video Playtime: The Gendering of a Leisure Technology.* London: Routledge, 1992.

Gray, Jonathan. "Crowds, Words, and the Futures of Entertainment Conference." *Antenna Blog*, November 15, 2011.

———. *Show Sold Separately: Promos, Spoilers, and Other Media Paratexts.* New York: New York University Press, 2010.

Greenberg, Joshua M. *From Betamax to Blockbuster: Video Stores and the Invention of Movies on Video.* Cambridge, MA: MIT Press, 2008.

Harries, Dan. "Watching the Internet." In *The New Media Book*, ed. Dan Harries, 171–82. London: British Film Institute, 2002.

Harvey, David. *The Condition of Postmodernity: An Enquiry into the Origins of Cultural Change.* London: Blackwell, 1989.

Hilderbrand, Lucas. "From the VCR to YouTube: An Interview with Lucas Hilderbrand (Part One)." *Confessions of an Aca-Fan*, April 14, 2011.

———. *Inherent Vice: Bootleg Histories of Videotape and Copyright.* Durham: Duke University Press, 2009.

———. "Reports on Digital Innovations in Arthouse Distribution." *Film Quarterly* 64.2 (2010): 24–28.

Hills, Matt. *Fan Cultures.* London: Routledge, 2002.

Holmlund, Chris. "Introduction: From the Margins to the Mainstream." In Holmlund and Wyatt, eds., *Contemporary American Independent Film*, 1–20.

Holmlund, Chris, and Justin Wyatt, eds. *Contemporary American Independent Film: From the Margins to the Mainstream.* London: Routledge, 2005.

Holt, Jennifer. *Empires of Entertainment: Media Industries and the Politics of Deregulation, 1980–1996.* New Brunswick: Rutgers University Press, 2011.

———. "Platforms, Pipelines, and Politics: The iPhone and Regulatory Hangover." In Snickars and Vonderau, eds., *Moving Data*, 140–54.

Hutcheon, Linda. *A Theory of Adaptation.* New York: Routledge, 2006.

Iordinova, Dina, and Stuart Cunningham, eds. *Digital Disruption: Cinema Moves On-Line.* St. Andrews, Scotland: St. Andrews Film Studies, 2012.

Jenkins, Henry. *Convergence Culture: Where Old and New Media Collide.* New York: New York University Press, 2006.

Johns, Adrian. *Piracy: The Intellectual Property Wars from Gutenberg to Gates.* Chicago: University of Chicago Press, 2009.

Johnson, Brian David. *Screen Future: The Future of Entertainment, Computing, and the Devices We Love.* Santa Clara, CA: Intel Press, 2010.

Karaganis, Joe. "Introduction." In *Media Piracy in Emerging Economies*, ed. Joe Karaganis. New York: Social Science Research Council, 2011.

Kernan, Lisa. *Coming Attractions: Reading American Movie Trailers.* Austin: University of Texas Press, 2004.

King, Geoff. *Indiewood, USA: Where Hollywood Meets Independent Cinema.* New York: I. B. Taurus, 2009.

Klinger, Barbara. *Beyond the Multiplex: Cinema, New Technologies, and the Home.* Berkeley: University of California Press, 2006.

———. "The DVD Cinephile: Viewing Heritages and Home Film Cultures." In Bennett and Brown, eds., *Film and Television after DVD*, 19–44.

Kompare, Derek. "Publishing Flow: DVD Box Sets and the Reconception of Television." *Television & New Media* 7.4 (2006): 335–60.

———. *Rerun Nation: How Repeats Invented American Television.* New York: Routledge, 2005.

Larkin, Brian. *Signal and Noise: Media, Infrastructure, and Urban Culture in Nigeria.* Durham: Duke University Press, 2008.

Lasica, J. D. *Darknet: Hollywood's War against the Digital Generation.* Hoboken, NJ: John Wiley & Sons, 2005.

Lefebvre, Henri. *Everyday Life in the Modern World.* Translated by Sacha Rabinovitch. New Brunswick, NJ: Transaction Publishers, 1984.

Lévy, Pierre. *Collective Intelligence: Mankind's Emerging World in Cyberspace.* Translated by Robert Bononno. Cambridge, MA: Perseus, 1997.

Livingstone, Randall. "The Myth of Classlessness in Apple's 'Get a Mac' Campaign." *Flow* 13.11 (April 8, 2011).

Lotz, Amanda D. *The Television Will Be Revolutionized*. New York: New York University Press, 2007.

McCarthy, Anna. *Ambient Television: Visual Culture and Public Space*. Durham: Duke University Press, 2001.

McDonald, Paul. *Video and DVD Industries*. London: BFI, 2007.

McDonald, Paul, and Janet Wasko, eds. *The Contemporary Hollywood Film Industry*. Malden, MA: Blackwell, 2008.

McMurria, John. "A Taste of Class: Pay-TV and the Commodification of Television in Postwar America." In Banet-Weiser, Chris, and Freitas, eds., *Cable Visions*, 44–65.

Mittell, Jason. "Narrative Complexity in Contemporary American Television." *Velvet Light Trap* 58 (2006): 29–40.

———. "Sites of Participation: Wiki Fandom and the Case of Lostpedia." *Transformative Work and Cultures* 3 (2009).

Moores, Shaun. "Media Uses & Everyday Environmental Experiences: A Positive Critique of Phenomenological Geography." *Participations* 3.2 (November 2006).

Mosco, Vincent. *The Digital Sublime: Myth, Power, and Cyberspace*. Cambridge, MA: MIT Press, 2004.

———. *The Political Economy of Communication*. 2nd ed. Los Angeles: Sage, 2009.

Murphy, Sheila C. *How Television Invented New Media*. New Brunswick: Rutgers University Press, 2012.

Newman, Michael Z. *Indie: An American Film Culture*. New York: Columbia University Press, 2011.

———. "Indie Culture: In Pursuit of the Authentic Autonomous Alternative." *Cinema Journal* 48.3 (Spring 2009): 16–34.

North, Dan. *Performing Illusions: Cinema Special Effects and the Virtual Actor*. London: Wallflower Press, 2001.

Owczarski, Kimberly Anne. "*Batman*, Time Warner, and Franchise Filmmaking in the Conglomerate Era." Ph.D. diss., University of Texas, Austin, 2008.

Parks, Lisa. "Flexible Microcasting: Gender, Generation, and Television-Internet Convergence." In *Television after TV: Essays on a Medium in Transition*, ed. Lynn Spigel and Jan Olsson, 133–56. Durham: Duke University Press, 2004.

Perren, Alisa. "Sex, Lies, and Marketing: Miramax and the Development of the Quality Indie Blockbuster." *Film Quarterly* 55.2 (2001–2002): 30–39.

Perren, Alisa, and Karen Petruska. "Big Hollywood, Small Screens." In Snickars and Vonderau, eds., *Moving Data*, 104–23.

Reiss, Jon. *Think Outside the Box Office: The Ultimate Guide to Film Distribution in the Digital Era*. Los Angeles: Hybrid Cinema Publishing, 2010.

San Filippo, Maria. "A Cinema of Recession: Micro-Budgeting, Micro-Drama, and the 'Mumblecore' Movement." *Cineaction* 85 (2011).

Schamus, James. "A Rant." In *The End of Cinema as We Know It*, ed. Jon Lewis, 253–60. New York: New York University Press, 2001.

Schatz, Tom. "The Studio System and Conglomerate Hollywood." In McDonald and Wasko, eds., *Contemporary Hollywood Film Industry*, 11–42.

Schiller, Dan. *How to Think about Information*. Urbana: University of Illinois Press, 2007.

Sconce, Jeffrey. *Haunted Media: Electronic Presence from Telegraphy to Television*. Durham: Duke University Press, 2000.

Seiter, Ellen. *Sold Separately: Children and Parents in Consumer Culture*. New Brunswick: Rutgers University Press, 1993.

Shaviro, Steven. *Post-Cinematic Affect*. Washington, DC: Zero Books, 2010.

Shimpach, Shawn. *Television in Transition: The Life and Afterlife of the Narrative Action Hero*. Malden, MA: Wiley-Blackwell, 2010.

Sickels, Robert C. *American Film in the Digital Age*. Santa Barbara: Praeger, 2011.

Silver, Jon, Stuart Cunningham, and Mark David Ryan, "Mission Unreachable: How Jaman is Shaping the Future of On-line Distribution." In Iordinova and Cunningham, eds., *Digital Disruption*, 133–42.

Snickars, Pelle, and Patrick Vonderau, eds. *Moving Data: The iPhone and the Future of Media*. New York: Columbia University Press, 2012.

Sperb, Jason. "A Few Thoughts on *Tron's* Blu-Ray Release." *Jamais Vu: Thoughts on Cinema and Media*, April 8, 2011.

Spigel, Lynn. *Make Room for TV: Television and the Family Ideal in Postwar America*. Chicago: University of Chicago Press, 1992.

———. *Welcome to the Dreamhouse: Popular Media and Postwar Suburbs*. Durham: Duke University Press, 2001.

Sterne, Jonathan. "Formatted to Fit Your Screen." *FlowTV* 15.5 (January 2012).

Striphas, Ted. "How to Have Culture in an Algorithmic Age." *The Late Age of Print Blog*, June 14, 2010.

———. *The Late Age of Print: Everyday Book Culture from Consumerism to Control*. New York: Columbia University Press, 2009.

Thompson, Kristin. "Do Not Forget to Return your 3D Glasses." *Observations on Film Art*, July 27, 2011.

———. "Has 3D Already Failed? The Sequel, Part 2: Real Dsgusted." *Observations on Film Art*, January 25, 2011.

Tryon, Chuck. "Digital Distribution, Participatory Culture, and the Transmedia Documentary," *Jump Cut* 53 (2011).

———. "Fan Films, Adaptations, and Media Literacy." In *Science Fiction Film, Television, and Adaptation: Across the Screens*, edited by J. P. Telotte and Gerald Duchovnay, 176–90. New York: Routledge, 2012.

———. "Pushing the (Red) Envelope: Portable Video, Platform Mobility, and Pay-Per-View Culture." In Snickars and Vonderau, eds., *Moving Data*, 124–39.

———. *Reinventing Cinema: Movies in the Age of Media Convergence*. New Brunswick: Rutgers University Press, 2009.

———. "TV Time Lords: Fan Cultures, Narrative Complexity, and the Future of Science Fiction Television." In *The Essential Science Fiction Television Reader*, edited by J. P. Telotte, 301–14. Lexington: University Press of Kentucky, 2008.

Turner, Graeme. "'Liveness' and 'Sharedness' Outside the Box." *Flow TV* 13.11 (April 8, 2011).

———. "Media, Community, and Zones of Consumption." *Flow TV* 15.3 (November 13, 2011).

Turow, Joseph. *Breaking Up America: Advertisers and the New Media World*. Chicago: University of Chicago Press, 2007.

Tzioumakis, Yannis. "From the Business of Film to the Business of Entertainment: Hollywood in the Age of Digital Technology." In *American Film in the Digital Age*, edited by Robert C. Sickels, 11–32. Santa Barbara: Praeger, 2011.

Ulin, Jeff. *The Business of Media Distribution: Monetizing Film, TV, and Video Content*. New York: Focal Press, 2010.

Valck, Marijke de. *Film Festivals: From European Geopolitics to Global Cinephilia.* Amsterdam: Amsterdam University Press, 2007.

Wasko, Janet. *How Hollywood Works.* New York: Sage, 2003.

Wasser, Frederick. *Veni, Vidi, Video: The Hollywood Empire and the VCR.* Austin: University of Texas Press, 2001.

Williams, Raymond. *Marxism and Literature.* Oxford: Oxford University Press, 1978.

———. *Television: Technology and Cultural Form.* New York: Schocken, 1974.

Winston, Brian. *Media, Technology, and Society, A History: From the Telegraph to the Internet.* London: Routledge, 1998.

Wyatt, Justin. "Revisiting 1970s Independent Distribution and Marketing Strategies." In Holmlund and Wyatt, eds., *Contemporary American Independent Film*, 199–212.

INDEX

ABOUT THE AUTHOR

CHUCK TRYON is an assistant professor in the English department at Fayetteville State University. He is the author of *Reinventing Cinema: Movies in the Age of Media Convergence*, published by Rutgers University Press, and has written articles for *Screen*, the *Journal of Film and Video, Popular Communication,* and the *Canadian Journal of Film Studies*.